Advances in
Teacher Education
Volume 2

Editors:

James D. Raths and Lilian G. Katz

Ablex Publishing Corporation
Norwood, New Jersey 07648

ISBN: 0-89391-275-1
ISSN: 0748-0067

Ablex Publishing Corporation
355 Chestnut Street
Norwood, New Jersey 07648

Contents

iii

Preface

A great deal has happened in education during the two years that have passed since we completed the preparation of the first volume in this series. A spate of national reports has been issued indicting the public schools, the teachers in them, and the professors who are responsible for their preparation. As one might expect, while the reports have been criticized for misstatements of fact, for wallowing in hyperbole, and for faulty characterizations of the problems facing contemporary education in the U.S., they have been accepted as essentially accurate and credible by the general public, by the politicians, and by many academics as well.

On the plus side, research in teacher education has finally been acknowledged as a genuine and respectable specialty by the American Educational Research Association. In June of 1984, the Association formally approved an application sponsored by a group of teacher education researchers for the formation of a special division (Division K) dedicated to the study of teacher education and teaching. We hope this good news comes in time to offset the grim repetitive charges contained in the national reports. With full standing as a division in the American Educational Research Association, teacher education research is more likely to flourish and prosper and gain the eminence and support it so richly deserves. This series of papers is similarly dedicated to the advancement of inquiry into teacher education. Each of the chapters in this second volume of *Advances in Teacher Education* addresses a critical topic in the field of teacher education, and we hope that readers will find the papers useful and pertinent to their own research interests.

Clark's chapter puts teacher education into perspective by taking up some of its recent history, policy issues, and structural and intrainstitutional factors that help to account for its present status. Based on this perspective, Professor Clark offers three propositions and a set of recommendations with which to redress the major issues in the field. In the second chapter Applegate presents a framework for the study of students' perceptions of their field experiences and offers researchers interested in working on such problems some major questions to be answered.

Ducharme addresses a relatively neglected area of research in the field of education in his paper on teacher educators. His analysis, description, and review of what has been said of teacher educators present researchers with a genuine challenge to seek further information and insight into the problems and predicaments faced by those responsible for educating the educators of the nation's children.

Acceptance of the central role of first-hand experience in the preparation of teachers is widespread and virtually unquestioned. But Feiman-Nemser and Buchmann's report of the findings from one of a series of studies of the role of experience in teacher education raises important questions about its pitfalls and limitations and provokes us to examine what kinds of experiences best serve what kinds of goals. In a discussion of teacher education in the Australian context, Hogben and Simpson address related issues by focusing on the relative value of theory versus practical training in the processes of becoming qualified to teach. Klinzing and Tisher's chapter argues that teacher educators can and should help their students to understand and maximize the potential contribution nonverbal aspects of their teaching behavior can make to their work.

Zeichner's contribution offers a detailed examination of individual as well as institutional factors that may influence the impact and effect of teacher education, particularly with respect to the teachers' perspectives on their work. Zeichner calls for further research to clarify the most powerful among the many factors that impinge upon the development of teachers' perspectives and how these multiple factors might be linked.

While only a few years ago the provision of early field experience for teacher education students was expected to solve many of the difficulties encountered in becoming a teacher, Waxman and Walberg's review of the available research on its effects suggests that once again, we were probably expecting too much. However, they suggest that the type and quality of the research reported to date on early field experience leaves many of the most important questions still unresolved.

Burden's paper is a review and analysis of the large and apparently expanding literature addressed to hypothesized developmental processes through which education students and teachers are said to pass. While this literature already includes several different "traditions" in terms of paradigms and methods, its popularity seems to suggest that it addresses issues of theoretical as well as practical interest to researchers.

Any educational enterprise faced with widespread criticism can be expected to turn its evaluation practices toward itself. Galluzzo's chapter is an exploration of the available literature in teacher evaluation. As he points out, teacher education evaluation is just beginning to emerge and appears to need our best efforts if it is to provide us with the information and insight required for genuine progress. Lastly, Griffin reviews the large research literature on student teaching and outlines a group of important issues in need of further analysis and investigation.

We believe the papers in this volume well represent the status of research in teacher education, and we are pleased to be able to present them to colleagues around the world who share our interest in this complex research area. We trust that the field will continue to flourish and to be animated by the investigation of problems as urgent and perplexing as those discussed in this volume.

James D. Raths
Lilian G. Katz

1

Transforming the Structure for the Professional Preparation of Teachers

David L. Clark
Indiana University

The preparation of teachers in the United States is conducted in a contextual environment so inimical to the production of excellent practitioners that teacher education institutions are facing the realistic possibility of extinction. This chapter will explore the ecology of this field from contemporary affective, structural, and political viewpoints. The exploration will cover familiar territory for the contextual environment has emerged over decades of policy and practice decisions. Exploration implies discovery. We need to discover ways to identify what is intolerable in this territory and to transform it. However, the exploration of the familiar leads infrequently to discovery. The essence of the current dilemma in teacher education lies in over familiarity with its contexture by practitioners and leaders. We have learned to live with the indefensible so long that we now defend it.

THE AFFECTIVE CONTEXT OF TEACHER EDUCATION

Proposition 1: Current national and state reform proposals for teacher education have exceeded the negotiated normalcy that controls the boundaries of calls for professional reform. Disestablishment of university-based teacher training programs is considered to be a practicable reform. Nothing is argued as better than something. Teacher education practitioners are losing a sense of personal efficacy and schools, colleges, and departments of education (SCDEs) are defensive and uncertain organizations.

This is not the first time that teacher education has been under attack nor are the current reformers the first who have called for the elimination of teacher training programs. However, the current situation is different and it

1

is more threatening. Support for disestablishment has a broader popular base. The attack comes during a period of quantitative recession. The reformers-by-elimination include executive and legislative offices and bodies that have the capacity to effect such changes.

Among a cluster of instances calling for partial or total disestablishment, New Jersey has provided the clearest example. Under the New Jersey plan, baccalaureate degree recipients who pass subject matter and competency (basic skill) tests become provisional teachers. The provisional status of a candidate continues through an internship year supervised by the state but operated by the school district. The intent of the plan is to provide an alternative route to a teaching career for individuals deemed qualified who have not completed teacher education programs.

New Jersey's plan is not only a useful example of disestablishment but illustrates what happens to a professional field when the bounds of normal dialogue about professional reform are broken. Extreme solutions are proffered by inexpert policy and decision makers with little concern about risk, since the policy maker has already judged the current situation to be contributory to the problem. The inexpertness of the proposers plus the search for quick remedies to long-standing deficiencies lead to the emergence and serious consideration of solutions to nonproblems or nonsolutions to problems. New Jersey has discovered a solution to a nonproblem. If teacher education were characterized by highly selective entrance requirements, onerous academic hurdles, and exclusive certification standards, one might imagine a pool of noncertified applicants who, given the opportunity, could become effective practitioners. But if there is one thing teacher education does not do, it does not place undue burdens of admission or course requirements on its students. To the contrary, in most schools, colleges, or departments of education across the country, the secondary teacher trainee completes only four education courses plus student teaching during the professional training period. The New Jersey proposal, in common with those in other states that are moving toward alternative routes to certification, allows baccalaureate degree recipients to avoid a training intervention which is so modest in scope that most observers of teacher education would cite its brevity as the problem. New Jersey is implementing a solution to a nonproblem.

Conversely, the plan could be labeled a nonsolution to a real problem. How do we attract more and better young women and men to teaching? By avoiding a 12-hour course requirement?[1] There are long-standing socioeconomic and professional factors that drive potentially able young practition-

---

[1] More recently, New York City dropped its preemployment requirement of six credits in education. The intent, according to the City's school system director of personnel, is to open "up the profession to liberal arts graduates" to "improve the quality of people coming into it" (Toch, 1984, p. 18).

ers away from teaching. They are difficult factors with which to deal. They do not yield to the simplism of alternative routes to certification. The basic problem to which the New Jersey plan is addressed is untouched by the solution.

There is a recent analog to the circumstance in which teacher education finds itself today. In the wake of the Coleman Report and the review of the research on school effects by Averch, Carroll, Donaldson, Kiesling, and Pincus (1972) for the President's Commission on School Finance, urban public schools found their existence as a viable educational tool in our society in peril. The popular interpretation of the day was that variations in student outcomes were due to variations in pupil characteristics and not to schooling. The short-range impact of these reports and of the attacks on urban education that followed them was a loss of a sense of efficacy by individual performers in the field and a loss of a sense of commitment from an organizational perspective.

Teacher education is experiencing this affective environment right now. Do not believe the argument of the nihilist that this is a period of opportunity. It is a period of danger. When all outcomes, including nonsurvival, are possible, the search for rootedness and stability overwhelms "the possible." Opportunities emerge in fields in which individual practitioners have a sense of personal efficacy; organizations are committed to a raison d'être; and there is tolerance on the part of supporters, critics, and clients for trials that may result in successes and/or failures.

Proposal 1

The current level of criticism by some reformists of teacher education is so destructive that the field needs to mount and support a critical rebuttal. And this rebuttal needs to be politically as well as intellectually defensible. When urban schools were facing their bleakest days, Ronald Edmonds (1979) challenged the popular notion that "schools made no difference" by noting, simply, that some did. Teacher educators are in a position currently to assert and defend a key proposition: that there is, and will continue to be, a growing body of knowledge about teaching which, if communicated effectively to teachers, will affect positively the performance of teachers. We need to parry those who advocate disestablishment by paraphrasing Edmonds' (1979) rebuttal (1979, pp. 22–23):

> How many effective teaching and learning tactics or strategies would you have to see to be persuaded that teachers must be taught the technical, human, and conceptual skills of instruction? If your answer is more than one, then I submit that you have reasons of your own for preferring to believe that teachers are better trained by ignoring the existing body of systematic professional education and knowledge. (pp. 22–23)

THE STRUCTURAL AND DEMOGRAPHIC CONTEXT
OF TEACHER EDUCATION

Neither politicians nor the public advocate the disestablishment of an agency or a field that is not already viewed as unproductive and vulnerable to attack.

Proposition 2: The contemporary attack on the field of teacher education is especially pernicious and dangerous because this social process subfield has long-standing structural and demographic characteristics that have impaired its productive effectiveness.

Viewing the Ordinary Anew

Before turning to a brief enumeration of those structural characteristics, let me remind you that we are attempting to discover our roots and their implications in all-too-familiar ground. To demonstrate how difficult that task may be, I want to refer you to a recent set of proposals for reform in teacher education by Bruce Joyce and Renee Clift (1984), reforms they called "The Phoenix Agenda." Before framing some propositions for reform, Joyce and Clift attempted to enumerate the common complaints about the field thusly:

- Teacher education draws poor students. The situation is getting worse.
- Teachers believe that their training was (is) poor.
- Teacher education institutions are separated from the knowledge base of education.
- The current process of learning to teach socializes teachers to a "practicality ethic" where survival concerns dominate.
- The current process of learning to teach results in a funneling of teaching styles and a movement toward the persistent recitation approach to teaching. (1984, pp. 5-6)

You will note shortly that I will identify an overlapping but somewhat different list of flaws. What I wish to call to your attention, however, are not the specific complaints or the proposals of the Phoenix Agenda but the reaction they elicited from a distinguished member of the teacher education community. Asked to provide a commentary, he noted that Joyce, "makes the usual complaints about teacher education" and that his list of reforms is, "all too familiar" to "those who have participated in the reform discussions of the past 20 years" (Imig, 1984, p. 19). He observed that "the National Center for Educational Statistics recently documented that 94% of schools of education are currently in the midst of significant change" (which

Joyce had apparently not examined) and that the Phoenix Agenda proposals were "mainstream" rather than "radical," having already been endorsed by the American Association of Colleges for Teacher Education (Imig, 1984, p. 19).

This commentary on the Phoenix Agenda missed the point. The Joyce and Clift complaints about teacher education, and of course, those that I will add, are "usual" because they are "true." The reform proposals are "familiar" because they have been recommended by thoughtful persons for a half century and not implemented. The indictment of teacher education is that the consensus among well-informed observers about problems and solutions has been evident for so long and the movement to reform has been so miniscule. Today, right now, the proposal offered by Dean Henry Holmes for the Harvard Graduate School of Education is as fresh as it was in 1928, i.e.:

> America has yet to be persuaded that the training of teachers is a highly significant part of the making of the nation. In requiring two years of graduate study for the degree of Master of Education, we are testing the seriousness of our national faith in the schools. (p. 897)

That faith has not yet been tested. I challenge you to view the following demographic and cultural characteristics of the field as if you were considering them and their implications anew—as if they were, as they are, *critical* to reform in teacher eduation.

1. Institutional Proliferation. Teacher education is everybody's business. Over 70% of the 4-year colleges in the United States operate state-approved teacher training programs. A few of these programs are dreadful on all counts—liberal arts education, subject matter major, and professional preparation. Many are substandard on one or more of these dimensions. This pattern of proliferation (a) dilutes the modest personnel and fiscal resources of the field; (b) impedes reform efforts that require upgrading of professional standards at the institutional level; and (c) divorces the bulk of the training programs from centers of knowledge production about education. The omnipresence of teacher education in higher education is linked to four other characteristics of the field: (a) the lack of selectivity of teacher education candidates; (b) the placement of this teacher training at the undergraduate level; (c) the low level of fiscal support for teacher training; and (d) the lack of a tradition of scholarly inquiry in the field. This pattern of proliferation does not represent a commitment to prepare excellent teachers for America's schools on the part of most of these participating colleges. It represents a commitment to serve the needs of their individual undergraduate populations. The majority of these institutions offer only a baccalaureate degree, and they are caught up in teacher education because they wish to compete evenly with other colleges for high school graduates.

Their professional staffs are not involved typically in knowledge production in education.

The commentary on the Joyce and Clift agenda noted, "the National Center for Educational Statistics recently documented that 94% of schools of education [Ed.: that would be circa 1,100] are currently in the midst of significant change...Teacher educators are deeply involved in the business of qualitative change" (Imig, 1984, p. 19). That image is absurd. Qualitative change is inimical to the best interests of the modal institution in teacher education in the United States. These colleges do not have the additional resources to support significant qualitative change. They do not have the faculty to implement those changes. They will respond to change in student or program requirements as they have responded in the past—by adhering to the minimum level of the state's certification requirements for teachers. In teacher education, the bulk of the small programs do not represent, as they are often portrayed, diversity and richness in training opportunities for prospective teachers. They represent a bland sameness that covers the country with mediocrity in preparation programs for educational professionals.

The current glut of SCDEs is inexcusable. To defend these programs as if they represented a level of aspiration for the field is to miss the point of the current situation. Eliminating proliferation is a keystone to attacking the weaknesses of the field.

2. The Undergraduate Connection. Donna Kerr (1983) struck exactly the right note in observing, "To be understood, the content, standards, and control of teacher education must be placed within the inhospitable (sometimes hostile) environment of undergraduate education...Teacher education can only be as good as its placement on the undergraduate level allows, and that is not very good" (p. 133, 139).

Why is the undergraduate connection so debilitating? Firstly, it limits the life space for teacher education. There is no realistic possibility that the professional training period for secondary school teachers can ever be expanded, nor should it be, in competition with either a subject matter major or a liberal program of studies. Second, the connection limits expenditures on professional training. Undergraduate programs compete within narrow limits for resources, and teacher education loses out or, at best, breaks even. An even break is a substantial loss when one is comparing the expense of professional training against general education.

As important as any single reason for breaking the undergraduate connection, however, is the bond between undergraduate program placement and institutional proliferation. You cannot stop one without stopping the other. All baccalaureate institutions will insist on the privilege of offering teacher education for as long as any are able to offer it. If no teacher education is offered at the baccalaureate level, the competitive advantage in recruitment will not govern an institution's interest in teacher education.

The integrity of the bond between proliferation and undergraduate placement and the relationship of this bond to the scope, funding, and admission standards for teacher education argue that breaking the connection is a national, not a state-level, necessity. Individual states might gain modest advantages by moving to a 5th-year program (California seems to have demonstrated that). However, attitudes, standards, and policies toward a professional field are determined, as Dean Holmes suggested, by the "national faith" in the significance of the enterprise.

3. The Invisible Intervention. The secret that teacher educators carefully withhold from critics, reformers, and usually themselves is that there is no significant program for training secondary school teachers in the United States. There are no demonstrable differences between secondary school teachers trained in SCDEs and those who walk in off the streets, because there is no major difference in the undergraduate training programs that they pursue.

Imagine, now, that you are an undergraduate student preparing to become a secondary school teacher. Sometime during your 4-year undergraduate program, you will take four basic courses in education—perhaps an introductory course when you are a sophomore; an educatioal psychology course when you are a sophomore or junior; a general methods course as a junior; a special methods course in your subject matter major in your senior year. Some states may be requiring a course in reading instruction or special education or computer science, or even a peculiar local requirement, e.g., that state's history. However, the total course requirements will not begin to match an undergraduate major in a subject field. Is it any wonder that the eight weeks of student teaching sticks out in your mind as the only noteworthy part of the program? All the elements of a professional training program are missing: a concentrated period of study in the area of professional expertise; socialization to the profession through intensive work and discussion with other trainees; mentorship with a clinical professor committed to the success of the trainee as a beginning professional; a chance to practice the application of one's professional skills in a variety of settings and real-world conditions.

Elementary education trainees receive better opportunities in their programs. However, the shortcomings in their programs are still striking. An emphasis on professional education course-work is hacked out of their undergraduate program in such a way that few have subject matter majors. These trainees typically still have limited practicum experiences, a weak mentor-trainee relationship, and no period of concentrated professional study.

There is no need to compromise among a liberal arts education, a subject matter major, and professional training for American teachers. We can have all those components and at a reasonable cost per trainee. We do have to stop defending what we now have. The current intervention is so inadequate in breadth and depth that it is not worth further evaluation. Its genesis and survival have been an unfortunate compromise with mediocrity among the academic community, the organized teaching profession, and the public. Lack of life space for professional teacher education is smothering the aspiration for excellence in the field.

4. The Quality of Teacher Trainees. Nothing is simpler to effect in most teacher training programs than an adjustment in entrance standards. Current demographic trends would seem to indicate that some such moves may be necessary and justified. The profession has always drawn the bulk of its recruits from the bottom third of college graduates, but during the period 1973–1982, the decline in SAT, ACT, GRE, and NTE scores of intended education majors dropped more sharply than the university student population in general (Borkow & Jordan, 1983, pp. 11–13). While the socioeconomic status of teaching and the structure of the teaching workplace may never draw consistently from the top one third of college graduates in the United States, the field can hardly expect to reform its ills with a personpower pool of trainees who have exhibited minimal academic performance. Intellectual curiosity and the attainments of scholarship are the essence of the teacher's life. The past and current academic quality of teacher trainees has been insufficient to sustain a move toward excellence in teaching. And the quality of entry-level trainees has an extended impact on the pool from which leadership personnel can be drawn for local school districts, state education agencies, and SCDEs.

There is no point in acting as if the field has had, has, or will have a fair share of the full range of the talent pool of college graduates at its disposal. While a longer-range effort is underway to make the field more attractive to academically talented entrants, a shorter range set of tactics and strategies could be employed to avoid the worst consequences of working with a less-talented pool. For example, we could avoid:

- Spreading trainers wastefully across 1,200 sites.
- Housing teacher education programs in colleges and universities with poor general academic standards.
- Avoiding responsibility for minimal entrance and selective retention standards for trainees.
- Choosing less academically able candidates for teaching positions when the talent pool contains apparently more able recruits (Kerr, 1983, p. 129).
- Restricting advancement to leadership positions to individuals with extended teaching experience.
- Limiting the range of professional opportunities for teacher-leaders in an individual school to a single classroom.

• Losing the more able among our initial recruits by structuring the teaching workplace in a restrictive and oppresive fashion (Schlechty & Vance, 1981, p. 10).

5. **Funding Teacher Education.** Expenditures for teacher training are geared to the cost of general undergraduate academic programs. Kerr (1983, p. 136) noted that in a 1977–78 study of 20 universities using an index of 1.00 to represent undergraduate education at universities, teacher education compared with other undergraduate fields thusly:

teacher education, 1.04
agriculture, 1.51
engineering, 2.07
nursing, 2.74

This long-standing pattern of inadequate, preservice, undergraduate support for teacher education has been aggravated by master's level "in-service" programs that drew students in great numbers based on state certification requirements, were easy to package as self-contained courses, and were frequently staffed by part-time, low-cost professorial personnel. For two decades, from 1955 to 1975, colleges with minimal baccalaureate level commitments found that master's level programs of training for teachers were too lucrative not to add to their portfolio of offerings. Whereas in most fields undergraduate education is used by research universities to offset some of the costs of doctoral study, in teacher education both baccalaureate and master's level programs served this purpose.

Additional expenditures would not solve all of education's training difficulties, but underfunding a program that has other major disadvantageous structural and demographic characteristics is akin to providing the least support to public schools serving disadvantaged school populations. Neither strategy makes any sense as a public policy and the outcome of such a policy is unerringly predictable.

6. **Intrainstitutional Factors Affecting Teacher Education.** SCDEs exist within a broader college or university setting. That environment has not been congenial to the search for excellence in professional training. As has been noted, most of the instruction provided to the undergraduate trainee is offered by an arts and science unit in the university. This necessity for professional, substantive, and liberal education for teachers has led reformers to argue for a university-wide commitment to teacher education. Such a pipe dream faces none of the realities of the university as an organization; an organization in which undergraduate studies and professional training are each low prestige areas; in which teacher education is a low prestige professional field; and in which teaching "service courses" for

other areas is the lowest prestige teaching activity. Nothing is more highly valued in the university than a commitment to research and development. But teacher education has always maintained a tenuous connection with the scholarly community, emphasizing the wisdom of the practitioner at the expense of a commitment to inquiry.

Without castigating educationists or teacher educators, teacher education has earned empirically the reputation it abhors. Why would an observant professor of mathematics not be cognizant of the fact that few able undergraduate students seek out teacher education, that the requirements for teacher certification are low, that most of her/his "good" students could not afford to stay in the field, that the university policy makers devote limited resources to the area, and that most professors of education produce precious little research and scholarly writing? And why after observing this for years ought not the individual attribute low prestige to the venture and those who pursue it?

The difficulty of modifying the intrainstitutional affect toward teacher education is increased by the fact that college professors are teaching at various levels of effectiveness with little or no technical training as teachers. They are protected against a common deficiency in their own training by the argument that there is nothing necessary to learn about instruction—at least nothing that cannot be learned adequately on-the-job.

7. The Commonalty of Teacher Education. The charm that teacher education held earlier in this century as the route to the professions for the common person has become its fatal weakness. It is easily accessible in every sense of that term: geographically proximate to the consumer, easy to enter, short in duration, optimally convenient to the remainder of the college student's academic program, easy to complete, inexpensive, nonexclusive (i.e., does not rule out other career options), and, until very recently, almost certain to result in placement in a secure, respectable professional situation. Teacher education has become Everyman. The parts fit together in an harmoniously ineffective fashion.

Proposal 2

Reform for teacher education has to be based on some affective changes in the reform community. First, having rejected disestablishment as an option, we must repudiate any attempt to portray the present pattern of teacher education as adequate, or nearly so, or in the process of acceptable reform. Such claims are not credible and lead us to defend the indefensible. Second, we must be unrelenting advocates of a broadly conceived program of structual reform that will, in turn, support long-range improvement in the quality of teacher education students, faculty, and programs. This means rejecting the argument that no particular reform is a necessary condition to comprehensive reform. Some are critical. The critical reforms needed to disrupt the deadening commonalty that has been accepted for teacher education are achievable:

1. Limit entrance to teacher education programs to postbaccalaureate students who hold a liberal arts degree with a subject matter major.
2. Require a minimum of one academic year of concentrated study and practice leading to the master's degree for preservice teacher preparation.
3. Modify standards for state accreditation of teacher education programs to ensure that institutions offering such teaching can exhibit a program that is "systematically organized, research-based, and practitioner-oriented" (Gideonse, 1984).
4. Increase the level of intrainstitutional funding for teacher education programs to that characteristic of other comparable postbaccalaureate fields of training.
5. Restrict admission to teacher education programs to students who have exhibited a reasonable level of academic proficiency in undergraduate studies and who assert, and have exhibited, a commitment to service and achievement appropriate to a professional field.

If this modest reform package could be implemented, the demography of the field would change sharply. Teacher education would be carried out in 200 to 300 colleges and universities. Life space for concentrated study would be provided. The minimal conditions of professional preparation programs would be met. The quality of candidates and trainers would be on the upswing. Curricular improvement in professional training would be stimulated by the improved conditions for study.

Are these proposals sufficient? No, just necessary! They represent a starting point toward the reform of teaching. There never will be adequate answers to the quality dilemma in education until teaching is a more satisfactory career economically and professionally. However, the bright spot for teacher educators in the near future is the possibility that they can initiate changes that, in and of themselves, will improve the quality of teachers and teaching in America's schools. What is required is revolutionary; but it is a gentle revolution.

THE CONTEMPORARY POLITICAL CONTEXT OF TEACHER EDUCATION

I have chosen to separate the political context for teacher education from the affect currently surrounding the field. The latter I interpret as an unfocused but widespread sense that teacher education is part of the problem, not part of the solution, in searching for improved teaching quality in schools. The former are those acts and actions that allow observers to document how the affect is being acted upon at the national and state levels by policy makers. Let me, then, offer a proposition on this point:

Proposition 3: Teacher education is experiencing federal disengagement and heightened national attention. Disengagement reduces the capacity of the field to respond. The focus of national attention demands response.

Teacher education is further advanced in the process of federal disengagement than other subspecializations in education. Recall how quickly this picture has changed. Do you remember EPDA? The Education Professions Development Act put the lie to the myth that no federal program can ever be terminated. This comprehensive investment in the education professions disappeared so completely and quietly that no reference is made to its existence in the 1983 *Handbook of Teaching and Policy*. Remember Teacher Corps and the National Education Association's "proprietary" legislation in teacher training, teacher centers? There may be sporadic efforts on the horizon to provide fellowship support for teacher education in areas of special need, e.g., science and mathematics, but the best bet at the present is to assume that attention to teacher education at the national level, if it is to be addressed at all, will be addressed by national, non-governmental associations and agencies. Such national initiatives will be supplemented by executive and legislative actions at the state level and program action at individual institutions of higher education.

National Calls for Reform

None of the national educational reform proposals ignored teacher education. The Congressional Research Service (Jordan, 1983) chose five diverse reports and analyzed their recommendations about teacher preparation, certification, and teacher education institutions. The reports included the National Commission on Excellence in Education, the Twentieth Century Fund, the Education Commission of the States, the National Science Board, and the Carnegie Foundation for the Advancement of Teaching. I have tried to classify the recommendations from the reports under a set of headings that reflect a frame of analysis appropriate to this paper:

1. *Proposals for SCDE role modification of schools of education*
   a. Limit number of education courses
   b. Expand role of liberal arts college
   c. Provide alternative routes to certification
   d. Increase number of content courses
   e. Expand field involvement in program design
   f. Move to 5-year program with the 5th year concentrating on professional education and field experience

2. *Manipulation of standards for trainees*
   a. Increase standards for admitting students to teacher education programs
   b. Increase performance standards in teacher education programs
   c. Increase standards for completion of teacher education programs
   d. Add postprogram examinations of competency for teacher certification
3. *Financial support for teacher training*
   a. Provide funds for targeted recruitment efforts (especially science and mathematics)
   b. Increase scholarship and loan provisions for teacher education candidates

Some general observations may place these recommendations in perspective:

- Although not noted in this list, all the reports paid attention to the workplace for teachers, advocating various systems of teacher recognition and incentives, e.g., major salary adjustments, master teacher and career ladder plans, targeted stipends for travel and study grants.
- All the reports reflected dissatisfaction with SCDEs and included references that made clear that they distrusted these units to offer and monitor high-quality academic experiences for teacher trainees or to lead the needed reform efforts in teacher education.
- None of the reports recommended federal disengagement from education generally or teacher education in particular. The recommendations emanating from the reports suggested that the needed action should focus first at the state level as adjustments are made in program requirements and standards of admission to teacher education and teaching (issues of accreditation and certification), and second, at the institutional level where the changes are administered and operated at the point of effective action.

First-Round Reformations

Congress has concentrated its efforts at reform in teacher preparation on the passage of a bill to support precollegiate mathematics and science education programs, including teacher recruitment and training provisions. The Department of Education funded a task force called the National Commission on Excellence in Teacher Education—supporting a proposal made by the American Association of Colleges for Teacher Education. The Department also entered into the support of 51 projects in state and local education agencies, universities, and other educational institutions to help those units design incentive pay plans for teachers. The most intensive reform activity has been at the state level where by the end of 1983 state education agencies, special task forces, or the state legislatures were proposing (in order of frequency) loan and scholarship provisions for teacher trainees, modified admission standards to teacher education programs, competency testing for teacher certification, and alternative routes to teacher certification (Walton, 1983, pp. 5–17).

An Assessment

The political action climate surrounding teacher education is mercurial. The flash points are spread across the country in state education agencies, state legislatures, and governor's offices. Disestablishment is still a politically visible, low-cost response to dissatisfaction with teacher education. For example, as this essay was being written, Pennsylvania's State Board of Education has given tentative approval to an "intern certificate" that would allow teachers to be employed without education course requirements. These "interns" would be required to pass a new set of examinations for teachers, except for the "professional knowledge" section.

What will occur over the next several years at the state level is difficult to predict. The staff of the National Commission on Excellence in Education predicts an explosive level of activity. They noted that by November, 1983, there were 165 state-level task forces working on educational reform. Forty-two states had reported initiatives in teacher preparation and/or certification (U.S. Dept. of Education, 1983, pp. 5–6). One might assume that this level of activity would have a geometric impact in future years.

On the other hand, it is easy to overestimate likely state-level activity. Translating executive or legislative intent into state-level programs of action is a cumbersome and uncertain task. The danger lies in its uncertainty. Perhaps the future will see thoughtful, well-considered efforts on the part of states to improve teacher education. However there are factors that would lead to the conclusion that this path is a less likely future than some other options. Teacher training institutions are viewed with suspicion and are a vulnerable target without a powerful constituency. Disestablishment, creating alternative routes to teacher certification, and the arbitrary manipulation of standards for admission to teacher education and/or teaching are actions with great appeal. They can be enacted and implemented by state authority. They are immediate and forceful. They cost little or nothing.

Proposal 3

Federal disengagement from teacher education is succeeding. The only issue at stake is how much, how soon. This does not suggest, however, that teacher education has no investment in the Federal/national scene. There are moves that can be made at a national level that will help the field:

1. *Jump on the most acceptable reform report.* The Carnegie Report was right in recommending a strengthened 5-year program for teacher preparation (Boyer, 1983). Building on this recommendation with its emphasis on a concentrated 5th-year program, teacher educators should concentrate on implementing a fifth year, master's level requirement for preservice teacher education.
2. *Ignore the current administration.* Teacher education has no powerful friends in the Reagan administration. There is no point in our behaving contentiously with the administration. However, trying to cooperate actively will simply divert us from our problems.
3. *Use friends in Congress.* The House and Senate will temper the process of disengagement. At the least they are interested in assisting in teacher recruitment and in scholarship and loan programs in areas of shortage and national need.
4. *Form effective alliances with professional friends.* Teacher education does have friends among professional educationists. Some of these current and potential allies have significant bases of political support. We should concentrate our efforts on helping potential friends in the National Education Association, the American Federation of Teachers, the American Association of School Administrators, the National School Boards Association, and specialized constituency groups such as Council for Exceptional Children and American Vocational Association to become well-informed and concerned about the improvement of teaching through teacher education. We have an honest chance to inform and convert our friends.
5. *Create national reform coalitions among teacher educators.* This is no time to hesitate to go beyond regularly constituted associations. The American Association of Colleges for Teacher Education and the Association of Teacher Educators have internal political constraints on their activities that limit their effectiveness on particular issues in particular time periods. Groups such as the Association of Colleges and Schools of Education in State Universities and Land Grant Colleges (ACSESULGC) and the ad hoc group of deans in "influential" universities that has been meeting at the Wingspread Conference Center are not similarly constrained. For the next decade much of the national leadership and spokespersonship will have to be assumed by the latter groups.
6. *Win one major national battle.* Focus on a concerted effort by the 50 states to move teacher education to a fifth-year (not 5-year) program. With the assistance of nationally recognized reformers, and

in combination with the Council of Chief State School Officers, National Conference of State Legislators, Education Commission of the States, National Governors' Association and the nationally based organizations of teachers and administrators, leaders in teacher education could make this change in program accreditation and teacher certification *the* reform of the 1980s.

Surely, however, the focus of action in teacher education has moved from the federal to the state level. Item 6 already noted one strategy teacher educators should employ in adjusting to this change. We should work diligently to highlight national concerns as the context within which state actions need to be taken. Policy options that are discussed and considered by state leaders in their national forums are more likely to reflect state-of-the-art information for policy makers than isolated state proposals. Teacher education needs the formation of intrastate coalitions and alliances that parallel those recommended in items 4 and 5.

SUMMARY

To this point, I have argued that:

1. We need to restore a sense of efficacy to teacher trainees, teacher educators, and the field of teacher education. We need to draw the line intellectually and politically against the nihilists.
2. We need to mount a reformist platform to redress critical, malleable, structural conditions in teacher education, i.e., reducing the number of SCDEs, moving teacher education out of undergraduate education, expanding the scope, power, and intensity of the teacher education training program, and increasing the fiscal support for professional preparation in teaching.
3. We need to join with our informed and friendly critics at the national and state levels to push a form of the Boyer plan, expand scholarship support, and create a lasting, broad-based coalition of concerned support for improvement in teacher education.

END NOTE

This entire analysis has assumed two propositions to be self-evident: (a) that there is and will continue to be a growing body of knowledge about teaching that, if communicated effectively to teachers, will affect positively the performance of teachers, and (b) that teacher education as a field of study and practice can and should flourish in inquiry-based departments of education committed to research, teaching, and school improvement. I would argue that anyone contesting either of these propositions is only pointing out limitations in current practice that can and will be overcome.

I believe that anyone accepting these propositios needs to go on to accept a special obligation to make them "true," i.e.:

- *To pursue with renewed vigor the linking of research on teaching, teacher effectiveness, and teacher education to teacher educators.* The current diffusion of research on teaching to classroom teachers can be argued to be more widespread than the diffusion of research on teaching to teacher educators. The critical contention that the university not only can but must train teachers assumes that university-based programs will integrate the burgeoning knowledge base about teaching with its teacher preparation program. The assumption that fewer sites for teacher education in knowledge producing institutions is integral to reform in teacher education relies on the integrity of knowledge production and knowledge use. That is our business.

- *To recommit ourselves to the tradition of scholarship and scholarly productivity in SCDEs.* The charge that the bulk of the baccalaureate institutions operating teacher education programs are divorced from the scholarly community rings hollow when many university sites are unproductive R&D centers. We must model the behavior we insist is necessary by increasing the quality and quantity of research productivity and integrating research and instructional programs.

- *To extend the scope of inquiry activity to include policy research and program-linked development activity.* Teacher education researchers have a special obligation to support the critical rebuttal of the nihilists in the policy arena. They need to increase their attention to research designed to generate policy options for teacher education (we have few now), to predict and then assess the outcomes of policy alternatives, monitor the field (both through census studies and evaluations of outcomes), and attend to the dissemination of accurate and compelling information to policy makers and practitioners.

- *To increase the level of outcomes-based development inquiry focused on teacher training programs.* If we are not designing and evaluating knowledge-based innovations, our work is incomplete. This emphasis on the "D" portion of R&D will assist us in (a) linking research on teaching to teacher educators; (b) generating policy alternatives; and (c) asserting a tradition of the necessity of scholarship in this field.

Proposition 4. If reformist teacher educators insist on conducting programs of reform within the present contexture for the professional preparation of teachers, they will fail. The failure to effect reform will lead ineluctably to an apprentice-style training program for teachers divorced from the university and the knowledge base about teaching.

Our current reform movements are in a nascent stage. They need to be pushed vigorously and quickly. No temporizing arguments, tactics, or strategies mounted for personal, political, or professional reasons should be brooked. Teacher education used up its slack time for reform over the past quarter century. Now we need basic structural reform.

REFERENCES

Averch, H., Carroll, S., Donaldson, T., Kiesling, H., & Pincus, J. (1972). *How effective is schooling? A critical review and synthesis of research findings.* Santa Monica, CA: Rand Corporation.

Borkow, N., & Jordan, K. F. (1983, November 7). *The teacher workforce: Analysis of issues and options for federal action* (Report No. 83-5775). Washington, DC: Congressional Research Service: The Library of Congress.

Boyer, E. (1983). *High school: A report on secondary education in America.* New York: Harper & Row.

Coleman, J. (1966). *Equality of educational opportunity.* Washington, DC: U.S. Government Printing Office.

Edmonds, R. (1979). Effective schools for the urban poor. *Educational Leadership, 37*(1), 15–24.

Gideonse, H. (1984, April 20). Memorandum to Association of Colleges and Schools of Education in State Universities and Land Grant Colleges members.

Holmes, H. (1928). The training of teachers and the making of a nation. *Proceedings of the Sixty-sixth Annual Meeting of the National Education Association, 66,* 897–906.

Imig, D. (1984). A commentary. *Educational Researcher, 13*(4), 18–19.

Jordan, K. F. (1983). *Comparison of recommendations from selected education reform reports.* Washington, DC: U.S. Department of Education, 1983. (Reprinted from Congressional Research Service: Library of Congress).

Joyce, B., & Clift, R. (1984). The Phoenix agenda: Essential reform in teacher education. *Educational Researcher, 13*(4), 5–18.

Kerr, D. (1983). Teaching competence and teacher education in the United States, In S. Shulman & G. Sykes (Eds.), *Handbook of teaching and policy,* New York: Longman.

Schlechty, P., & Vance, V. (1981). Do academically able teachers leave education? The North Carolina case. *Phi Delta Kappan, 63*(2), 106–112.

Toch, T. (1984, May 16). Education courses waived for teachers in New York City. *Education Week, 3,* 1, 18.

U.S. Departmeant of Education. (1983, November). *Meeting the challenge: Recent efforts to improve education across the nation.* Washington, DC: U.S. Dept. of Education.

Walton, S. (1983, December). States' reform efforts increase as focus of issues shifts. *Education Week, III*(13), 5–18.

2

Undergraduate Students' Perceptions of Field Experiences: Toward a Framework for Study

Jane H. Applegate

Kent State University

Field experiences are widely accepted as a principal means for learning to teach. Both practicing teachers and students in preparation programs believe that experiencing a classroom of pupils first-hand is necessary and may be sufficient for teacher education. Increasingly field experiences are being added to traditional course work in philosophy and history of education and educational psychology as well as to general and special methods courses. Students point to these experiences as the lifeblood of their programs. Though teacher educators have accepted and proliferated more and earlier field experiences, they frequently wonder what these experiences teach. For the purposes of this discussion "early field experiences" refer to those experiences which occur in school settings prior to student teaching. Research on early field experiences is still relatively limited. Most of the empirical work completed on early field experiences has depended (perhaps unintentionally) upon students' perceptions of those experiences. The perceptions that students develop throughout their preparation to teach result from the interactions they have with people, from courses they take, and from the experiences they have in schools. Such perceptions may form the basis of attitudes and values about teaching, undergird teaching perspectives, and guide decision-making about classroom practice for years to come.

The purpose of this chapter is to review two areas of study which may contribute to further understanding of students' perceptions of field experiences. These areas—influences which shape perception and results from previous studies of students' perceptions—may be useful in building a framework to guide future study.

To begin this review, let's first look at a typical field experience in teacher education:

Pat enrolled in "Introduction to Education" in her first semester in college. The course was designed to acquaint prospective teachers with school life from the teacher's point of view. To accomplish that goal students were placed with practicing teachers 3 hours a day for 10 weeks. During the remaining weeks of the semester students discussed what they had done and what they learned from the experience. When Pat learned about the time she would spend in school she was thrilled. Pat had wanted to teach high school English since her class with Ms. Wilson in the ninth grade. Because of the memory of that experience, she requested a ninth-grade English class for her field assignment. Instead Pat was placed with a fourth-grade teacher in a self-contained classroom. When she voiced disappointment to her professor, she was told that at this point in her career she needed a broad experience and that since there were mostly elementary education majors in her class, all students had been placed in one elementary building. That way they would have one another for support.

They all went together on the first visit to the school, met the principal, and toured the building. They were told that they were to assist the teacher with any projects assigned. They were also told to keep a journal about the experience. For the next 10 weeks, Pat went to the building each afternoon. On the third day her teacher sent her home to change clothes. The teacher told her if she wanted to be a teacher she must dress like one. Her typical college-student jeans and sweater would not be appropriate. To Pat this meant she'd have to go back to her dorm after her 11:00 a.m. art class and change clothes every day. She'd also have to ask for more money from her parents for new clothes. The rest of the week she observed the teacher. She also observed the second week and the third. She looked at the fourth graders, she looked at text books, she looked at bulletin boards, desks, windows, plants, and the floor.

Pat was bored. She finally called her professor and told her what was happening. The professor advised Pat to ask the teacher if there was anything she could do to help. Pat felt the teacher didn't like her or she would have already included her in classwork. Nevertheless, she would do as the professor suggested. The teacher gave Pat some spelling papers to grade; she also asked her to take inventory of the science equipment and clean the science center. Everyday for the next 3 weeks Pat graded papers—homework papers, quiz papers, practice papers, and tests. She never knew teachers assigned so much paperwork or that students spent so much time working with paper. The teacher seemed pleased that Pat was doing the grading. Pat secretly wondered how the teacher knew what the pupils were accomplishing if she graded all the papers.

With 2 weeks left in her field experience the teacher asked Pat if she would like to teach a lesson. Pat was terrified. What would she teach?

How would she do it? Should she try to teach like the regular teacher or should she try to do something which was comfortable to do? The teacher asked Pat to bring a lesson plan to her the next day. A lesson plan? What's that? What should she do? Who could she talk to about this? Pat called home. She asked her mother if she could drop out of school. She was not ready to be a teacher. She tried to remember what she had done as a fourth-grader. How had her teacher taught her? Was there anything memorable about the fourth grade? Yes. She remembered once the teacher gave everyone in the class a picture clipped from the newspaper with no title or caption. She had to write a story about the picture. That would do. Pat wrote down the idea and took it to the teacher. The teacher talked through the idea with Pat. How much time would the lesson take? What materials would she need? What did she want students to learn from this activity? How would she grade the finished papers? Pat didn't know there were so many decisions to make. The next week she taught her lesson. The fourth graders were responsive; they seemed especially well behaved. Pat's enthusiasm was restored. She had taught her first class in her first semester of college. She felt successful, but she knew she had a lot to learn.

After the experience she thought about the 10 weeks she had spent in that classroom. She wished she had been allowed to do more than grade papers. But she didn't really know if she felt ready to do much more. Sitting in the back of the room was comfortable. Being in front of the class was scary. She surely didn't have enough memories from childhood to keep her in lesson plans for the rest of her life. The university professor asked many questions about the experience that Pat had not considered: What were the pupils' interests and abilities? Did the teacher have routines that were followed? How did the teacher deal with misbehavior? Were handicapped pupils or minority pupils treated differently than others? How did the curricula reflect the values of the community? What special skills did the teacher have? Did the teacher enjoy her work? What extra school duties did the teacher have? Do you still want to be a teacher? Pat had more to think about. Though her attitude about becoming a teacher was more tentative than it had been initially, Pat decided to stay in the teacher education program. She received an "A" in the course.[1]

Pat's experience is not unlike the experiences of other students in field-based courses. For her, the experience brought new personal and professional insights. From the initial placement to the concluding reality of teaching a class, perceptions of self, school, profession, and program were gathered and sorted. As noted by Fuller and Bown (1975), the experience of becom-

---

[1] The case was compiled from the anonymous writings of students, cooperating teachers, and university faculty members as part of the Applegate and Lasley research as well as from the author's observations.

ing a teacher involves coping with three types of perceptions: internal perceptions, or feelings and motives, self-observation, or awareness of self in situation, and external self-evaluation, or sense of competence. The student in field experiences gathers all three types of perceptions. For Pat, expressions of those perceptions came through conversations with others and the writing she did in her journal. Inferences were drawn and decisions made. The impact of the experience forced a confrontation with past and present simultaneously. Private feelings and hunches became public. Reflection on the experience created an awareness about herself as a teacher that had not previously existed.

But what knowledge can be drawn from Pat's perceptions of her field experience? What has she learned? What influenced the perceptions she reported? How did her report of those perceptions affect the meaning she gave to them? How can her experience and those of others in teacher preparation be useful in shaping future knowledge about field experiences? Consider what might have influenced her perceptions of that experience.

INFLUENCES WHICH SHAPE STUDENTS' PERCEPTIONS

A field experience as part of teacher preparation is in many ways like other experiences designed to affect human thought and behavior. Consider, for example, a visit to an art gallery. When an individual tours a gallery he is surrounded by a set of sensations from which meanings are formed. For an individual, some art is attractive; other art is not. Judgments made about the value of a work for an individual arise from several influences. Aestheticians may point to technique, culture, history, medium, fantasy or personal attributes of the artist himself to shape the judgments made in relationship to the art object (see Coleman, 1968, for a description of aesthetic judgments). Likewise when undergraduate students in teacher education enter field experiences several factors influence students' perceptions of those experiences.

First, university students bring to field experiences a level of understanding and a degree of mastery of the *techniques or skills of teaching.* Can they write lesson plans? Can they organize a sequence of instruction? Can they write on the board legibly? Can they operate a film projector? Can they develop appropriate computer software to complement a reading lesson? Can they reinforce appropriate student behavior? Whatever teaching skills are taught by teacher education programs and whatever degree of competence and confidence students hold may affect perceptions of field experiences. Many people interested in teaching as a career have had a variety of experiences working with children or youth prior to entry into formal teacher preparation. Whether they have worked in summer playground programs, taught crafts on weekends to neighborhood children, or volunteered assistance in day-care centers, students of teaching are developing their teaching skills without formal instruction or feedback. If a student has had no technical training, what are appropriate expectations for field experiences that are part of formal preparation? If a student has completed 80% of his professional course work, should those expectations be different? The technical mastery of teaching skills and the expectations held by university instructors and cooperating teachers as well as by the students themselves may shape perceptions of the experience.

A second consideration is the *culture* within which the experience occurs. For teacher education students in field experiences, an understanding of two cultures is required: the culture of the university and the culture of the school. University students have a special set of characteristics defined by the university experience. For freshmen, there is often a separation from the past, a new living environment, a new peer group, a new set of roles and expectations. Likewise at each level of university life new challenges are posed: getting course work sequenced, meeting grade requirements, securing part-time employment, looking for a mate, becoming self-sufficient. The perceptions of university students about course work or career may be influenced by maturation and life transitions. Likewise, when the university student enters the public school classroom, teachers and administrators in the building may assume the university student knows all there is to know about school life. The culture of the school requires a particular set of behaviors from its professional staff. Such attributes as time, dress, parking places, and the types of subjects discussed in the teachers' lounge are all part of a school's norms and standards. Such cultural attributes and the degree to which teacher education students can grasp them may influence perceptions of the experience as well.

University students also bring with them to field experiences *personal histories* related to schooling. Perceptions about teaching and learning have been evolving since the early years of life. Expressed perceptions about current experiences in schools may be reflections of past experiences. Criticism or praise expressed about an experience may be a result of unconscious comparison with one's own schooling experience. Even the memory of teachers in earlier years can influence the choice of teaching as a career or the behaviors that students demonstrate during field experiences. One's traditions shape expectations. If, for example, a teacher education student has had experiences as a pupil with particular methods of discipline, then those previous experiences may have some impact on the way the university student interacts with pupils during his own field experiences.

A fourth consideration which might influence perceptions is the *image* one holds of teachers and teaching. Both consciously and subconsciously people collect and store images of teachers beginning early in life. Teachers are central characters in books for young children; they are frequently portrayed on television in both humor and drama. Much writing has been done about teachers and the conditions of schools in the popular press. Talk of teachers and schools occurs around dinner tables. Visual and verbal images are formed and may affect the expectations students hold about the teachers and teaching. When university students enroll in field-based courses they may imagine themselves as a Kotter or Coach Reeves. Their perceptions of the field experiences may draw upon the best or the worst, depending upon the images they hold.

A fifth set of influences on one's perceptions is the *personal attributes* of the individual. The sum total of what one brings to an experience—a person's intelligence, health, age, cognitive style, values, personality, gender, motivation, interests and abilities—all play some part in capturing sensations and making meaning from them. Notably the works of Kohlberg (1969); Harvey, Hunt, and Schroeder (1961), Perry (1970), and Loevinger (1976) have provided new theoretical frameworks with which to view the personal attributes of prospective teachers. The studies of Schlechty and Vance (1983) have focused upon demographic and academic characteristics. Perry's work intimated a relationship between cognitive development and personality development; he also suggested that a prospective teacher's cognitive complexity may affect the way in which perceptions about classroom activities are gathered. Hunt (1977) determined that prospective teachers learn differently and that the way teachers learn can significantly influence the ways they teach. Schlechty and Vance (1983) have looked at trends in the academic ability of prospective teachers and suggest that students in teacher preparation are less able than their counterparts studying other disciplines. The perceptions gathered by students during field experiences are undoubtedly affected by their personal attributes.

A final set of influences which may affect students' *reported* perceptions is *the way perceptions are gathered.* Just as the art enthusiast is attracted to and repelled by particular media, so, perhaps, may the student in a field experience be attracted to or repelled by the methods researchers use to study students' perceptions. Several different research strategies have been used with differing effects. Largely studies of students' perceptions have been descriptive compilations of opinions, self-reports, and subjective judgments. The most frequently used method for data gathering has been the questionnaire. (See, for example, Yarger, Howey, and Joyce, 1977; Morrow and Lane, 1983; and Gantt and Davey, 1973). The use of questionnaires has allowed educational researchers to gather a great deal of information from students in a relatively short amount of time. Researchers may influence students' perceptions through the questions they ask. Whether students have considered the attribute of social interaction in a high school classroom or not, if asked on a questionnaire to rate the quality of social interaction observed during their field experience, they are more likely than not to respond to the item. Perceptions have also been gathered through personal interviews. (See, for example, Fuller, 1969, and Thompson, 1982.) Through face-to-face dialogue questions about hopes, aspirations, and anxieties can be asked in such a way as to elicit accurate information. The interview also permits probing into the context and reasons for answers to questions. Again, the questions interviewers ask are critical. In an interview situation the verbal fluency of the student may affect the student's response. A student who might not trust the interviewer or might not feel comfortable in the interview context may color the perceptions verbalized to give the interviewer what the student thinks he/she may want. A third strategy for eliciting students' perceptions has been personal writing. (See, for example, Applegate & Lasley, 1983, 1984a). Students are frequently asked to keep journals, diaries or logs of their activities and perceptions during field experiences. But for research purposes open-writing, journal keeping or recording critical incidents are somewhat controversial as tools for data collection. Because some sudents are not comfortable writing and because rules for data analysis are frequently disputed, open writing as data is less frequently used. Each of these methods has its own strengths and shortcomings. In the study of students' perceptions of field experiences the methods used are not neatly fixed. It is important, though, to consider the relative impact that method may have on breadth and depth of data gathered, that medium may influence perception.

These six types of influences may direct both students' interpretations of events and researchers' interpretations of perceptual data. When students describe or judge an event which took place as part of a field experience, with which lens are they viewing? Likewise, as researchers analyze and interpret findings from studies of students' perceptions, are their assumptions clear? The range of circumstances, variables, and stances toward working with perceptual information present difficult challenges to educational researchers and teacher educators. For students' perceptions to be valued and valid, these types of influences must be considered.

WHAT STUDIES TELL ABOUT STUDENTS' PERCEPTIONS OF FIELD EXPERIENCES

Findings from studies of students' perceptions can be clustered into four domains: what students tell about themselves, what students tell about the schools in which they work, what students tell about the profession of teaching, and what students tell about their preparation for teaching.

What Students Tell About Themselves

My experience in the school today was so confusing. I don't know now if teaching is for me. I went into the classroom prepared to work with a reading group, and the teacher sent me on errands all over the building to gather equipment he needed for a science lesson later in the day. Other teachers in the building treated me like a go-fer. I really felt like I didn't belong.

When students in teacher education programs reflect upon their early experiences in schools much of what they say is related to themselves. The studies of Fuller (1969) demonstrated that student teachers have concerns with self. Students entering teaching are concerned about survival: "Where do I stand? How adequate am I? How do others think I'm dong?" (Fuller, 1969, p. 214).

Ironically, though, according to the study of Book, Byers, and Freeman (1983), students entering teacher education programs expressed a relatively high level of confidence in their overall ability to teach immediately: "Some 24% stated that they were highly or completely confident in their ability to teach ... This level of confidence is bothersome in that it supports the idea that many students do not feel a need for professional knowledge to be successful" (p. 10). Perhaps one thing field experiences do for students is help students examine self-confidence, realistically assess the teacher's role, and review teaching as a career choice.

Different hypotheses were offered by both Scherer (1979) and Hardy and Mershon (1981) with regard to confidence. Scherer studied the relationship between early field experience and student teachers' self-concept and performance. She wanted to see if early field experiences affected subsequent performance in student teaching and if self-concept was a predictor of performance. Her findings indicated that students who participated in early field experiences had more and earlier self-doubt at the *beginning* of student teaching but at the conclusion of student teaching had significantly less self-doubt; also the self-esteem of the field experience group was significantly higher. No differences were found on performance ratings. Hardy and Mershon (1981) tested students' perceptions of learning preference against preference for field-based coursework. They found that students who selected field-based courses perceived themselves as more independent and collaborative in their learning styles. Students in field-based courses were found to be more confident in their learning abilities, more cooperative, and more interested in working with others.

Thompson (1982) in interviews with 113 students at different points in their teacher preparation found that gains in self-knowledge were a major outcome of field experiences. When students were asked, "What did you learn from your field experiences?" a major category of responses was "understanding of self." Typical comments listed were, "I gained confidence in myself," "I learned more about myself with the interaction with students," "I have found out I really want to be a teacher" (p. 19). She concluded by speculating that "perhaps early field experience provides a vehicle for the development of self-knowledge and self-confidence" (p. 27).

In support of that speculation, Applegate and Lasley (1983) found that, in fact, students expect that field experiences will be a vehicle for self-study. When students were asked to express their expectations for forth-coming field experiences, they described the experience as an opportunity to better understand their own abilities, affirm their career choice, develop their confidence, and test their implicit theories about teaching.

Together these studies indicate that students perceive field experiences as an opportunity to learn about themselves, to explore career decisions, to test their confidence, and to assess their skill levels. It is not clear, at this point, how these learnings are accomplished, only that in students' eyes they are. It appears that the assessment of confidence in teaching is ambiguous, though important. Are field experiences useful in developing confidence or are students who participate in field experiences the confident students? Is the relationship between confidence and performance worth pursuing? Students seem to believe feeling confident about one's ability to teach is necessary for success.

What Students Tell About the Schools in Which They Work

> I wish everyone could see the classroom where I was assigned for my field experience. The teacher is *neat*. Everything is in its place. The bulletin boards are perfect, the desks are perfect, the children sit perfectly. It almost doesn't seem natural for fourth graders to be so good. Mrs. Pierce really has everything under control.

Students in field experiences also gather perceptions about the schools, pupils, and teachers with whom they work. Thompson (1982) found that second to learnings about self, students reported that field experiences gave the opportunity to gain "real world" knowledge. That knowledge took three categorical forms: (a) understanding differences and similarities in pupils; (b) knowledge of the teaching process; and (c) development of ability to work with other adults. Such statements as, "I saw a wide range of student abilities," "I saw the day-to-day situations a classroom teacher faces," "Teaching involves a lot of clerical work," and "I learned how to get along with fellow teachers" were typical of those reported by students in her study.

Harp (1974), building upon Fuller's thesis, suggested that earlier field experiences would provide a basis for earlier role acceptance. His study focused upon the relationship between early field experiences and the concerns of students preparing to become teachers. Fuller's "concerns statements" were administered at different time intervals during a freshman field experience. The results of the study indicated that the concerns of students matured significantly during the full quarter of the experience. More frequent concerns about pupils and their progress were evident in statements such as these: "I am concerned that children are not having enough opportunity to be creative and imaginative" and "Slower students are placed in slower groups but little help is available for each student" (Harp, 1974, p. 372).

In a different type of study, Poole (1972) wanted to identify particular elements of students' perceptions of field experience through an analysis of students' reports of their experiences in schools. A questionnaire focusing upon students' experiences with cooperating teachers, with the principal of the school, with other staff, with the physical arrangements within the school, and with contacts with fellow students was developed. A factor analysis of the data gathered from 523 students revealed six categories of perceptions: experience of a well-organized, supportive situation; experience of criticism; good working relationships with other staff; lack of support; good working relationship with fellow students; and good, informed working relationships with cooperating teacher and pupils. Of these factors, the establishment of a good working relationshp with all people involved in the situation was determined as the most important learning from the field experience.

Applegate and Lasley (1983, 1984a) in their studies of expectations and problems of students in early field experiences noted that the expectations students hold and the problems students express are very different. In the study of students' expectations, six factors were identified: expectations for assessing the profession, expectations for observing models of professional practice, expectations for acquiring insights and ideas, expectations for practicing teaching skills, expectations for understanding various school and classroom settings, and expectations for dealing directly with students. The researchers concluded that many of these expectations which deal with the activities of teaching were shaped by the expectations of college faculty. That is, if teacher educators expect students to observe particular phenomena or practice particular skills, that is what students think they will learn and do. Reported problems by students following field experiences suggest that students' actual learnings are quite different from their expected learnings. The 7-factor analysis of reported problems indicated that students in field experiences had the following problems: (a) problems with managing students; (b) problems working with the cooperating teacher; (c) problems dealing with the specific needs of students; (d) problems dealing with students' time problems; (e) problems timing and pacing students' activities; (f) problems with workload; and (g) problems with clear communication. While expectations were highly related to the tasks of teaching, problems were primarily focused upon interpersonal relationships. Students never anticipated problems with pupils, yet much of their writing focused upon that particular area of concern.

When these studies are synthesized, one can see that as students describe what they are learning about schools and pupils, these learnings are heavily influenced by interpersonal relationships. Students' reports are of observations and interactions with the people in the setting. Their talk is primarily about the pupils in the classroom. Perhaps that is because that role remains their strongest identity. Virtually nothing is said about curriculum. What is taught is either not noticed or is taken for granted in the given situation. Little is said about instructional strategies, except in relationships to pupil conduct or interest. The affective nature of the classroom takes precedence over the cognitive.

What Students Tell About the Profession of Teaching

> The teacher I'm working with is always on the go. I don't think she sits down all day. Even between classes she's working. Yesterday she ate lunch during a committee meeting and then stayed after school to coach volleyball. At that pace, I don't know how I'll make it.

A third cluster of perceptions reported by teacher education students is about the profession of teaching. Perceptions in this area seem different from those gathered about the acts of teaching; what teachers do is somewhat different from what it means to be a teacher. Book, Byers, and Freeman (1983) included in their assessment of students entering teacher education programs a series of questions about the goals of teachers. Students were asked to rank order the following goals in terms of importance: student achievement, student self-concept, and classroom environment: "The number of students who believed that enhancing students' self-concepts was the most important goal (of a teacher) was considerably higher than the corresponding number who selected promoting academic achievement and nearly double the number who selected creating a good learning environment" (Book et al., 1983, p. 11).

Gibson's (1976) study of the effects of field experiences on the development of perspectives about teaching pointed to field experiences as central to socialization into the teaching profession. Eighteen students were interviewed 17 times during their 3-year preparation program. Particular emphasis was given to questions about field experiences, expectations, impressions, preparation, and learning. Students reported that teaching was physically and mentally exhausting and that they felt generally unprepared for teaching, seeing little relationship between college course work and school activity. Students reported attempting to behave in the classroom in a way they thought was expected of them by the school and college rather than doing what they thought appropriate. In concluding, Gibson (1976) stated, "It is clear from this study that the majority of students are able to visualize themselves as teachers before entering college. The process of professional socialization is such as to give sharper focus to this identification, but also to expose the student to experiences during training which cause her to question her identification and commitment" (p. 249).

While Thompson (1982) noted it difficult to separate statements about "commitment to the profession" from statements about "knowledge of the 'real world' of teaching," comments related to learning from field experiences about the profession of teaching were these: "Teaching is more than an 8:00–3:00 routine," "Teaching is a very demanding field and requires a lot of energy," and "I do realize now there is more to be learned, and this will come with further experience."

Field experiences provide students contact with practicing teachers. Those teachers, in turn, give students glimpses of the teaching life. Students soon realize that there is more to teaching than giving and getting information. The notion of professionalism, though, is still spurious. Students see it related to time, energy, enthusiasm, and commitment. Again, affect and satisfaction seem to be a pervading theme from students' perceptions.

What Students Tell About Their Preparation for Teaching

> Yesterday the professor in social studies methods told us to practice probing questions during our field assignment today. I wasn't really sure what he meant by that, but when I got to the classroom and told my cooperating teacher what I was supposed to do, he laughed and told me not to worry. Any question would be fine. I still don't know what a probing question is, but I guess that's not important. What is important is being out in the school doing something.

A final cluster of perceptions reported by teacher education students relates to the preparation program for teaching. As stated by Newlove and Fuller (1971), "Prospective teachers, convinced that teaching is the most practical experience of all, beg for classroom experience in their education courses" (p. 335). Much of the research in this area has focused upon the impact of programs on people rather than the impact of people on programs. Teacher educators have traditionally viewed students as passive and receptive; the integration of field experiences into courses and programs has encouraged students, to some degree, to become more active in their development as teachers.

Cooper (1983) described six types of data collected for the purpose of program evaluation: (a) teacher characteristics and demographic data; (b) teacher effectiveness; (c) program effectiveness; (d) program characteristics; (e) contextual variables; and (f) pupil outcomes. When reviewing studies about students' perceptions of field experiences, students refer primarily to program effectiveness.

Yarger, Howey, and Joyce (1977) gathered perceptual data from over 2,200 students in 175 teacher-training institutions about their preparation to teach. As part of the study, students reported seeing cooperating teachers and college supervisors as quite similar in educational experience and views concerning education: "Particular congruence was noted in the perceived views of both groups concerning the amount of time that should be spent in student teaching, the evaluation of student teachers, views of the teacher education program and views concerning innovation . . . Students perceive they are evaluated jointly by the cooperating teacher and the college supervisor, and they believe that the evaluation is based upon their ability to demonstrate teaching skills" (Yarger et al., 1977, p. 35). In addition, with regard to supervision of field-based course work, this study noted that students perceived no consistency in supervision and that much of the supervision was casual. Again, the study reinforced the perceived value of student teaching as the most critical part of their preparation.

Even before students are engaged in teacher preparation they have culled expectations about the way they should be prepared. Book, et al. (1983) found in their study that students expect on-the-job training and supervised teaching experiences to be the most valuable sources of their professional knowledge. From a rank-ordered list students indicated that their third choice would be preparation in their major field of study; fourth, courses in instructional methods; fifth, courses in educational psychology; sixth, their own experiences as K–12 students; seventh, self-directed reading; and finally, courses in the social–philosophical foundations of education.

During teacher preparation students are frequently asked perceptions or reactions to particular phases of their programs. Researchers look at effects of one type of program approach on subsequent courses. Marso (1971) wanted to see if students participating in field-based course work would have different attitudes toward their teacher preparation than those who participated in traditional campus-based courses. He also wanted to see if student achievement would be consistent between the two groups. Daily logs were kept by students in the field-based program. Both groups were given the Minnesota Teacher Attitude Inventory and a self-constructed opinion scale about teacher preparation. Marso (1971) concluded that students in the field-based program:

> had many relevant and meaningful experiences that favorably increased their attitude toward teaching and students; led them to rate more highly their senior education block courses, to consider teaching in slum–poverty-type schools, to feel more sure of their decision to teach or not to teach; and made them feel more prepared to be a teacher. All of this occurred without any apparent loss of academic achievement in the traditional sense (p. 198)

Hedberg (1979) shared similar questions in his study of the effects of field experiences on achievement in educational psychology. He looked at the achievement levels of two groups of students enrolled in an educational psychology course, one section of which was field-based, the other campus-based. There were no significant differences between the groups on an examination constructed to measure knowledge, comprehension, and application of psychological concepts. Students in the field-based course perceived it positively enhancing their group of psychological concepts and their applications.

Students' perceptions of field experiences are also gathered from students as recent graduates through follow-up studies. One example of such a study was conducted by Lynch and Kuehl (1979) who studied responses of 120 graduates to a question about changes recommended for program improvement. Former students voiced opinions about what they thought of their professional preparation and about what they thought of teaching as a career. With regard to their preparation program, field experiences were mentioned as the most important component of the program. Former students were critical of overlapping content in both general education and professional education classes and suggested more time in field experiences in place of some required education courses. Graduates also suggested that university professors associate with teachers in public schools more frequently in order to "ensure relevancy and make preservice and inservice university coursework more meaningful" (Lynch & Kuehl, 1979, p. 21).

Students anticipate experience as part of their preparation to teach. They know they will have it, they look forward to it, they value it and after they leave the college campus they recount it as the most significant part of their program. Unfortunately, research to date, has not gotten much beyond describing students' satisfaction with the experience.

A SYNTHESIS AND A SUMMARY

Presented in this chapter were two areas useful for the design of a framework to guide the study and interpretation of students' perceptions of field experiences. First, six types of influence were discussed: mastery of skills or techniques of teaching, the culture of the experience, personal history, medium, teacher image, and the attributes of the individual. Then a series of studies were reviewed, based upon the outcomes of the studies: what students tell about themselves, what students tell about the schools in which they work, what students tell about the profession of teaching, and what students tell about their preparation. Together these areas—influences and outcomes—can be examined to create a base from which future research can be guided.

The studies described in this review, while attempting to assess students' perceptions, have been carried out primarily in isolation. Many have concluded with superficial findings related to the satisfaction students feel in fieldwork. But, because field experiences have "always been the heart and mind of teacher preparation" (Haberman, 1983, p. 105), studies of students' perceptions related to field experiences are a worthy investment in the future of teacher education. For too long such study has been random and "guided at best by folk wisdom and unevaluated experience, and has been noncumulative in building a growing body of reliable, replaceable information" (Shutes, 1975, p. 85).

Consider, for a moment, how these areas might be used to begin a plan of inquiry: A matrix with cells interfacing influences and findings might be developed (see Fig. 1). Drawing from the findings of previous studies, a recurring outcome in the self-knowledge category was the concept of confidence in teaching. For that concept to be meaningful, it must be interpreted. Questions might be raised related to types of influence:

- Is confidence in teaching related to one's mastery of technical skills?
- Is confidence in teaching related to the culture of the school in which the experience occurs?
- Is confidence in teaching related to one's prior teaching experiences?
- Is confidence in teaching assessed through students' writing about self as teacher?
- Is confidence in teaching related to one's image of a confident teacher?
- Is confidence in teaching related to one's personality characteristics or learning style or intelligence?
- Do the technical skills of a student and the student's personality affect the student's sense of confidence?

FIGURE 1 A framework for interpeting perceptual data

INFLUENCES		Self-Knowledge	Findings from Previous Studies		
			The Schools in Which Students Work	The Profession of Teaching	Teacher Preparation
	Skills or Techniques of Teaching				
	Culture				
	Personal History				
	Medium				
	Image				
	Personal Attributes				

Such questions might stimulate a line of inquiry which could serve to build an understanding of the attributes of self and experience which foster confidence in teaching. Likewise other earlier results could be examined.

Needed for clarity in the study of students' perceptions is focus and follow-through. Isolated studies void of context will only contribute to the ambiguity and contradiction which characterizes the area of research in field experiences. This chapter has been a review of two areas which could contribute to a long range plan of research. It is also a plea for a more concerted focus toward understanding what students experience, how they experience it, and what meaning they make from such experience. It is hoped that research on students' perceptions of field experiences will continue and that the influences which shape perceptions as well as the methods used will be considered in light of this discussion.

REFERENCES

Applegate, J. H., & Lasley, T. J. (1982). Cooperating teachers' problems with preservice field experience students. *Journal of Teacher Education, 33*(2), 15–18.

Applegate, J. H., & Lasley, T. J. (1983, April). *What undergraduate students expect from preservice field experiences.* Paper presented at the annual meeting of the American Education Research Association, Montreal, Quebec.

Applegate, J. H., & Lasley, T. J. (1984a, April). *Perceived problems of students in early field experience.* Paper presented at the annual meeting of the American Education Research Association, New Orleans, LA.

Applegate, J. H., & Lasley, T. J. (1984b, April). What cooperating teachers expect from preservice field experience students. *Teacher Education,* 70–82.

Austin-Martin, G., Bull, D., & Molrine, C. (1981). A study of the effectiveness of a pre-student teaching experience in promoting positive attitudes toward teaching. *Peabody Journal of Education, 58*(3), 148–153.

Book, C., Byers, J., & Freeman, D. (1983). Student expectations and teacher education traditions with which we can and cannot live. *Journal of Teacher Education, 34,* 9–13.

Coleman, F. J. (1968). *Contemporary studies in aesthetics.* New York: McGraw Hill.

Cooper, J. (1983). Basic elements in teacher education program evaluation: Implications for future research and development. In K. R. Howey & W. Gardner (Eds.), *The education of teachers.* New York: Longman.

Fuller, F. F. (1969). Concerns of teachers: A developmental conceptualization. *American Educational Research Journal, 6*(2), 207–226.

Fuller, F. F., & Bown, O. (1975). Becoming a teacher. In K. Ryan (Ed.), *Teacher education* (The 74th yearbook of the National Society for the Study of Education). Chicago, IL: University of Chicago Press.

Gantt, W. N., & Davey, B. (1973). Pre-student teachers react to field-supplemented methods courses. *Educational Leadership, 31,* 259–262.

Gibson, R. (1976). The effect of school practice: The development of student perspectives. *British Journal of Teacher Education, 2*(3), 241–250.

Haberman, M. (1983). Research on preservice laboratory and clinical experiences: Implications for teacher education. In K. R. Howey & W. E. Gardner (Eds.), *The education of teachers.* New York: Longman.

Hardy, C. A., & Mershon, B. (1981). Field-based vs traditional teacher education: A study of learning style preference. *Teacher Educator, 16*(3), 23–36.

Harp, M. W. (1974). Early field experiences: A maturing force. *Elementary School Journal, 74*(6), 369–374.

Harvey, O. J., Hunt, D., & Schroeder, H. (1961). *Conceptual systems and personality organization.* New York: Wiley.

Hedberg, J. (1979). The effects of field experience on achievement in educational psychology. *Journal of Teacher Education, 30*(1), 75–76.

Hunt, D. E. (1977). Learning/teaching styles in S.U.G. In F. Dubois (Ed.), *Conference in multiculturalism in education.* Ottawa: Mutual Press.

Kohlberg, L. (1969). Stage and sequence. The cognitive-developmental approach to socialization. In D. Godlin (Ed.), *Handbook of socialization.* Chicago, IL: Rand McNally.

Loevinger, J. (1976). *Ego development.* San Francisco, CA: Jossey-Bass.

Lynch, H. L., & Kuehl, R. (1979). Recent graduates have definite ideas on how to improve teacher education programs. *Teacher Educator, 15*(3), 16–21.

Marso, R. N. (1971). Project interaction. A pilot study in a phase of teacher preparation. *Journal of Teacher Education, 22*(2), 194–198.

Morrow, J. E., & Lane, J. M. (1983). Instructional problems of student teachers: Perceptions of student teachers, supervising teachers and college supervisors. *Action in Teacher Education, 5*(1-2), 71–78.

Newlove, B. W., & Fuller, F. F. (1971). The 15-minute hour: A brief teaching experience. *Journal of Teacher Education, 22*(3), 335–340.

Perry, W. G., Jr. (1970). *Forms of intellectual and ethical development in the college years: A new scheme.* New York: Holt, Rinehart, & Winston.

Poole, C. (1972). The influence of experiences in the schools on students' evaluation of teaching practice. *Journal of Educational Research, 66*(4), 161–164.

Scherer, C. (1979). Effects of early field experience on student teachers' self-concepts and performance. *Journal of Experimental Education, 47*(3), 208–214.

Schlechty, P., & Vance, V. (1983). Recruitment, selection and retention: The shape of the teaching force. *Elementary School Journal, 83*(4), 469–487.

Shutes, R. (1975). Needed: A theory of teacher education. *Texas Tech Journal of Education, 2,* 94–101.

Thompson, L. L. (1982, March). *Faculty and student perceptions of early field experiences.* Paper presented at the annual meeting of the American Education Research Association, New York, NY.

Yarger, S., Howey, K., & Joyce, B. (1977). Reflections on preservice preparation: Impressions from the national survey. *Journal of Teacher Education, 28*(6), 34–37.

3
Teacher Educators: Description and Analysis

Edward R. Ducharme
University of Vermont

INTRODUCTION

To begin bluntly: Teacher educators are among the least welcome guests at the educational lawn party of the establishment of higher education. Depending on where one seeks commentary and criticism, he can hear or read the following assertions about teacher educators: They are antiintellectual. They do or attempt things better left undone. They mystify the obvious. They have no academic standards. They give everybody A's. They have no academic content to teach. They use jargon destructive of the English language. They produce publications of no merit. And so it goes.

> much of the concern about education in graduate schools of education touches on one aspect or another of the nation's public schools, including that of preparing teachers and administrators for those schools. It is widely known in academia that, generally, those teachers and administrators score lower on the graduate record exam (GRE) and other measures of scholarly talent than to aspirants for the Ph.D. in, say, physics or the professional degrees in law and medicine. The knowledge easily translates into second-class citizenship at universities for students of education and for their professors, whether or not those professors deserve such a label because of their research and teaching and whether or not the G.R.E. is, in fact, the ideal instrument for finding the right people to do the daily work of the schools. (Howe, 1982, p. vii)

Howe's observations reflect a present-day view of teacher education, a view in a state of flux depending on what is current in the nation's concerns about young people and schooling.

The general public sees SCDE (schools, colleges, departments of education) faculty as those who provide preparation for jobs that do not exist,
those responsible for what some see as the deplorable state of the public
schools. When SAT scores or reading achievement levels decline SCDE
faculty are accused of having trained prospective teachers poorly. When
the SATs of undergraduates entering teacher preparation programs decline, SCDEs are accused of having low standards of admission. When a
public school teacher or group of teachers presents a curriculum or approach distasteful to the local community, SCDEs are blamed for not
having prepared people for such sensitive issues. When first-year teachers undergo any sort of trauma, they blame the SCDE faculty for not
teaching them about the real world. When new social pressures such as
mainstreaming or multiculturalism emerge, SCDEs must include these
emphases in the curriculum. When significant learning problems
emerge, SCDEs are asked to provide research and remedy. (Ducharme
& Agne, 1982, p. 31)

The link among teacher educators, schools, teachers, and children and all
that goes on among and between them is, of course, not new. It is deeply
rooted in teacher education's beginnings in America.

Teacher educators are often talked about but rarely studied. They are
not well-defined with respect to academic content responsibilities, institutional roles, and professional status. Among the issues that vex the group
are the following:

- *Second-class institutional citizenship:* Teacher educators, perhaps
  both as a result of their own actions and some prejudices from
  others, have generally low status on campuses.
- *Little legitimacy:* The campus institutions rarely acknowledge more
  than a *pro forma* kind of legitimacy for teacher educators; increasingly, field practitioners are questioning their legitimacy.
- *Vague raison d'être:* Obviousiy linked to the preceding, this issue
  confounds the profession. Uncertain or vacillating about purpose,
  teacher educators often appear vague about precisely why they
  exist.
- *Lack of a central organization or agency:* There are, to be sure,
  organizations such as the American Association of Colleges for
  Teacher Education (AACTE) and the Association of Teacher Educators (ATE); but neither these nor any other group has been able to
  form a coherent organization to help shape and define, to support
  and nurture.
- *Tentative scholarship and research:* Despite a plethora of legitimate
  questions for scholarly inquiry, teacher educators often produce
  publications that lack substance, cogency, and scholarship. Left
  currently unresolved is the question of whether this condition results

from lack of interest or lack of ability. Sometimes one is forced to recall Koerner's harsh words of two decades ago:

> It is an indecorous thing to say and obviously offensive to most educationists, but it is the truth and it should be said: the inferior quality of the Education faculty is *the* fundamental limitation of the field, and will remain so, in my judgment for some time to come...There is still a strong strain of anti-intellectualism that runs through the typical Education staff. Despite their increasingly frequent apostrophes to academic quality. Until the question of the preparation and the intellectual qualifications of faculty members is faced head-on in Education, the prospects for basic reform are not bright. (Koerner, 1963, pp. 17–18)

Despite its present uncertain status, teacher education in America began with some noble aspirations, aspirations that perhaps introduced the tone of ambiguity to follow as teacher educators moved to formal higher education.

> I answer briefly, that it was my aim, and it would be my aim again, to make better teachers, and especially, better teachers for our common schools; so that those primary seminaries, on which so many depend for their educatiion, might answer, in a higher degree, the end of their institution. Yes, to make better teachers; teachers who would understand, and do their business better; teachers, who should know more of the nature of children, of youthful developments, more of the subjects to be taught, and more of the true methods of teaching; who would teach more philosophically, more in harmony with the natural development of the young mind, with a truer regard to the order and connection in which the different branches of knowledge should be presented to it, and, of course, more successfully.
>
> Again, I felt that there was a call for a truer government, a higher training and discipline, in our schools; that the appeal to the rod, to a sense of shame and fear of bodily pain, so prevalent in them, had a tendency to make children mean, secretive, and vengeful, instead of high-minded, truthful, and generous; and I wished to see them in the hands of teachers, who could understand the higher and purer motives of action, as gratitude, generous affection, sense of duty, by which children should be influenced, and under which their whole character should be formed. (Peirce, 1851, p. 65)

The above remarks are from a letter by Cyrus Peirce, the principal of the first public normal school in America, to Henry Barnard. The latter had asked Peirce to describe his aims in establishing his normal school.

In his remarks, Peirce, writing in 1851, either directly or implicitly hit upon the issues that have dominated and continue to dominate much discussion in teacher education. He wanted teachers to know more about the nature of young people, the subjects to be taught, the methodology to be used; he wanted kindly disposed people who would guide the young through pure motives and not through fear of violence. He went on in his letter to show how even individuals with appropriate subject matter knowledge will need skill and power to teach. He said teachers in the schools should avoid memorization and foster understanding. In order for teachers to have the proper skills and attitudes, Peirce argued, there was a need for normal schools staffed by the best faculty. One could go on at length describing what Peirce wanted his normal school to be; the observations have a contemporary relevancy.

His letter, written early in the history of formalized teacher education in America, contains ideas and principles that are both the glory and bane of teacher educators; the glory when carried out powerfully and persuasively, the bane when weakly applied and broadly misunderstood. He was among the first to articulate the perennial tension between theory and relevance, terms invented later to describe the conditions of being a teacher educator, conditions that continue to befuddle the profession. More than anything else, however, his remarks show concern for student learning, growth, and development that were to mark teacher education in its journey from small normal schools to large universities. Peirce's observations make it easier to comprehend teacher education's continual stops and starts, first toward affective, personal development, then toward cognitive development, then toward a combination of both. Teacher educators appear to have had difficulty figuring out what they are or should be.

A PROBLEM OF DEFINITION

Who or what is a teacher educator? Not an easy question to answer. Both the variety of institutions having teacher education programs and the ranges of roles and responsibilities of the faculty at these institutions make definition difficult.

In a recent study, Carter (1984) defines a teacher educator as

> a faculty member in a tenure track who taught at least one required undergraduate professional education course during the preceding twelve months. (pp. 125–126)

This definition works well for Carter in her study of 28 teacher educators and has applicability for many in the profession. But a broader definition is required for dealing with teacher educators in a more global context.

For several years, a colleague and I have engaged in a study of the education professoriate in America in the 1980s (Ducharme & Agne, 1982).

We originally began our work by focusing on teacher educators but quickly found the term unsatisfactory. It rarely captured enough people's professional lives. For example, we discovered that one individual might spend part of his life teaching principles of reading to students in elementary education and another part of his life leading a doctoral seminar in educational research; another spends a portion of his time in supervision of student teachers, another portion teaching a professional ethics course to students in the nursing program, and a final portion doing a research project on the impact of a recently enacted Magnet Schools program. For these and other reasons, we determined to use the term *professor of education* even though we grant that it, too, has its definitional problems. On the positive side, however, the term enables the inclusion of a wide range of individuals involved in teacher education.

The close connectednesss of the two terms is of long standing. It has been argued that all of the education professoriate has its roots in teacher education.

> Historically at least the central function of this emergent profession (education professoriate) was the training of teachers and other practitioners. The era in which professors of education came into existence as a subprofession was perhaps more unusual in the history of national education than we have realized. The unparalleled expansion of formal schooling which occurred in the United States between 1860 and 1930 created an almost instant demand for literally hundreds of thousands of teachers. . .

> This great multiplication of practitioners of teaching and school management in America occurred at the time when there were no significant numbers of highly qualified practitioners to prepare the necessary number of novices through an apprenticeship system. (Borrowman, 1975, pp. 57–58)

The near inseparability of the terms *teacher educator* and *professor of education* is writ large in the 1975 publication by the Society of Professors of Education edited by Ayers Bagley and entitled *The Professor Education: An Assessment of Conditions*. In particular, the essay "The Education Professoriate: A Historical Consideration of Its Work and Growth" (Johanningmeier & Johnson, 1975) shows how the roots and development of the professor of education are inextricably tied to teacher education.

In this chapter, I use the term teacher educator in a broader sense than that person who works specifically on a day-to-day basis with prospective and practicing teachers. While I will use the term teacher educator, much of my commentary is applicable to the larger group known as professors of education: *They are those who hold tenure-line or "hard money" positions*

*in schools, colleges, and departments of education (SCDEs), teach begin-
ning and advanced students in professional education, and conduct research
or engage in scholarly studies germane to professional education.*

The preceding is, at best, a loose definition. There are, on most higher
education campuses, education faculty members who teach and conduct
scholarly studies in areas that, at first glance, appear irrelevant to teacher
education; e.g., the senior faculty member in international education who
conducts research in educational practices in developing countries. Yet I
would contend that the seeming misfit between their work and teacher education is a result of the profession's lack of a capacity to synthesize and
integrate such studies rather than the innate irrelevance of the studies themselves. I would further contend that these individuals are, indeed, teacher
educators. Professional myopia causes artificial distinctions that are harm-
ful to the profession.

Teacher educators come in all shapes and sizes. The very variety confounds efforts to generalize. Everyone has his own classification system. I
like the following:

1. *School Person:* Has generally spent considerable time in the lower
   schools prior to (IHE) appointment; tends to find examples from
   practical experience; not disdainful of scholarly pursuits but not
   enthusiastic either; believes all education professors would be better
   off if they took a turn in the field occasionally; seeks validation
   and meaning from practitioners; avoids institution of higher education (IHE) committees and related activities; believes schools are
   the ultimate testing ground for IHE efforts.
2. *Scholar:* May or may not have spent time in the lower schools prior
   to IHE appointment; spends much time in scholarly pursuits anal-
   ogous to literary and historical studies in more traditional academic
   areas; deprecates knowledge acquired solely through experience,
   may articulate a theory-practice fusion; seeks IHE-wide responsibilities.
3. *Researcher:* Most likely had no experience in lower schools prior to
   IHE appointment or, if he or she has had such experience, rarely
   acknowledges it; committed to "pure" research activities; expresses
   disdain for practical solutions not rooted in research results; seeks
   out relationships with the IHE faculty in research-oriented disciplines; likely to hold the Ph.D.
4. *Methodologist:* Almost always has had considerable experience in
   lower schools prior to IHE appointment and is proud of the experience; committed to the marriage of theory and practice; does some
   professional writing generally limited to how-to articles loosely
   linked to educational theory; believes work is misunderstood by
   colleagues; spends much time in lower schools.

5. *Visitor to a Strange Planet:* Usually from the lower schools; somehow ended up at an IHE; remains ambivalent about both the lower schools and IHE; often locked in at the associate professor level; most likely appointed to IHE during the 1960s growth period; spends little time in scholarly work and occasionally deprecates the effort of those who do; pays little attention to IHE norms for behavior and performance.

These categories may be made clearer through the following descriptions of three composites of faculty members serving in teacher education programs.

Professor Irene Welstrum has been on the faculty of Greenmore College for 15 years. She came to Greenmore as a "fresh Ed.D." with doctoral study in education from a major state university. Her dissertation was the report of a study of problems of brain-damaged children in acquiring basic reading skills. Prior to her doctoral work, Professor Welstrum had been an elementary school teacher in one of the innovative, progressive school districts in the state.

At Greenmore, Professor Welstrum *is* the teacher education program with the addition of two part-time faculty, recent retirees from the nearby public schools. She teaches courses in educational foundations and teaching methods, and she conducts seminars for student teachers. She rarely has any opportunity to "use" her doctoral training; she has published two articles since finishing her doctoral work. The first was adapted from her dissertation research; the second was in the vein of a homily on teacher education programs in literal arts colleges. She is a member of the college admissions committee, the local AAUP chapter, and the President's Committee on Professional Women. Mildly respected by her colleagues and enormously well-liked by her students, Professor Welstrum intends to finish out her career at Greenmore.

Professor Maurice Lawton has been at Colburg State College for nine years. Previously, he had taught physical education in high school, been an assistant principal and principal, and, finally an associate superintendent. He earned his Ed.D. degree while serving as a school administrator and attending graduate school part time during the school year and full time during the summer. He received his degree in secondary curriculum. Other than an occasional printing of his informal remarks at workshops or conferences, no word of his has ever been in print anywhere. He almost appears to pride himself on this condition, saying that he never was much for theory, that he always was more of a doer than a thinker. He appears to be locked in as an associate professor for the rest of his career, a condition he says does not bother him. Students like him, but when asked, they rarely can recall what it is he taught them. He himself says that he believes in "more informal learning, less book-stuff and more down-to-earth reality." He is a willing member of any committee for which he is appointed. When asked what he does, he laughs a bit self consciously and says that he gets kids ready to face those devils in the high schools.

Professor Norman Williams has been a member of the faculty at State U. for 19 years. Earlier he had gone directly from undergraduate school where he had majored in mathematics to an M.S. program in psychology and from there to a Ph.D. program in educational psychology. During his first several years he taught learning theory to undergraduates planning to teach. More recently, he has taught only doctoral students in educational psychology. He publishes two or three articles annually, has authored two books, frequently presents at national conferences, and occasionally provides consultation services for fee to government and industry.

These three sketches in no way exhaust the possible range of SCDE faculty types, but they suggest, to a degree, how varied in background, preparation and training, workload, scholarship, attitude toward work, level of students taught, and relationship to theory and practice they can be. Beyond a general concern with education, membership in an SCDE faculty, and likely connection between their work and the preparation of educational professionals, they have little in common. But they are all teacher educators, either directly or indirectly. Their inclusion under the rubric of teacher educators makes manifest the problems of definition.

TOO MANY PLACES

The range of interest, knowledge, preparation, commitment, and skill implicit in the previous remarks suggests how difficult it is to achieve a sense of commonality among teacher educators. The lack of commonality has many causes, not the least of which is the wide range of institutions in which they work. The size goes from what Dean Richard Wisniewski of the University of Tennessee terms the "one-monk school" to the multifaceted, fully developed state university. Presently, there are slightly under 1,400 institutions in the United States that prepare teachers. That number and the implied variety of professional preparation raise many issues for observers and commentators on teacher education in America:

> What strikes a visitor from Europe is the remarkable variety of institutions and patterns within which such undergraduate teacher education takes place. It is possible to become a teacher in the United States by following programmes in a large number of fairly small liberal arts colleges, with no strong or over-riding commitment to this particular task. Many more intending or possible teachers follow structurally similar programmes in schools or departments of education within larger universities. (Judge, 1982, p. 32)

Almost *any* higher education institution can develop a teacher preparation program. There are, to be sure, standards such as the National Council for the Accreditation of Teacher Education (NCATE), state department of education reviews, and sundry other essentially *pro forma* "quality control" processes. However, the very number and diversity of institutions in the "approved" category suggest "ease-of-entry" into the professional preparation world. Thus one finds this previously cited wide range of individuals serving in ill-defined SCDEs, individuals somewhat uncertain of their own status and purpose, while others appear to prosper and offer arguments for the high value of small programs in, for example, liberal arts colleges (Travers, 1980). In the final analysis, very few higher education programs are prevented from offering programs in teacher education.

The purpose of these remarks is not to suggest the abolition of programs at any of the wide range in the nearly 1,400 institutions that prepare teachers. Rather, it is to suggest that the sheer number of institutions itself makes governance difficult, a common culture unimaginable, and professional sequence highly unlikely. The lack of commonality might be comforting to a group, large or small, at any institution which seeks to try something new. But it can also be discomforting to individual teacher educators seeking a sense of comradeship and identity with individuals and other places.

Teacher education in America embraces a very broad range of institutions. Public and private (some church-related), large and small, single purpose or multipurpose, urban, rural, and in between, baccalaureate, graduate, or both, almost exclusively oriented toward research or engaging in none at all. This array has organized itself in a variety of ways. But half the institutions training teachers belong to AACTE as you well know. Less than half submit themselves for accreditation by the National Council for the Accreditation of Teacher Education. Further subdivisions occur in the form of the Association of Independent Liberal Arts Colleges of Teacher Education (AILACTE), Teacher Education Council of State Colleges and Universities (TECSCU), and the Association of Colleges and Schools of Education in State Universities and Land Grant Colleges and Affiliated Private Universities (ACSESULGC/APU). Another smaller group of research-oriented universities has been operating for some years under the title of the Deans' Network. Individual teacher education faculty organize themselves through the Association of Teacher Educators (ATE). This organizational variety, overlapping sometimes but also leaving out significant numbers of institutions and teacher education faculty, frequently reflects strongly held differences of opinion about where to go and what to do in teacher education, to say nothing of education generally. (Gideonse, 1983, p. 110)

Thus teacher educators live and work in a variety of places that defy commonality; they may belong to organizations composed of individuals whose common theme is difference.

LACK OF AN ACCEPTED KNOWLEDGE BASE

Teacher educators are a troubled lot. Much of their trouble may come from a lack of genuine, agreed-upon academic knowledge base. James Koerner (1963), that unmentionable critic of teacher education of the 1960s, may have stated the theme of these conditions more accurately than even he thought:

> Education as an academic discipline has poor credentials. Relying on other fields, especially psychology, for its principal substance, it has not yet developed a corpus of knowledge and techniques of sufficient scope and power to warrant the field's being given full academic status. (p. 17)

Howsam, Corrigan, Denemark, and Nash, writing 13 years later, came to a quite different, much more optimistic conclusion.

> Teacher education is well though the decade within which it promises to come into its own and into its profession; tremendous progress is being made. Its acceptance within the profession and within the university appears imminent. (Howsam et al., 1976, p. 40)

Despite nine years of development since the Howsam observation, it does not appear that teacher education has produced an accepted knowledge base, an agreed upon core of research and scholarship seen as central to all perspective professionals. Its acceptance on equal terms with other academic studies does not appear imminent in 1986. The continued resistance or reluctance of teacher educators to define and accept with any precision the area of their knowledge and skill will continue to trouble their work.

Howsam, himself, writing in 1982, cites knowledge development and professional incapacity to respond.

> From the late 1960s to the present substantial progress has marked the efforts to build a validated knowledge base for the practice of teaching...There is little evidence, however, that individually or collectively the practitioners are pursuaded. Unless and until the *conviction* and *power* reside in the same place, there is little prospect of rapid development towards a profession which is rooted in the capacity to deliver trained expertise to a needing public. (p. 2)

Teacher educators, then, unlike many higher education faculty, have little common agreed-upon knowledge. They came from a tradition built largely from conventional wisdom, pragmatism, anecdotal prescriptions, and personal testimonials. For years, there was little more than custom and tradition to validate what teacher educators did. Consequently, there were and there continue to be significant differences of opinion about appropriate knowledge and practice beyond what seemed to have "worked" for professors when they were in the schools. Sizer (1975) has commented tellingly on this condition:

> Education is full of clever professors who lack the finesse which only first-hand experience can give. That some do not see the scholarly lacunae this lack causes is distressing; that others who do see it deride it is lamentable.
>
> At the other extreme are the education professors who come to the university from careers wholly in practice. All too often when a person so experienced becomes a professor, he adapts the Old Dog mode, passing on his tricks to the New Dogs, lecturing on the techniques he used to get his former job in the field done. (p. 339)

Because such views, beliefs, and practices have rarely been anchored anyplace but in the professor's mind, there is likely to be a considerable range of practice and procedure advocated from campus to campus. Nor is much of anything likely to be of a sustaining quality. An academic discipline that relies heavily on outdated "wisdom from the field" and ignores emerging knowledge will not prosper in higher education in the 1980s and beyond, nor will its practitioners feel comfortable in an environment characterized by and sustained by groups with traditions of shared, research-based knowledge and practice.

OBSCURE FUNCTIONS

Perhaps because teacher educators are unsure of their knowledge base, they also are tentative and uncertain about their functions. In one of their many assertions in *Educating a Profession* (1976), Howsam and his colleagues stated that "Teacher education is the preparation and research arm of the profession" (p. 41). The bald simplicity of the statement has a certain appeal.

But, quite clearly, teacher educators are not and cannot be responsible for all of the preparation program for teachers. One recent critic of teacher education argues that, to the contrary, none of the program of the preparation of teachers should be the province of teacher educators, because there is no basis for anything beyond liberal studies:

> liberal education should constitute the formal educational preparation of teachers; it should be handled by professors of academic disciplines that make up the liberal arts (including, of course, mathematics and science), rather than by professors of education. (Spillane, 1982, p. 21)

Such a posture, not a unique one, leaves no function for teacher educators in SCDEs; it leaves functions only for those who have no desire to be called teacher educators, namely, professors in the academic disciplines.

Fortunately for teacher educators, there are relatively few who would take this extreme view despite some present-day activity in a few states to develop quick-fix certification programs for liberal arts graduates interested in teaching. Most, even a few severe critics, see the place for professional knowledge in the preparation of educational professionals.

Gideonse (1982) has produced a concise and specific list of what prospective teachers ought to know and what they ought to be able to do.

- different instructional approaches, including use of existing and emerging media;
- the relationship between diverse characteristics of learners and instructional strategies;
- curriculum models and theories, especially in subjects for which a given teacher will be responsible;
- small-group processes;
- professional responsibilities and obligations;
- consultation skills to work with other professionals, including knowledge of their roles and of the organization and administration of schools;
- parent/professional relations (including community relations;
- a capacity for inquiry and design to meet the specific needs of individual learners, including diagnosis, instructional and curricular design, and evaluation skills;
- classroom and behavior management;
- self-awareness, or the ability to be in touch with oneself. (p. 16)

Surely in this rich panoply of skills and knowledge there are functions for teacher educators of all stripes and persuasions. What is needed is an agreement on the above or some equally broad conception of what teachers ought to know. There is clearly a function for teacher educators in each of the specifics enumerated by Gideonse. Teacher educators clearly, in this era of educational reform, ought to clarify what their appropriate functions are and why they are uniquely qualified to fill these functions. Otherwise, they face a withering array of responsibility. Having failed to declare responsibility for a specific set of functions and come to a collective agreement on what they are, teacher educators could be left with little function.

Currently, even the view that SCDE teacher educators ought to do the training of teachers and educational professionals is being subjected to challenge. Perhaps as remnants of the 1960s belief in the wisdom in the field, certainly as a result of teacher educators' behavior during the 1960s and 1970s when they relinquished part of their training responsibilities to the field, recently there have been increasing challenges to the perogatives of university-based teacher education.

> University-based teacher educators must recognize and accept the fact that there are professionals working in educational agencies who are every bit as qualified as we—and perhaps more so—to be teacher educators. (Backman, 1984, p. 3)

Backman has merely brought the point, made by many others, to its most succinct and pointed form. Whether true or not, the implicit sentiment has to be very troubling to teacher educators.

Spillane (1982), a high-ranking school administrator of long standing and holder of a doctoral degree in education, would remove the internship supervision totally from the control of teacher educators:

> An internship—during which the prospective teacher engages in actual classroom practice under the tutelage of a master teacher—is the best introduction to the profession. Pedagogical training ought to be in the hands of administrators and master teachers in the schools. (p. 21)

When one recalls that the field internship is frequently the most valued experience in the prospective teacher's preparation, then he realizes even more how much to the quick Spillane's contention would cut teacher educators. Teacher educators have specific skills, knowledge, and attitudes to bring to bear on the training of educational professionals. They, by virtue of where they are and their professional backgrounds, have the capacity to help school people blend idealism, knowledge, pragmatism, and purposes.

> The university's most singular contribution to the preparation of public school educators must be to keep alive in young people a sense of idealism and critical social vision. Public and professional resistance to this function of the university will continue to stiffen as political disenchantment and personal impotence intensity, and cries for accountability fill the air. Nevertheless, now, more than ever, educators need "sustaining themes" to order their experiences and to make sense of their lives. Sustaining themes are valuable for teachers, not because they can be converted to useful techniques in classrooms, but because they represent a faith in larger societal ideals and purposes—the reasons why most educators choose to enter their profession in the first place. Unfortunately, these purposes tend to recede from consciousness the more we struggle daily to endure in our professional settings. (Nash & Ducharme, 1974, p. 107)

The heyday of the Performance Based Teacher Education (PBTE) movement that occasioned this comment, is, fortunately, over; but the giveaways
of professional responsibilities have not ceased.

That teacher education is the research arm of the profession is an
appealing sentiment for teacher educators. The past record of teacher educators in qualitative research directed at professional practice has been,
however, a mixed one at best. Clark (1978) is quite clear on the record of individual practitioners:

> However, the reader should not infer from this presentation that SCDEs
> are hotbeds of educational R and D productivity. Although they com-
> pete well with other educational agencies, individual faculty productivity
> is still disappointing. (p. 5)

Some of the reasons for this "disappointing" productivity will be commented on subsequently. For the moment, it is sufficient to suggest that individuals uncertain about their function are not likely to excel at anything.
Teacher educatorss are not the exception.

ROLE AND STATUS IN HIGHER EDUCATION AND SOCIETY

Teacher educators may often not feel at home on IHE campuses even though
they may have struggled very hard to get there. They do not command the
kind of respect that others in academe receive:

> So far as I can tell, the legitimacy of the professors of education has
> never been fully granted by either practitioners, other kinds of profes-
> sors, or indeed, by the public at large. So long as the shortage of practi-
> tioners are acute and sharply felt, all groups tolerated professors of
> education as a necessary if somewhat embarrassing nuisance. At least on
> most major university campuses the prevailing mood has been that
> someone on the campus should do the teacher training job and since
> only the professors of education would take it on, they must be toler-
> ated. (Borrowman, 1975, p. 58)

The "business" that educators conduct remains suspect on major and
minor campuses. The generally low esteem for teacher educators from academics for the more traditional fields is transferred to all associated with
education:

> However hard they may wriggle, schools of education remain just that:
> schools of education. They are associated, especially but by no means
> exclusively in the minds of other academics, with the ill-regarded busi-
> ness of teacher education. They may be guilty of little or none of that

prejudice themselves, but that isn't the point. They remain leaders of a poor and motley bunch, known to attract only the weaker students. (Judge, 1982, p. 56)

Fuller and Bown (1975) have argued that teacher educators have generally low status:

Teacher educators have, by and large, humble social-class origins and low status in comparison with their academic colleagues. They more often hold paying jobs while working toward a degree, enter the faculty later, perhaps with the Ed.D., and so are less likely to have acquired the scholarly credentials valued by academicians. Their work is likely to to conative rather than the cognitive pursuits esteemed by other faculty. Worst of all, the knowledge base of education is considered by academicians to be largely exogenous. These personal and occupational differences compound the historical problems of status experienced by normal schools turned colleges of education. (p. 29)

The Ducharme-Agne data bear out the above generalizations; over 60% of their sample of more than 1,000 are the first generation to be college educated; 38% of their fathers had less than a high school education; approximately 30% of their mothers had less than a high school education. Seventy-seven percent went to a college at an institution fewer than 300 miles from their homes. There is perhaps a parallel upward-mobility characteristic of both SCDE teacher educators and lower school teachers who have traditionally used teaching as an entry point into a higher rung on the middle-class ladder.

We can estimate that in an occupation now numbering over two million members somewhere around six hundred thousand persons have crossed the boundary between blue-collar and white-collar work. Teaching appears to be one of the more important routes into the middle class. (Lortie, 1975, p. 38)

The ease of entry into teaching in the lower schools, effectively described by Lortie, produced a situation whereby virtually anyone with a bachelor's degree, a modicum of intelligence, and some determination could become a teacher. Individuals in American society have rarely, if ever, been precluded from entry into teaching because of quality issues. Even in the 1970s, when there was an excess of candidates for the positions available, applicants were not excluded because they were not good enough but rather because positions were not available. Currently, with shortages again appearing, quality is still not the issue. This general ease of entry situation has led to the somewhat oversimplified view that "anyone can become a teacher." There may be a parallel view that nearly anyone with a degree can become a teacher educator, particularly when the "rules" for behavior are seen as vague or nonexistent. Surely the move to higher education represents another rung or two of further movement on the social status ladder, even if the movement is accompanied by second-class citizenship within the institution. They may garner what respect accrues from society generally for the title of professor; but within the institution itself, they may be seen as suspect professors.

Howsam et al. (1976) hypothesized a number of reasons why teacher education has a less-than-secure place in higher education:

1. Failure to overcome the "normal school" image and the hard feelings that were engendered when normal schools were incorporated into or became colleges and universities.
2. An assessment on the part of the academic community that teaching is and will remain a semiprofession and is, therefore, lower on the academic totem pole than the disciplines or the other professional schools. Other marginal units on campus have a similar or more aggravated circumstance.
3. Negative "spin-off" from the ongoing competition for the time of students in teacher education.
4. Difference over whether teaching is an art or a science.
5. Conscious or unconscious realization that to accept teaching as a profession would require teachers in higher education to undergo professional preparations or admit inadequacy as teachers.
6. Failure of teacher education to assert its uniqueness and to develop a distinctive presence on campus.
7. The ongoing closeness of government influence through accreditation and certification which characterizes teacher education and does not characterize other university units.
8. The absence of any outside force which is concerned enough to come to the aid of teacher education politically or institutionally. Most notable is the professional organizations which logically could be expected to do so but do not. (p. 60)

Teacher educators arrive on campus as professors at an older age than professors in other fields (Ducharme & Agne, 1982), a condition that may account for their difficulties in role definition. A further difficulty may be caused by the nature of what they were doing prior to coming to higher education. There is considerable evidence that, generally, teacher educators have had much experience in the lower schools prior to coming to higher education (Ducharme & Agne, 1982, p. 32). Using a smaller, more geographically concentrated sample, Carter (1984) has concluded much the same thing; namely, that upward of 75% of teacher educators have had several years of experience in the lower schools.

And while this experience may well suggest that teacher educators have much in common with lower school educators and administrators, their presence on higher education campuses suggests something else. They are different enough to have sought out or been sought out for advanced degree work that would eventually take them to the campus. Katz, Raths, Irving, Kurachi, Mohanty, and Sani (1982) contend that teacher educators are not well-accepted either at the university or by professionals in the field.

Wisniewski (1984) speculates on the possible impact of public school experience on the scholarly behaviors in education faculties.

> Most education faculties have had extensive public school experiences. To what degree does this fact explain the value placed on scholarship? Would schools of education be stronger if fewer members of the faculty had public school experiences? Such a shift might increase education's status on campus, but what would be the impact on the practicing profession? To what degree do persons transitioning from one social system to another, i.e., public schools to universities, successfully internalize the norms of the academy? Given that scholarship is not highly valued in the public schools, is this the primary reason why only some professors are scholars? (p. 10)

Who can say with any certitude what the impact of one's prior experience is on one's current performance? Yet surely a period of 5 to 7 years spent in the lower schools, at the beginning of one's career, coincident with what developmental theorists suggest is a high point in one's profession of idealism, must have considerable impact. And when we join the experience of all individuals in a given SCDE, we have scores of years of experience acquired at critical points in individuals' lives. What might be some of the carry-over effects?

- *Adherence to the work ethic of schools.* Schools are, among other things, places where individuals are nearly always under pressures to get things done immediately. The clock is relentless. One is always on call. Transported to higher education, former school professionals work long hours (Ducharme & Agne, 1982, p. 32).
- *Belief in individual work with students.* Good schools are characterized by individuals who spend much time with students, in part, because they believe in the efficacy of individuals working with others.
- *Suspicions about theories and research.* School practitioners are rarely the most enthusiastic consumers or supporters of theory development and research and scholarship productivity. As a residue of their experience in the lower schools, teacher educators may

carry some of this view with them to higher education. Their own work, occasionally done with an accompanying minimum of traditional research and scholarly techniques and practices, is not necessarily an adequate antidote to these feelings.

SCHOLARSHIP AND RESEARCH

Teacher educators appear to be caught between two conflicting worlds. The first is the old world caricatured by people who had, by whatever process that seemed appropriate, been judged effective and gone on to university studies to acquire a doctorate or, equally often, been hired out of the public schools by a local college or university to work with undergraduates. Long on experience and sure of their views, these individuals taught and continue to teach their students using their own past as their source of pedagogy. The new world is caricatured by more recently appointed faculty who are likely to have undergone more vigorous graduate work, more inclined to believe in research, disposed to teach from a set of beliefs or principles anchored in some research. Some would argue that the first set of individuals continues to do the major bulk of the teaching while the second group assume the research function or burden.

It is not clear whether or not teacher educators are good scholars on their campuses. Certainly much of the research that affects school and should affect teacher education is not done by teacher educators. Ducharme and Agne (1983) contend that, from a purely quantitative view, teacher educators publish as much and perhaps more than their colleagues in other units. Schwebel (1982) contends differently, as do Roemer and Martinello (1982). All contend that more must be done, and that quality is as much an issue as quantity. Yet one wonders about the degree to which issues of such long standing ever are changed to any significant degree. It may well be that teacher educator's position on campuses will remain suspect.

Teacher education is a field of inquiry, if that is not too strong a word, characterized by debate as to the supremacy of theory or practice. The resultant tension has not always been a good thing for teacher educators. The continuing tension between theory and practice produces not only lack of clarity and focus of professional goals; it also contributes to serious overstatements of the value of one over the other, and to one being denigrated or ignored by the holder of the opposite view.

> One cannot, I think, overstate the propensity of speculative minds to lose all perceptions of reality nor the tendency of practitioners to lose their preception of possibility. (Borrowman, 1975, p. 60)

> Today, we still seem to be struggling with our historical legacy, trying to balance theory with relevance; vacillating between conceptions of teaching and the teaching of competencies. We have yet to find a way of

showing that all our activities, practical and theoretical, are but various and necessary forms of the process of maintaining free and public schools. (Johanningmeier & Johnson, 1975, p. 15)

This inability to achieve a balance or to demonstrate and argue effectively the appropriate dominance of one over the other may contribute to some of the problems in scholarship. At the very least, it contributes to the vague and sometimes contradictory nature of the scholarship.

Teacher educators are in a difficult position with respect to scholarly productivity, the traditional hallmark of the university professor. It has been noted that professors of education, as a general rule, rarely follow up on the work begun during their doctoral studies. Indeed, for some who have produced projects rather than the more traditional research-based dissertation, there may be nothing, in fact, to follow up on.

> The development of precision, clarity, and systematic research design has brought with it a great specificity, which seems to be increasing in the major universities that prepare education faculty. The dissertation topics chosen seem to lose interest, since (1) no faculty member could be found who had ever pursued his dissertation with follow-up on even related research, and (2) no faculty member was using the knowledge gained in his dissertation in some active way in the field. (Haberman & Stinnett, 1973, p. 138)

Haberman and Stinnett's observations in 1973 still appear relevant in 1985. Thus one of the norms of university behavior may prove to be unusually difficult for teacher educators who may lack training, disposition, and knowledge to do sustained scholarship of the traditional mode.

Yet, teacher educators living in academia must, it appears, submit to the same rules and guidelines that all faculty must. Oh, to be sure, there are those who argue that some teacher educators ought to be in the same category of the university professor who does surgery and demonstrates surgery for students but does neither research nor any other scholarly activities. Yet such an individual becomes a full professor. There are many reasons why this system works well for medical faculty, not the least of which are the power, financial importance, and public prestige of medical schools generally. Even in the best of times for education faculty, the public has never come close to granting education the esteem it bestows on medicine. Teacher educators had best not rely on any quick turnarounds in public view or in university differentiation.

SOME CONCLUDING OBSERVATIONS

Teacher educators might conceivably continue on as they are. To do so would be to err seriously. A professional campus-based group cannot, in the 1980s, continue on without function, body of knowledge, status, and the other indicators that accompany life at colleges and universities. How might teacher educators in the next few years forge a worthwhile identity after decades of nonstatus? Not easily.

The very ambiguity in the role and function of teacher educators, the mixed perception others have of them, the lack of focus, and the rest of the characteristics alluded to in this chapter all indiate the need for redefinition and for assimilation. Perhaps a descriptive chapter might contain an argument for what might be, given the context of what is. What are some things that might be? I would offer the following:

- *A commitment to quality scholarship.* Two conditions suggest why this is paramount: (a) the oft-cited lack of quality scholarship by the majority of teacher educators, and (b) the current availability of a much broadened range of research practices amid the presence of a national commitment to knowledge based on sound data. It is simply irresponsible to continue to ignore these issues in the 1980s.
- *A commitment to a reasoned consensus.* There is a growing body of knowledge about how people learn, what a positive learning environment is, and what precedes what in learning complexity. Teacher educators must be aware of the gathering body of knowledge, involved in its growth, learned in the research, and potent in the teaching.
- *A commitment to a campus presence.* By and large, teacher educators live and work on campuses, or, at the very least, they draw their salaries from campus-based institutions. This condition implies mightily that teacher educators be a vital part of institutional affairs committees, research, governance, and the like. They must make known what they do and how the work contributes to the purpose of the university in the development and spread of knowledge.
- *A commitment to a national representative organization.* As indicated, Gideonse and others have shown that no national organization truly speaks for teacher educators. One wonders whether this condition is a result of the organizations' behaviors or the individual's behaviors. I side with the latter. It is difficult if not impossible for an organization to represent individuals and institutions who are uncertain as to whether or how they want to be represented. For whatever enemies of teacher educators exist, the old maxim "Divide and conquer" has no applicability. There is virtually nothing to divide.
- *A commitment to clear articulation and demonstration of role and function.* Were it not so tragic, it would be comic that teacher educators cannot, some 140 years after Peirce's letter to Barnard, state their role and function and demonstrate that their interventions are

truly efficacious in the development of powerful teachers in the lower schools. One still attends conferences in which minor studies of modest events are purported to show that such-and-such a technique might provoke a 5% increase in student-initiated questions rather than demonstrations that the approximately 40-plus semester hours of professional education courses that elementary education majors takes produce a clear, positive impact on teacher performance and pupil achievement.

- *A commitment to inquiry.* This commitment flows from the last. An academic, professional group must demonstrate its commitment to honest, scholarly inquiry into the issues that confront it. Teacher educators have not done this, and the results are manifest. Research has languished, professional development has stagnated, and custom and tradition have prevailed.
- *A commitment to collaboration.* Teacher educators cannot, on their own, produce teachers of merit and quality. The effort requires the combined work of those in other academic units beyond teacher education. Teacher educators, on most campuses, will have to change their behavior patterns and, perhaps, even their beliefs.

Even were all of these to occur, plus whatever thoughtful "commitments" others in the profession might develop, one cannot guarantee an easy path for teacher educators. Decades of history are in the way of whatever progress and development might occur. One can envision a future several decades from one in which a description not unlike that in this chapter is written. One hopes such is not the case. Rather, one hopes that the latent power and energy in teacher education come to the fore to produce a different picture, a new history.

REFERENCES

Backman, C. A. (1984). Moving teacher education towards the twenty-first century: Reflections of a new dean. *Journal of Teacher Education, 35,* 2–5.

Borrowman, M. L. (1975). About professors of education. In A. Bagley (Ed.), *The professor of education.* Minneapolis, MN: University of Minnesota.

Borrowman, M. L. (Ed.). (1965). *Teacher education in america: A documentary history.* New York: Teachers College Press.

Carter, H. (1984). Teachers of teachers. In L. Katz & J. Raths (Eds.), *Advances in teacher education.* Norwood, NJ: Ablex.

Clark, D. L. (1978, March). *Research and development productivity in educational organizations* (Occasional Paper, No. 41): The Ohio State University; National Center for Research in Vocational Education.

Durcharme, E. R., & Agne, R. M. (1982). The education professoriate: A research-based perspective. *Journal of Teacher Education, 33,* (6), 30–36.

Fuller, F. F., & Bown, O. (1975). Becoming a teacher. In K. Ryan (Ed.), *Teacher Education NSSE Yearbook*. Chicago: University of Chicago Press.

Gideonse, H. (1983). *In search of more effective service*. Cincinnati, Oh: Rosenthal.

Gideonse, H. D. (1982). The necessary revolution in teacher education. *Phi Delta Kappan. 64*, 15–18.

Haberman, M., & Stinnett, T. M. (1973). *Teacher education and the new profession of teaching*. Berkeley, CA: McCutchan.

Howe, H. (1982). Forword. In H. Judge, *American graduate schools of education: A view from abroad*. New York: Ford Foundation.

Howsam, R. R., Corrigan, D. C., Denemark, G. W., & Nash, R. J. (1976). *Educating a profession*. Washington, DC: American Association of Colleges for Teacher Education.

Howsam, R. B. (1982). The future of teacher education. *Journal of Teacher Education, 33*, 2–7.

Johanningmeier, E. V., & Johnson, H. C., Jr. (1975). The education professoriate: A historical consideration of its' work and growth, in A. Bagley (Ed.), *The professor of education*. Minneapolis, MN: University of Minnesota.

Judge, H. (1982). *American graduate schools of education: A view from abroad*. New York: Ford Foundation.

Katz, L. G., Raths, J. D., Irving, J., Kurachi, A., Mohanty, C., & Sani, M. (1982). *Reputations of teacher educators among members of their role-set*. Paper presented at the annual meeting of the American Educational Research Association.

Koerner, J. D. (1963). *The miseducation of american teachers*. Boston, MA: Houghton Mifflin.

Lortie, D. C. (1975). *School teacher: A sociological study*. Chicago: University of Chicago.

Nash, R. J., & Durcharme, E. R. (1974). The university can prepare teachers: An unfashionable view. *Educational Forum, 39*, (1), 99–109.

Peirce, C. (1965). Letter to Henry Barnard, in M. L. Borrowman (Ed.), *Teacher education in America*. New York: Teachers College Press.

Roemer, R. E., & Martinello, M. L. (1982). Divisios in the education professoriate and the future of professional education. *Educational Studies, 13* (2), 203–223.

Schwebel, M. (1982). Research productivity of education faculty: A comparative study. *Educational Studies, 13* (2), 224–239.

Sizer, T. R. (1974). On Myopia: A complaint from down below. *Daedalus, 103* (4) 332–340.

Smith, B. O. (1980). Pedagogical education: How about reform? *Phi Delta Kappan, 62* (2), 87–91.

Spillane, R. R. (1982). Some Unfortunate Assumptions. *Phi Delta Kappan, 64*, 21–22.

Travers, E. F. (1980). The case for teacher education at selective liberal arts colleges. *Phi Delta Kappan, 62* (2), 127–131.

Wisniewski, R. (1984). *The scholarly ethos in schools of education*. Unpublished manuscript, University of Tennessee, Knoxville.

4

Pitfalls of Experience in Teacher Preparation*

Sharon Feiman-Nemser
Margret Buchmann
Michigan State University

There is a common belief in the educative value of firsthand experience. We say things like "That was a real learning experience," "Practice makes perfect," "Experience is the best teacher," and "Let experience be your guide." Common sense casts experience as both the means and the content of important learnings.

This implicit trust in firsthand experience is particularly evident in discussions about learning to teach. Teachers claim that most of what they know about teaching came from firsthand experience. In short, they learned to teach by teaching. When teachers look back on their formal preparation, they generally cite student teaching as its most valuable part. In deference to this belief, preservice teacher education gives more and more time to classroom experiences, while inservice programs stress teachers sharing their experiences with one another.

* This work is sponsored in part by the Institute for Research on Teaching, College of Education, Michigan State University. The Institute for Research on Teaching is funded primarily by the Program for Teaching and Instruction of the National Institute of Education, United States Department of Health, Education, and Welfare. The opinions expressed in this publication do not necessarily reflect the position, policy, or endorsement of the National Institute of Education (Contract No. 400-81-0014).

A modified version of this chapter appeared under the same title in *Teachers College Record,* 87(1), Fall 1985, 53–65.

Sharon Feiman-Nemser is the coordinator of the Knowledge Use in Learning to Teach Project and an associate professor of teacher education. Margret Buchmann is the coordinator of the Conceptual-Analytic Project and an associate professor of teacher education.

But is experience as good a teacher of teachers as most people are inclined to think? To answer this question, one must take into account commonly used informal strategies of inference and judgment, the immediate impact of personal memories and classroom realities, the instructional purposes of teacher educators, and the normative context of schools as institutions.

This chapter focuses on the contribution of firsthand experience at the preservice level of learning to teach. The discussion rests on a broad view of learning to teach as a process that begins before formal teacher preparation and continues afterward. This means that preservice field experiences are part of a continuum that includes powerful early experiences with parents and teachers as well as the learning that inevitably occurs on the job. Learning from firsthand experience in preservice education is influenced by past experiences of schooling which shape subsequent learning from teaching.

To set a concrete frame of reference for our discussion, we begin with three vignettes that describe specific occasions for firsthand experience at the preservice level and in elementary schools. More and more, preservice programs are providing exploratory field experiences so that future teachers can encounter the realities of classroom life early in their formal preparation. The first vignette describes such an opportunity. The second vignette illustrates another trend—linking field experiences with foundations courses. The third vignette is about student teaching, the most familiar way of giving preservice teachers first hand experiences with schools and classrooms. While the three students that figure in these occasions are fictitious, the vignettes are based on observations and interviews.

Each vignette is followed by a commentary in which we explore what the imaginary student is learning from the experience. The commentary is guided by three questions. First, what is the preservice teacher learning in the here and now? We look at potential learnings—insights, messages, inferences, reinforced beliefs—about being a teacher, about pupils, classrooms, and the activities of teaching. We are interested in a particular type of inappropriate learning, which we call "pitfalls." Second, how do these lessons of experience relate to the central purpose of teaching, that is, helping pupils learn things? Third, to what extent do these lessons foster the capacity to learn from future experience?

The conceptual and behavioral traps which we call pitfalls are present in all three vignettes. The discussion highlights each of them in turn. It is based on studies of the social psychology of judgment, reinforcement theory, research on teaching and teacher education, and the educated imagination of a teacher educator with a philosophical bent and a philosopher interested in teacher education.[1]

---

[1] The inferences and generalizations in our discussion are based on the following: Buchmann and Schwille (1983); Anderson (1981); Becker (1972); Dewey (1904/1965); Feiman-Nemser (1983); Little (1982); Nisbett and Ross (1980); Platt (1973); Sarason (1982); Tabachnick, Popkewitz and Zeichner (1980); Wilson, (1975); and Zeichner (1980).

The scenes that follow deal with learning from experience in the pre-service phase of learning to teach. The expectation that something will be learned in these different occasions is probably justified. Yet not all learning is productive or desirable. Thus the question of whether we want future teachers to learn all the lessons of experience must be examined.

VIGNETTE 1: EARLY FIELD EXPERIENCES

Every Thursday at 8:15 a.m., Karen catches the bus to Central School, where she spends the day in the fourth grade. Even though Karen is only a sophomore, she has always wanted to be a teacher because she loves children. She is excited about being a teacher's aide this term. This is the first time Karen has been inside an elementary school since she was a pupil, and she is surprised at how modern the building is and how knowledgeable the fourth graders seem. She had wanted the children to call her Karen, but the teacher introduced her as Miss Miller, which feels a little strange.

In the morning Karen works with Tommy on his spelling list. While the teacher runs a reading group, she helps individual pupils with their seatwork. At recess, Karen goes outside with the children and usually ends up playing with the same three girls. At lunchtime she swaps experiences with other university students enrolled in the same introductory education course. During the silent reading period after lunch, Karen talks a little with the teacher and then marks papers. She can see that some pupils understand their work better than others. The teacher has asked Karen to do a bulletin board on careers and to take the class to the library. Karen really feels like a teacher walking the class to and from the library.

Commentary

In trying to make sense of her first field experience, Karen naturally thinks about how this setting resembles the ones she remembers from her own schooling. Her judgment about the pupils implies a comparison with the past and thoughts about the future. Not only does she feel that they know more than she did at their age, she also feels apprehensive about whether she will know enough to teach these children. Yet much of what she sees is familiar. Past experience helps in making sense of spelling lists and reading groups, recess and bulletin boards, seatwork and ditto sheets. Actually, her familiarity with these classroom practices gives her a feeling of competence. Classroom life is not all that strange to Karen, even seen from the other side of the desk. Many things are fixed in the school day, and classroom activities have inherent and predictable patterns. Caught up in memories that help her understand much of what is happening around her, Karen identifies teaching with things she already knows. Still, there is a lot to learn, but Karen is unsure about how to define it and how to go about learning it.

The fact that she prefers to be called Karen and plays with the same three children at recess suggests that she feels more like a pupil than a teacher. Yet getting the class to and from the library without mishap gives her a sense of what it will feel like to be in charge and have students do what she wants. A sense of power gets added to some sense of competence; acting like a teacher, Karen sees pupils acting in their matching roles. "Should the teacher be an authority or a friend?" Karen wonders. How she resolves this issue will depend on what is modeled in the classroom and on the expectations she holds and encounters at the university and in the schools.

Similarly, what Karen makes of her observation that the children differ in their understanding will depend on how the teacher handles errors and misunderstandings and whether teacher educators explain the pedagogical significance of errors. The observation she makes about the children's written work relates to the heart of teaching: helping students learn things and looking for what they have learned. Will this observation be turned into questions which Karen actively tries to answer in further field experiences and in her professional course work? It probably will be, if Karen has the inclination and capacity to connect classroom experience with formal knowledge and to learn from further experience by thinking about it. These capacities are central to teaching, but they must be learned. Most teachers do not bring an inquiring disposition to their preparation, and immersion in the classroom tends to preclude inquiry. Since it is unlikely that the habit of inquiry will be acquired on the job, it is important to cultivate it at the preservice level and reinforce its role in teaching.

In early field experience, *unquestioned* familiarity is a pitfall, because it arrests thought and may mislead it. People generally do not recognize that their experience is limited and biased, and future teachers are no exception. The "familiarity" pitfall stems from the tendency to trust what is most memorable in personal experience. Karen approaches her early field experience with preconceptions about what classrooms are like and what teachers do. She has a selective interest, and her perceptions are personal and affectively charged. Ideas and images of classrooms and teachers laid down through many years as a pupil provide a framework for viewing and standards for judging what she sees now. Such frameworks will fit with social traditions of teaching and schooling; they have the self-evidence and solidity of the taken-for-granted.

Fundamental facts of classroom life, such as that teachers *are* in charge, may impress Karen; however, she may not relate this fact to the central tasks of teaching, unless someone helps her to do so. One can learn to be in charge without learning to teach children something. Classroom experience in itself cannot be trusted to deliver lessons that shape dispositions to inquire and to be serious about pupil learning. On the contrary, it may block the flow of speculation and reflection by which new habits of thought and action are formed.

VIGNETTE 2: CLASSROOMS AS LABS

As a sophomore Tom had an early field experience much the same as Karen's. Now he is a junior halfway through his preservice program. This term, in conjunction with his educational psychology course, Tom spends one after-noon a week in a second-grade classroom. Because he is only there for half a day, he does not know all the pupils' names. He is not even sure that they know his name. Nor is he sure of the classroom routines. Most of the time, he observes. He is supposed to focus on three pupils whom the teacher has identified as in some way different from the others.

Tom spends 15 minutes observing each pupil. His assignment is to de-scribe what they are doing during academic activities, to note the specifics of their behavior, and the setting in which it occurs. At first Tom thought this would be easy. But it is hard to watch and write at the same time, and he is not sure about what to write down. In her feedback, the university in-structor said that Tom should try to be more objective and avoid so many inferences. Instead of noting that his focal pupil is not paying attention, he should describe what he sees, that is, that D. goes to the pencil sharpener, returns to his desk, stares out the window, and so on.

Tom's difficulties stem in part from the fact that by the time he arrives, the class is already busy at work. His three focal pupils are at their desks doing assignments, and Tom has trouble figuring out what they are supposed to be doing, let alone whether they understand it. He does notice differences, though, in their ability to concentrate, tendency to move around and talk to neighbors, and accuracy of work. Tom looks forward to the time after recess. Then his assignment will get easier, because he can hear what the teacher says. Still, for the last two weeks, the class has been rehearsing for Parents' Night, which doesn't strike Tom as a very academic activity.

In his educational psychology course, the instructor said that focused observation can help one learn to think like a teacher. It gives teacher candi-dates practice in noticing differences in children's responses to instruction and that, in turn, can help them decide whether pupils are learning some-thing. Tom can see that he is beginning to pay closer attention to children's behavior, but he is uncertain about the value of writing such detailed notes. Certainly when he is a teacher he won't be able to watch individual pupils for 15 minutes at a time. He would rather work with the pupils and find out about their learning that way. Because he is in the classroom for such a short time, Tom cannot become an integral part of the action. Also, getting in-volved would keep him from concentrating on just those things that he needs to practice for his university class. His observation assignment is meant to set him apart from what is going on. The children rarely approach him for help and the teacher does not count on Tom's assistance. It is Tom who is the learner, and what he learns are ways of seeing, not of acting.

Commentary

Tom's learning experience is largely shaped by the instructional purposes of his course in educational psychology. He appears to be learning how to take detailed notes on individual children's responses to academic activities. Based on practice and feedback, he will become more adept at distinguishing description from judgment and at providing some context for observed behavior such as the teacher's purposes, the instructional task, or expectations for social interaction, Over time he should also begin to see patterns in the behavior of individual pupils and differences among them. In that sense he is developing tools to see how children respond differently to instructional activities. The question is whether Tom himself relates this growing awareness to his future work as a teacher.

Is Tom learning habitual ways of seeing, or is he acquiring a skill that he is capable of applying to specific situations? In the first case, there may be some transfer once he is actually teaching. That is, Tom will continue to look for differences in student responses to instruction. In the second case, Tom will have to decide whether teaching calls for the application of observational skills. He must come to believe that this kind of observation can (indeed should) inform instructional decision making. In other words, this "academic" skill must become part of his conception of teaching.

In either case, a lot depends on what happens with his observations, both in the classroom and in his foundations class. Building habitual ways of seeing requires instruction and reinforcement. Tom will need help in thinking about what these observations mean and what they imply for action. He can get that help from two sources—the classroom teacher and his university professor. Suppose the teacher shows Tom that she, too, is a classroom observer, even though she does not have the luxury of observing in the way Tom does. Suppose she talks with him about what his data may mean, encourages him to observe the same children in nonacademic activities to round out his impressions of them, tells him when she can afford to observe, and explains how observation helps her to decide what to do. Suppose on the other hand, that the teacher lets Tom go about his business without paying much attention to him, seems to ignore or miss the kinds of observational cues he is picking up, and treats the business of lengthy note taking as somehow irrelevant. Clearly these two alternatives would communicate quite different messages about the role of observation in teaching and learning to teach. Note that the second alternative is liable to reinforce any beliefs about the irrelevance of academic learning for teaching that Tom might already hold.

Chance also plays a role. The cooperating teacher's conception of her work may include observation. Ordinarily, she makes time to act on this conception. This class of second graders, however, happens to be exceedingly diverse and lively. The teacher is busy keeping order while doing her best to adapt assignments for individual pupils. She cannot respond as fully as she would like to all pupils, let alone spend time with Tom.

Classrooms are busy places, and Tom sees that the teacher must attend to many things. The observational skills that he is developing are related to helping children learn. Without training in how to look and what to notice, it is easy to miss important clues about pupil responses to instructional activities. Tom can afford to concentrate on mastering this way of looking precisely because he is not responsible for what goes on. But there is a pitfall. If Tom does well in this assignment, he will have the gratification of a good grade. But this immediate reward is indigenous to the university culture, not to the culture of schools and teaching. The very structure of Tom's assignment shows that university learning and classroom teaching are worlds apart.

Tom's experience illustrates what we call the "two-worlds" pitfall. In teaching, observation is a means, not an end. Ways of seeing do not imply ways of acting. Tom may succeed in becoming a skilled observer, but this will not guarantee that he will know how to act wisely on what he notices. Nor will further classroom experience in itself activate the acquired skills in situations that call for observation. Tom will need help to see how what he has learned as a university student can shape his thought and action as a teacher. His university instructor may tell him that learning to look is important in learning to teach. Will Tom come to see observation as a valuable tool for the work of teaching, or as something he must do, this term, for a course requirement?

The two-worlds pitfall has at least two aspects. The norms and rewards associated with Tom's formal professional preparation fit with the academic setting. Doing well at the university brings immediate and highly salient rewards, which may not have much to do with success in teaching. On the other hand, the pressure to adapt to the way things are in schools is great. Moreover, this pressure will resonate with common-sense notions of teachers and classrooms acquired through the personal experience of schooling. Confronted with such pressure, academic learning is liable to evaporate, regardless of its worth. Its availability in memory depends on attributions of relevance and connections to particular instances that have personal meaning and felt significance. Its availability in action depends on know-how in adapting the learning to concrete situations.

VIGNETTE 3: PRACTICING TEACHING

It is spring. Sue has just begun her third week of student teaching in a fourth-grade classroom. Today, she is supposed to take over the morning activities. Since Sue has been watching the teacher for the past two weeks, she has a good idea about what the morning is like, and that makes her feel fairly comfortable. In addition, the teacher explained what lessons she should cover and gave Sue the teacher's guides to follow. This morning Sue is planning to play Simon Says after the reading lesson. She puts the math assignment on the board just like the teacher does and calls the first reading group to the front of the room. She calls on children in turn to read the story and then asks the questions spelled out in the guide. Everything goes smoothly, and Sue thinks with some elation that she can actually teach.

Next week Sue will take over for the entire day, which means that she will also teach spelling, science, and social studies. She plans to have a spelling bee for Friday. This will generate a lot of noisy excitement, because the pupils enjoy competing with each other. In science she will teach a unit on batteries and bulbs that the science methods teacher showed her; she wonders how the children will like discovering things on their own. So far she has not seen any science instruction in this classroom, but her cooperating teacher said she could try out this unit. Some movies have already been ordered for social studies, so the day will be pretty well filled. Sue hopes that she can keep the pupils busy and that she won't have to discipline anyone. She is eager to see if she can get through a whole day on her own. The outcome will mean a lot to her. Sue stands at the threshold of doing the work of teaching in earnest. Whatever will help her to come out of this experience in one piece will impress her as tried and trustworthy.

Commentary

So what does it prove if Sue can make it on her own in student teaching? In the first place, it shows that she can keep the system running, which is how Sue basically sees her task. She is confident, because she knows what happens in the morning. She believes that she can step into the teacher's shoes and do what her cooperating teacher does. Moving children through the daily schedule is, of course, part of the teacher's responsibility, but a real teacher also has to decide what that schedule will be, how the children should be grouped, and what assignments to put on the board. The point is that student teaching occurs in somebody else's classroom; this makes the requirements for action in student teaching fundamentally different from those that fall on the teacher.

Making it on one's own in student teaching is not the same as learning to teach. Sue's confidence is not well-founded; she does not see clearly that the givens around her were shaped and established over time and that, for the real teacher, there is a good deal of uncertainty to contend with. Classroom structure has to be created, and it can take different forms. Sue's personal experiences as a pupil and her experiences in the field do not provide a reliable sample of the variation in classroom environments. What can be experienced first hand is necessarily limited and likely to be biased. Just because experiences seem plausible does not mean they are trustworthy. Sue's belief that she knows how classrooms work will be difficult to dispel, because it grows out of things she has seen and participated in; these experiences are vivid and cathected. Yet inferences and generalizations based on firsthand experience are frequently unwarranted or at least premature.

One can see why Sue thinks she is learning to teach. She rehearses behaviors that she identifies with teaching and that mostly are familiar to the class. She and the cooperating teacher will see children at work, perhaps happily and with excitement. It is unlikely that her cooperating teacher will fail to commend her performance. Student teachers are particularly sensitive to things that bring about a feeling of success. Going through familiar routines and being praised will produce that feeling, independent of whether practices lead to student learning.

Sue's confidence is partly based on her observations in this classroom. But vivid memories of her own schooling also help her figure out what to do and how to structure the time and activities. This applies, for instance, to the spelling bee. Teachers often use competition as an incentive to get children through boring tasks. Unless Sue is helped to see the possible long-term consequences of such instructional strategies—shaping pupil conceptions of the purposes of classroom life in terms of rewards extrinsic to learning, for example—she may continue to think of a spelling bee simply as a "fun thing to do." If no one requires Sue to practice making and justifying instructional decisions or to consider the consequences of given actions in a specific practical context, she may get confirmed in a view of teaching as filling time, keeping children busy, perpetuating familiar practices without considering their consequences for pupil learning, in the short *and* long run. Classroom experience alone, whether past or present, cannot justify what teachers do, nor teach teachers to think about their work.

Sue has the impression, common to many teacher candidates, that student teaching is the time to put it all together, the definitive test of the relevance and practicality of formal preparation. In this context, it would be important to know what motivated Sue to try out the elementary science unit on batteries and bulbs. Was Sue's decision impelled by an interest in science and a belief that children should understand how their everyday world works? Or was it motivated by a desire to try out something new and neat (being "creative" is a characteristic of student teachers that teachers and teacher educators often judge favorably). The problem is that the discovery approach to science teaching rests on a view of knowledge that presupposes a deep understanding of subject matter and children's learning.

Sue has never seen the teacher in this classroom teach science. Has Sue seen any demonstration of "open" pedagogy in science? Without understanding the value and limits of "messing about," she will have no basis for deciding when and how to intervene in order to nudge children's learning along.

What will the experience be like, and what will Sue learn from it? Various scenarios are possible. The children could cooperate in this new kind of learning because the activities are fun, and the teacher could compliment Sue on her creativity. On the other hand, Sue could be unable to manage hands-on discovery learning, and the teacher could be displeased with the commotion and the amount of time being taken. While it is not clear whether *either* scenario would promote science learning in the pupils, *both* have potential for teaching Sue some things about teaching—if she is helped to articulate the lessons of this experience. Just as the pupils must make sense of their experiments with batteries and bulbs, so Sue must think about what happens in relation to pupil learning. In the first case, this means looking for evidence of student learning. In the second, it means figuring out what went wrong and what to do about it without rejecting the whole approach forever. (While it may be too complicated now, discovery learning is worth another try.)

Before one can assess what Sue has learned from her student teaching experience as a whole, one needs to know about the teacher's intentions as well as those of the university staff. Perhaps the teacher has judged that Sue needs a lot of guidance as she takes over a block of time. Or it may be that the teacher is not much inclined to have her classroom schedule altered, especially at this time of year. Has Sue been encouraged by the university staff to fit herself into the teacher's overall plan and propose mostly activities that do not alter what is going on in this classroom? The university staff realizes that teachers need to keep their classrooms running and appreciates how easily even routines that have been established over time and with care can be upset.

This analysis illustrates the "cross-purposes" pitfall. The legitimate purposes of teachers center on their classrooms; classrooms are not designed as laboratories and do not operate to further the purposes of learning to teach. Almost necessarily, the teacher will see the teacher education student's attention to the way things are as praiseworthy. It is functional from the point of view of classroom life. Yet, without instructional intervention, Sue's adaptiveness to the here and now may be dysfunctional for the long-range purposes of learning to teach. Learning from further experience presupposes acting with understanding. Attending to the immediate requirements for action in established settings does not foster the capacity to learn from further experience. Nor is one's success at this task a reliable predictor of success at running one's own classroom for the purposes of pupil learning.

CONCLUSION

The three vignettes illustrate three pitfalls that must be overcome, if preservice field experience in classrooms is to serve the broad purposes of learning to teach. At best, field experience in teacher preparation means learning things that are only part of the job of teaching. Once they begin teaching, Tom, Karen, and Sue will quickly see that they do not know all there is to know about teaching. The more serious problem is getting into pitfalls or learning things that are inappropriate in any teaching situation and that will be reinforced on the job. The familiarity pitfall arises from the fact that prospective teachers are no strangers to classrooms. The two-worlds pitfall arises from the fact that teacher education goes on in two distinct settings and from the fallacious assumption that making connections between these two worlds is straightforward and can be left to the novice. The third pitfall arises from the fact that classrooms are not set up for teaching teachers: It's a case of being at cross-purposes.

These pitfalls arrest thought or mislead prospective teachers into believing that central aspects of teaching have been mastered and understood. Premature closure comes from faulty perceptions and judgments that are supported, even rewarded, by trusted persons and a salient setting. For Tom, this setting is probably the university classroom; for Karen and Sue, the elementary classroom. What makes these perceptions pitfalls is that future teachers get into them without knowing it and have a hard time getting out. What makes them even more treacherous is that they may not look like pitfalls to an insider, but rather like a normal place to be. Clearly, help from the outside is necessary on both counts.

Overcoming the Pitfalls

The familiar is the most salient and the least amenable to inquiry. Overcoming the familiarity pitfall requires a break with the taken-for-granted and a recognition that the familiar and the real rest on social and mental constructions. Future teachers cannot be expected to recognize that what they know about classroom life is only part of a universe of possibilities. They need help in seeing how their personal history and experience of schooling influence their perceptions of classrooms in a way that makes it difficult to appreciate alternatives. Both ends and means must be considered. A larger and more flexible vision need not result in a rejection of traditional or familiar ideas and practices. There is, however, a big difference between mere habit and customary action that is understood and seen in perspective. Furthermore, plain thinking and empirical research do sometimes show that traditional ways of doing things are not always sound or effective. Overcoming the familiarity pitfall should keep future teachers from confusing what is with what can be or should be, and heighten their receptivity to new data.

Overcoming the two-worlds pitfall requires acknowledging that the world of thought and the world of action are legitimately different. Each has its unifying purposes and a potential for making a contribution to learning to teach. In other words, one does not overcome the two-worlds pitfall by eliminating it. The goal of professional education is acting with understanding. Neither understanding nor action by itself will suffice, and belief alone does not produce action. Teacher education students need help in seeing how understanding can clarify and shape ways of doing. They also need instruction in judging ways of doing and in adapting them to particular settings as well as to their own capacities. Teacher education students cannot be expected to make the crucial distinction between enlightenment and application in considering the uses of knowledge in teaching. This is where teacher educators must take responsibility for their students' learning.

Finally, there are two ways to overcome the cross-purpose pitfall. One is to identify learning to teach with adaptation to whatever classroom and school setting the student teacher is placed in. The more desirable alternative is to work toward a closer fit between the purposes of classroom life and those of learning to teach. This would require structural and normative changes in schools, changes that would enable teachers to study their practice together and get rewards for doing so. If schools became places where teachers as well as pupils learned, then future teachers would learn to teach in classrooms where their cooperating teachers were also students of teaching.

In such a setting, chance and the press for action would not decide what student teachers learn. The give and take of conversation among persons at different places in learning to teach would expand the universe of concrete alternatives and overcome the limits and biases of personal experience. Thus, future teachers would get the message that learning to teach is a lengthy, ongoing process that other people care about, a process in which one's own experiences provide only some of the data.

REFERENCES

Anderson, D. C. (1981). *Evaluating curriculum proposals.* New York: Wiley.

Becker, H. S. (1972). A school is a lousy place to learn anything in. *American Behavioral Scientist, 16*(1), 85–105.

Buchmann, M., & Schwille, J. (1983). Education: The overcoming of experience. *American Journal of Education, 92,*(1), 30–51.

Dewey, J. (1965). The relation of theory to practice in education. In M. L. Borrowman (Ed.), *Teacher education in America: A documentary history.* New York: Teachers College Press, Columbia University. (Original work published in 1904)

Feiman-Nemser, S. (1983). Learning to teach. In L. Shulman & G. Sykes (Eds.), *Handbook on teaching and policy.* New York: Longman.

Little, J. W. (1982). Norms of collegiality and experimentation: Workplace conditions of school success. *American Educational Research Journal, 19*(3), 325–340.

Nisbett, R., & Ross, L. (1980). *Human inference: Strategies and shortcomings of social judgment.* Englewood Cliffs, NJ: Prentice-Hall.

Platt, J. (1973). Social traps. *American Psychologist, 28,* 641–651.

Sarason, S. B. (1982). *The culture of the school and the problem of change* (2nd ed.). Boston, MA: Allyn & Bacon.

Tabachnick, B., Popkewitz, T., & Zeichner, K. (1980). Teacher education and the professional perspectives of student teachers. *Interchange, 10*(4), 12–29.

Wilson, J. (1975). *Educational theory and the preparation of teachers.* Slough, England: NFER Publishing Co.

Zeichner, K. (1980). Myths and realities: Field-based experiences in preservice teacher education. *Journal of Teacher Education, 6,* 45–55.

5

The Role of the Practicum in Teacher Education: A Particular Point of View

Donald Hogben
Ken Simpson
Flinders University of South Australia

In a recently published Australian report entitled *The Practicum in Teacher Education* (Turney et al., 1982), the authors make the following statement early in their first chapter:

> Ideally conceived the practicum is a purposeful series of supervised professional experiences in which student teachers apply, refine, and reconstruct theoretical learnings, and through which they develop their teaching competencies. The practicum is an integral part of the programme of teacher education contributing to the achievement of its aims and closely related to its content components. (p. 1)

As it stands, this statement seems straightforward enough; one finds little immediately to argue with. However, as the report unfolds, and as one examines more closely central notions such as "theoretical learnings," "teaching competencies," and "teacher education," it becomes very clear that the meanings attached to such expressions can and do vary considerably. These variations have profound implications for the role of the practicum.

In this chapter we examine some central notions of the kind identified in the previous paragraph, particularly as they bear upon the nature and significance of the practicum. In so doing we shall draw upon our experience with the Bachelor of Education degree offered by the School of Education at Flinders University of South Australia. This degree has been substantially restructured over the past few years and, in the course of this restructuring, serious consideration was given to its basic purpose and to the place of the practicum within the overall program.

Although some readers would perhaps find a detailed account of this particular degree program interesting as such, we actually devote very little attention to specific program details. Rather, we focus on the sorts of major issues which concerned us in our planning and which must be of concern in any teacher education program, even though their final resolution in particular programs may differ markedly from ours. In the course of this portrayal we make no attempt at any sort of detailed, comprehensive review of relevant literature, which is now very extensive. Nor do we discuss any other teacher education programs or practices. Because the report referred to previously does contain a thorough review of the literature, both Australian and overseas, and because it contains at least some reference to the themes we shall be pursuing, we shall quote from it at a number of places in order to illustrate certain points. Generally, however, too much concern with other approaches is counterproductive. A condition of useful discussion is the establishment of a context of discussion coherent in its own terms, rather than the attempt to combine incompatible positions (see Simpson, 1981).

Although we write from within an Australian context, we believe that what we have to say may well apply equally in many other places. Our familiarity with teacher education in Britain and the United States suggests that the issues and problems in at least these countries are very similar to those we address from Australia.

PROGRAM PURPOSE AND AUTHORITY SOURCE

Despite the generally acknowledged central place of the practicum in teacher education degree programs and the consistent research finding that students typically regard the practicum as the most important component of such programs, it continues to present serious problems for program planners and remains for many students a threatening, confusing, frustrating, disappointing experience. The literature (including the Australian already referred to) abounds with discussion of the practicum and its problems, and the personal experiences of the present authors have certainly included encounters with most of the standard concerns. Practica are frequently difficult to organize, relations between training institutions and schools are sometimes strained, the roles and responsibilities of supervising school teachers vis-à-vis staff from institutions are often unclear and, despite the acknowledged importance of the practicum, it nevertheless remains for many university and college education faculty something they would be relieved to see as outside their sphere of responsibility.

While many of the problems with the practicum are indeed quite serious and are extremely difficult to overcome satisfactorily, we take the view that a good many of them are in fact secondary difficulties and would largely disappear from teacher education programs, if the central task of identifying program purpose were seriously addressed and resolved. We now consider this issue in some detail, arguing the necessity for a clearly formulated understanding of central thrust of any given program. But, since not all programs of teacher education can nor should pursue the same ends, it follows that there must be practica designed for distinctly different major purposes. This does not mean, of course, that such programs may not share a number of features.

A satisfactory answer to questions about the purpose of any particular program presupposes that some authoritative basis upon which choice of purpose can be defended has been accepted. At various times Flinders University School of Education has invoked a variety of bases, the choice being determined by the contingent features of the occasion or the particular idiosyncrasies of the people who happened to be involved. Decisions tended to be pragmatic, and the principles were accordingly flexible. And we have every reason to believe that the state of affairs would be a fairly accurate portrayal of the situation obtaining in a very large number of teacher education programs operating today. Once we decided that a major program difficulty was the absence of a firm, authoritative base and that we did indeed need a clear point from which to start, there followed fairly readily agreement that the starting point lay with the nature of the institution of which we are part: the university.

Notwithstanding the existence of more-or-less powerful influences on universities and colleges, there is a reasonably clear sense in which they are in control of their programs; and they are certainly responsible, and perhaps accountable, for the quality of these programs. Attempts to abdicate this responsibility cannot succeed, for should authority be transferred to some outside group such as, for example, a professional teacher organization, the university would remain accountable for *this* decision and would need to justify it appropriately.

We know of no cases where universities or colleges have fully abdicated control or allowed significant program components to be determined solely by outside groups. However, there are many programs of teacher education wherein such abdication, or something very close to abdication, has occurred in the case of the practicum. Certainly in the case of the Flinders's Bachelor of Education degree, it was true until fairly recently that the supervising classroom teachers, school principals, and deputy principals were very largely responsible for planning the students' school experiences and evaluating their performances. Education faculty did indeed visit the students in the schools, but such visits served an essentially public relations or liaison function. Although the University faculty retained the right to determine the final result of each student's practicum, the reports received from supervising teachers and other school personnel were heavily relied upon. Turney et al. (1982) surveyed teacher education institutions across

Australia and reported a variety of practices concerning the allocation of responsibility for practicum organization, student supervision, and final assessment. While noting that a number of institutions insist that they must retain the major responsibility for student practicum assessment, they concluded that

> an increasing number of institutions rely heavily on the supervising teacher's evaluation reports. (Turney et al., 1982, p. 181)

The following statement from one university teacher education program is cited:

> the major advising and assessing roles belong to the Master Teachers (supervising school teachers)...who know best the school situation in which they and the student are working. (Turney et al, 1982, p. 181)

Such a statement not only makes quite clear where the major responsibility for student assessment is taken to lie, but it also clearly reflects the program purpose: to prepare school classroom teachers committed to a particular set of beliefs and practices. The Flinders's program is differently oriented, and the nature of the difference is explicated in the remainder of this chapter.

Despite what some of the comments made so far might suggest, the central thrust of Flinders University Bachelor of Education since its restructuring still remains, in some sense (which we clarify later), teacher preparation with a focus on the elementary school. This aim presupposes some view of teacher roles, which, if the University is to retain authority and control of the program, must be determined by the University. To this we now turn.

THE ROLE OF THE TEACHER

The immediately obvious way for any institution preparing teachers to proceed is to *specify* the role of the classroom teacher, and, on the basis of that specification, to identify the kind of preparation that role requires, hoping, perhaps, to show that the kind of preparation required is one that the particular institution is admirably fitted to provide. But diversity of opinion invariably intervenes: The role of the teacher is variously conceived, and these various conceptions can stretch teacher role to overlap with roles normally clearly distinguished from that of the classroom teacher. On various lines of extension, the teacher's role overlaps that of driving instructors, dancing teachers, and training officers in industrial or commercial enterprises; that of authors, publishers, and media producers; that of clergymen, social workers, and psychiatrists. Accounts of the role that identify it with the whole of this field make it unplayable; accounts that select from the field are open to criticism for their sins of omission.

Specifying the role of the teacher is no simple task. This fact has been recognized recently in a number of reports of inquiries into teacher education in Australia. The year 1980 saw the completion of a national inquiry into teacher education chaired by Emeritus Professor Auchmuty (1980), and the publication of state inquiries from New South Wales (Correy, 1980), South Australia (Gilding, 1980), Victoria (Asche, 1980), and Western Australia (Vickery, 1980). All reports considered the practicum and contained some discussion of teacher role, noting particularly how it appears generally to have broadened and become more complex in recent years. The South Australian inquiry, for example, referred to submissions it had received and discussions its members had held in schools, which had repeatedly thrown up contrasting opinions regarding the "proper" role of the classroom teacher.

> On the one hand, there are those who hold that teachers are now being asked to undertake a variety of tasks beyond those formerly seen as their province and for which they have been insufficiently prepared. This, it is argued, should be recognised in changes to their professional development programmes [including the practicum] and to their conditions of service. On the other, it is contended that many of the tasks teachers are being asked to deal with are quite outside, and interfere with, their legitimate function and constitute a tendency which should be resisted, or even reversed, so they can resume a role more obviously centred on classroom work. (Gilding, 1980, pp. 1–2)

Against this sort of background, we see no way of satisfactorily specifying *the* role of the teacher, except that it be specified in the most formal way; that is, in a way which offers a pattern to which any acceptable account of teacher role should conform, rather than a specification of substantive practices, principles, or purposes. If the role were to be specified in substantive rather than formal terms, then one is obliged, we believe, to recognize a very large number of alternatives requiring different forms of preservice preparation. We have proposed (and this proposition has been accepted and underlies much that takes place in Flinders University B.Ed. program) that teacher role should be *formally specified*. This formal specification identifies as central to the role of the teacher the making of well-grounded decisions of a particular kind. Despite our coming down in favor of formal role specification, we fully recognize that the alternatives of giving either a formal or a substantive account of the teacher's role have considerable overlap. The substantive option requires that alternative roles be identified and how they are played out demonstrated; perhaps, for a number of reasons, with one particular alternative being identified. The formal option, of the kind referred to previously, requires an account being given of the sort of decisions in question and the contexts in which such decisions might be grounded. Of course, the satisfaction of such a requirement does in fact involve a consideration of the content of the substantive option. If one calls the body of belief which supports a particular role description or account an *educational theory,* one could say that the major difference between the formal and the substantive options is that the former requires a concern with extratheoretical and metatheoretical issues, while the latter does not.

Before taking up in more detail a consideration of teacher education within universities, and in particular the Bachelor of Education degree at Flinders University, some further fairly brief remarks about theories and roles seem warranted. For those readers interested in a detailed account of "educational theory" underpinning much of the B.Ed. program restructuring and the place of the practicum, such an account has been provided by Simpson (1982). In our view, a lot of confusion in teacher education can be traced to lack of clarity over what is understood by "educational theory." Much of this confusion probably results from the demarcation of "theory" from "practice," and the failure by many writers and planners of teacher preparation programs to recognize the existence and significance of *practical theories.* Discussions of the practicum either in the general literature or in university and college handbooks and brochures, seem almost invariably to contain some comment similar to "Organized school experiences will attempt to integrate the practical and theoretical aspects of the degree program." A chapter devoted to problems of the practicum in the report by Turney et al. (1982, pp. 24–26) includes a section headed "Theory–Practice Dichotomy" in which the authors observe:

> The need to relate the experiences of the practicum with other more theoretical components of the teacher education programme has been a growing concern of many teacher education institutions, and programmes specially designed to integrate theory and practice are gaining impetus. (p. 25)

Educational theories should be clearly distinguished from psychological theories, sociological theories, and the rest; and they should be recognized as practical theories. Such recognition removes the theoretical–practical dichotomy and forces the acceptance of the view that classroom practice in fact *exhibits* educational theory. This is so, because a practical theory is one in which a general purpose is developed into specific actions, and/or specific actions are justified relative to some general purpose. By definition, a practical theory necessarily combines normative and empirical components, the normative component providing the basis of the identity of a particular theory. Theories are logically ordered, and, ideally, basic normative rules entail executive decisions. The most obvious distinction between educational and other practical theories is in terms of the *general purpose:* The distinction between a program of public education and one of public health or transport, for example, is best drawn in terms of the general purpose of the program. The role of participants or practitioners in a practical program should be specified in terms of the categories of decision that they are required to undertake in the implementation of the program; it is thus to be specified in terms of the purpose involved.

It seems obvious enough and true enough to say that the role of teachers will be differently specified in terms of different theories. Of course, to assert this requires that one be able to say what are the characteristics of a purpose or of a theory which make that a distinct educational purpose or theory. In other words, there must exist criteria for putative educational theories. These criteria will have to establish conditions of *kind* and of *adequacy;* that is, they will have to establish the nature of an educational purpose together with the requirements of a complete or adequate statement of a purpose of that sort. They will thus constitute an account of an educational theory, and hence of teacher role, which is formal in the sense that it does not generate specific prescriptions for action but provides rather the formal framework within which such prescriptions can be generated on the basis of substantive purposes.

THE UNIVERSITY AND TEACHER EDUCATION

In the course of providing formal accounts or descriptions of the kind elaborated previously, one would naturally offer such examples of alternative substantive educational theories as were available. Since time in preservice programs is limited and theories are indefinitely complex, one might well concentrate on that theory which was most commonly used; or at least, upon the theory/theories which came closest to providing an account of what was currently occurring in schools. Despite the fact that the substantive option appears to be the most commonly adopted in colleges and universities providing programs in teacher education, Flinders School of Education is moving against a preoccupation with this orientation. Located as it is within a university, and given the nature of its faculty and its involvement with continuing research, it is very well suited to the formal option. The formal option is, in effect, the study of educational theories, a pursuit which can with benefit include observation of and experience in classroom teaching, but which is not primarily concerned with the encouragement of any particular form of classroom practice, or the pursuit of any particular classroom goals; except, of course, its own. Any *particular* educational theory represents a closure of prior questions; thus to exhibit a theory is not an academically demanding task. The examination of attempted closures in the metatheory is just the sort of task with which a research-oriented institution such as Flinders University might be expected to be engaged. If one can also argue, as we believe we can, that the formal option does indeed prepare students to meet a pressing need of the education enterprise, one is well on the way to an account of the point of one's educational programs, which would both justify their place in a university and support their claim to serve as qualifying students for teaching, among other things.

We commence the required argument by contrasting the natural interest of universities, as suggested, with that of schools; and in the process we shall make some preliminary comments on the teaching practicum. Our comments on schools are necessarily somewhat oversimplified and general. We feel sure, however, that readers will nevertheless find in our account a recognizable state of affairs.

Universities, in contrast to elementary and high schools, have a choice between formal and substantive options in their concern with the study of education. Schools must express a particular theory; or, one might say, schools *are* expressions of particular theories. We don't mean to say by this that any given school will profess and follow some complete and consistent theory. Such is rarely, if ever, the case in practice. The point is just that any given school does *something;* and to the extent that what it does is done purposefully and consistently, it is the expression of a theory. A school thus exhibits patterns of behavior and, from its point of view, it is more important that a teacher (or a student practicing teaching) *fits* the pattern than that he or she *interprets* or *values* the patterns in any particular way. Schools typically have no interest in metatheory or in theories other than those which they express; unless perhaps, things go so drastically wrong that they lose a sense of the pattern of their activities, in which case one might wonder whether they should still be called "schools." Indeed, it may only be if something goes wrong that a particular school would show any interest in the theory it expresses; and even then the interest may be expressed by teachers comparing dispositions to act rather than enunciating principles of action. One might say: A school is concerned with an educational theory only as it is expressed in practice; a university such as Flinders is concerned with theories—contributory theories and metatheory—and with practice only as an expression of a theory.

This isn't necessarily a criticism of schools. It appears to us perfectly appropriate that they should run that way. And in societies that are highly conservative, stable, and homogeneous, schools do appear to run well in that way. In such "steady states," given that any significant aspect of theory must be reflected in an aspect of practice, then correct practice is not only valuable in itself but also a sufficient criterion of theoretical grasp. And, any student who successfully models his or her behavior on that of a competent teacher can be regarded as theoretically and practically trained. On the assumption of a high degree of stability and homogeneity, the chance of significant theoretical diversity, or at least of the serious promulgation of diverse theories, is slight. The practice models offered to students will be familiar and congenial, and the practices acquired by students during their training will travel well in space and time. However, it is clear that contemporary western societies do not accord well with this description. We are being continually reminded from all quarters that we are living in times of rapid change; established authority of nearly every kind (political, religious, moral, intellectual) is being questioned, and many current economic and social trends are unlikely to be halted or reversed. The Director General of the South Australian State Education Department has recently spoken on the theme of the schools vis-à-vis societal change. He concluded:

> I believe, therefore, that the schools should not endeavour to reinvent societies, but to reflect their needs and aspirations. In doing so schools must change. Inevitably, there will be disagreements about what are, in fact, the needs and aspirations of students, and about the adaptations that are made by schools. (Steinle, 1981)

To a certain extent schools are protected from the effects of rapid change, despite the unseemly haste which occasionally characterizes the adoption of fads by schools in some places. School systems actually possess enormous inertia. Any school, in a sense, spans about a century: It is influenced, through the conditioned expectations of its older teachers, by some 50 years of the past, and it influences, through its conditioning of potential teachers among its pupils, some 50 years of the future. Lortie (1973, 1975) has drawn attention to the fact that training in education seems to have a relatively low impact on teacher attitudes and behavior. He stresses the influence school pupil experience exerts, and believes that "the protracted exposure to potent models leads teachers-to-be to internalize...modes of behavior which are triggered in later teaching...To a considerable extent future teacher behavior is rooted in experiences which predate formal training" (Lortie, 1973, p. 487). Research conducted with Bachelor of Education degree students at Flinders prior to the restructuring of the degree (see, for example, Hogben & Petty, 1979a, 1979b) and, more recently with students preparing to be high school teachers through the same institution (see Hogben & Lawson, 1983, 1984), has provided some support for Lortie. However, despite the overall stability of attitudes of students and beginning teachers, revealed through the research at Flinders, some quite marked changes have been detected. The powerful influence of what Lortie (1975) has termed "apprenticeship-of-observation" cannot be denied, but the protection against change and new experiences is not complete by any means. Teachers are confronted with tasks that they have not practiced and certainly lose faith in some practices in new situations. Practices are changed or adopted, often in an ad hoc fashion; and teacher education students may not find the patterns familiar or congenial. They may also develop well-founded doubts about the capacity of models to travel. On the whole, modeling, with or without some explicit recognition of the theory the model is supposed to express, cannot be better than a partial answer to the question how to prepare teachers. A teacher must expect to make many conscious decisions in more-or-less unfamiliar contexts. This requires more than habits of action—and we certainly do not wish to deny the importance of habits in many day-to-day classroom situations. And it requires more than the ability to state a theory. It requires, in addition, an understanding of the way in which that theory is distinct from other theories and the resources its background supporting theories provide for identifying and explaining situations, so that the theory can be brought to bear upon them. It would be nice to think that all teachers possessed this capacity; plainly they do not. It is our view that it is very important that at least some should, and it is a capacity that the Flinders University B.Ed. degree program is aiming to develop through its concern with formal theory.

THE ROLE OF THE PRACTICUM

The wide range and variety of aims or goals found in statements about teacher education programs, and/or reflected in the sorts of activities they support, can be reduced to three basic orientations. These orientations or purposes, expressed in very broad terms, appear to be: (a) to produce graduates who are good at what the schools currently do; (b) to produce graduates who are good at what the schools ought to be doing; and (c) to produce graduates who are good at deciding what ought to be done. From what we have said so far in this discussion, it will be clear that the third broad purpose is that pursued in our Bachelor of Education degree. Since the practicum forms an integral and essential component of the degree program, its function must be to support this basic purpose. Therefore the Flinders practicum might be said to be to afford students the opportunity to develop their understanding of educational theory by planning courses of action on a theoretical base and to analyze observed practices and behaviors in a theoretical context. Of course, these become complementary activities when the actions taken and the observations made occur in the same classrooms. This work involves: (a) the attempt to identify at least one theoretical context— that which the classroom instantiates; (b) analysis and discussion of that context as far as it can be identified; (c) perhaps the identification of an alternative theoretical context as one in which the student would choose to practice in that setting; and (d) the use of one of those contexts as a basis for the student's teaching activities. In practice, the Flinders students work in at least three different schools over the final two years of the program and are expected to reveal an increasing capacity to undertake these tasks satisfactorily. The students are required to maintain detailed observation records and detailed plans of teachings undertaken.

With such activities reflecting the central purpose of the program, the record of the student's practicum must include a reflective account of the instantiated theory related to specific observations; may include an account of an alternative theory which the student is employing (or would employ in a similar situation); and must include an account of the student's teaching activities which relates them to the theory stated. Satisfactory performance in these respects, together with displayed ability to use the appropriate theoretical terms in the given concrete situations, is the basis of a passing grade for the practicum.

This account of the place and nature of the practicum raises questions concerning the roles and responsibilities of supervising classroom teachers vis-à-vis those of practicum supervisors from the University: indeed the overall relationship between the cooperating schools and the University's School of Education. Quite clearly, the roles and relationships differ markedly from those commonly obtaining in Australia and elsewhere and certainly differ in quite fundamental respects from the situation reflected in the quotation from Turney et al. (1982, p. 181) which we cited in the section entitled "Program Purpose and Authority Source." Clearly, for the Flinders University Bachelor of Education practicum to function as intended, the School of Education must provide students with a framework of understanding of educational theory within which they can attempt to satisfy practicum requirements and within which their work in the schools can be assessed. This is accomplished through the lecture and seminar program conducted at the Univeristy. During the practicum, University supervisors must assist students in meeting the requirements and, of course, must play the major role in their assessment. This is accomplished through a careful examination of the students' recorded work, discussion of this work with the students, and regular observation of the students' classroom activities.

Under such a scheme, the supervising classroom teachers are not answerable to the School of Education, and they do not form part of its teaching force. From the School of Education's point of view, they are in a very real sense part of the subject matter. Cooperation from supervising teachers, is of course, quite essential. It would be at best difficult, and at worst impossible, for students to meet our practicum requirements, if their supervising teachers were unable or unwilling to devote time to discussion with them.

The Bachelor of Education degree at Flinders University is considered primarily as a *qualification for teaching* and not as a guarantee of acceptable classroom performance; that is, the award does not certify performance as a teacher. This has clear and important implications for the practicum and for any reports or references written for students on the basis of their practicum activities. That we do not see our degree as certifying performance as a teacher does not, of course, mean that the School of Education has no interest whatsoever in such performance. From all that we have said so far, this is quite clearly not the case. What we do wish to stress is the distinction between "qualification for teaching" and "performance as a teacher." It so happens that the registering authorities in Australia consider the possession of the Flinders Bachelor of Education degree (a qualification for teaching) a sufficient basis for provisional registration as a teacher. Full registration is typically granted upon the completion of one year's acceptable teaching performance. But such a situation need not necessarily obtain. It would be quite possible for the University to award the degree to a student whose teaching performance, from the school's point of view, is considered unsatisfactory. A student's school performance may be of a kind and of a standard sufficient to satisfy the University's demands, and yet the student may not have modelled any observed behavior nor indeed exhibited any patterns of behavior which inclined any supervising teacher or school principal to certify, through a report or reference, that he or she would be a desirable employee. It would be wrong in our view for the University to withold its award in such a situation, though perfectly correct for the schools with which the student was associated through the practicum to withold a reference which might be used to secure employment. Conversely, it would be quite wrong for the University to grant its award to a student who had obtained glowing reports and references from the schools, but who had failed to establish to the University's satisfaction that he or she had an adequate grasp of educational theory as we have defined it.

CONCLUSION

Job-oriented modeling conceptions of the practicum are common in Australia and elsewhere. Quite clearly, such conceptions are of interest to the employers, to the graduates of teacher education programs, and also to the schools who cooperate with the training institutions in the mounting of practice. However, we have argued here that such conceptions are not those best suited to the university, and they are of doubtful value anyway. We have supported this argument with an account of the sort of thinking which is underpinning the Bachelor of Education degree program presently offered within the School of Education at the Flinders University of South Australia, and, in the course of this account, we have outlined what we take to be an academically significant conception of the practicum. Since students can quite readily display job capacity, and secure employment references, in the course of their practicum academic exercises, there is certainly no need for us to disavow, or seek to eliminate this function of the practicum.

REFERENCES

Asche, K. J. A. (1980). *Teacher education in Victoria*. (Interim Report of the Committee of the Victorian Enquiry into Teacher Education). Melbourne: Government Printer.

Auchmuty, J. J. (1980). *Report of the national inquiry into teacher education.* Canberra: Australian Government Publishing Service.

Correy, P. M. (1980). *Teachers for tomorrow.* (Report of the Committee to Examine Teacher Education in New South Wales). Sydney: Government Printer.

Gilding, K. R. (1980). *Report of the South Australian enquiry into teacher education,* South Australia: Government Printer.

Hogben, D., & Lawson, M. J. (1983). Attitudes of secondary school teacher trainees and their practice teaching supervisors. *Journal of Education for Teaching, 9,* (3), 249–263.

Hogben, D., & Lawson, M. J. (1984). Trainee and beginning teacher attitude stability and change: Four case studies. *Journal of Education for Teaching, 10* (2), 135–153.

Hogben, D., & Petty, M. F. (1979). Early changes in teacher attitude. *Educational Research, 21,* (3), 212–219.

Hogben, D., & Petty, M. F. (1979). From student to primary school teacher: Attitude stability and change. *South Pacific Journal of Teacher Education, 7,* (3 & 4), 92–98.

Lortie, D. C. (1973). Observations on teaching as work. In R. M. W. Travers, (Ed.), *Second handbook of research on teaching.* Chicago, IL: Rand McNally.

Lortie, D. C. (1975). *School teacher: A sociological study.* Chicago, IL: University of Chicago Press.

Simpson, K. (1981). The definition of curriculum. *Curriculum Perspectives, 2,* 23–26.

Simpson, K. (1982). The identity of educational theories. *Educational Philosophy and Theory, 14* (2), 51–59.

Steinle, J. (1981, November). *Should schools endeavour to re-invent society or should they reflect it?* Public lecture delivered at the Flinders University of South Australia as part of the series "The Education of South Australia" arranged by the School of Education.

Turney, C., Cairns, L. G., Eltis, K. J., Hatton, N., Thew, D. M., Towler, J., Wright, R. (1982). *The practicum in teacher education: Research, practice, and supervision.* Sydney: Sydney University Press.

Vickery, R. L. (1980). *Teacher education in Western Australia.* (Report of the Committee of Inquiry into Teacher Education appointed by the Minister for Education in Western Australia). Perth: Government Printer.

6

Expressive Nonverbal Behaviors; A Review of Research on Training with Consequent Recommendations for Teacher Education

Hans G. Klinzing
University of Tuebingen, West Germany

Richard P. Tisher
Monash University, Australia

INTRODUCTION

The terms nonverbal behavior and nonverbal communication are often used interchangeably. Strictly speaking nonverbal behavior denotes the broad category of behavioral or physiological responses other than words. The category includes a wide range of phenomena, for example, coverbal behaviors such as gesture, facial expression, eye gaze; paralanguage, such as tone and pitch of voice, rate and length of speaking, errors in speech; proxemics, such as distance between speakers, use of space; and features such as appearance (attractiveness, dress), smell and the arrangement of the physical environment. Nonverbal communication includes all of the preceding features and, in addition, involves the transmission and interpretation of messages which depend upon the nature of the environment and the shared codes, or meanings about that environment. Nonverbal communication involves interpretation of messages linked with nonverbal behaviors.

Anthropologists, psychologists, sociologists, and linguists have, for more than half a century been interested in nonverbal communication and have produced a large number of research reports.[1] It is only within the last two decades that educationists have begun to take greater note of the important role of nonverbal behavior and communication in the teaching process. That interest, however, has resulted in a number of important payoffs, as the reviews of Smith (1979) and Woolfolk and Brooks (1983) attest. A number of correlational and experimental studies indicate that nonverbal behaviors like eye contact, gestures, vocal inflections and body movement, and combinations of nonverbal behaviors depicted by "enthusiasm," "animation," and "variation of stimuli," can have positive effects on students' motivation, attention, rating of the teacher, immediate recall, and achievement.[2] On the other hand, there are some studies that indicate that high frequencies of given nonverbal behaviors have negative effects in lessons such as reducing pupils' attention to lesson content and consequently their achievement (Brophy & Evertson, 1974b). There are others that show that when students are involved in inquiry–discovery, or discussion, or practicing tool skills (Bettencourt, 1979; Brophy & Evertson, 1974a), or when the lesson content is intrinsically interesting (Land, 1980; Williams & Ware, 1976), nonverbal behaviors have little influence on outcomes. Be that as it may, the weight of the evidence is such that the role of teachers' nonverbal behaviors in enhancing pupils' attention, interest, motivation, and achievement has been established. As a consequence there are implications for preservice and inservice teacher education to develop teachers' awareness about nonverbal behaviors and their effects and to help them to express themselves nonverbally. How teachers' awareness about nonverbal behaviors is to be enhanced and how they are to be trained to be judicially expressive nonverbally can be deduced from a number of studies that have assessed the effects of nonverbal behavior training programs with trainee and experienced teachers. Findings from training studies in counseling and psychotherapy also contain implications for teacher training.

PURPOSE AND ORGANIZATION OF THIS REVIEW

An objective of this review of research on projects attempting to enhance the quality or the quantity of teachers' nonverbal behaviors was to ascertain whether any consistent guidelines could be formulated for nonverbal behavior training programs. Detailed searches through the ERIC document

---

[1] The research studies include those in anthropology by Birdswhistell (1970), in sociology by Goffman (1963), in psychology by Dittman and Llewellyn (1968), Ekman and Friesen (1972), Hall (1966), Scheflen (1976) and Sommer (1969), and in "speech" by Ehrensberger (1945) and Woolbert (1920).

[2] Sixteen correlational and 18 experimental studies were located in which relationships between non-verbal behaviors and student or audience outcomes were studied (see Klinzing et al., 1984a). The studies include those by Conners and Eisenberg (1966), Fortune (1967), Kaufman (1976), Rosenshine (1968), and Williams and Ware (1977).

collection, dissertation abstracts, reports, and bibliographies yielded over 700 references on the training of teachers about nonverbal behaviors. Of these, only 64 were judged to be relevant to the purposes of this review which is directed to procedures for increasing individuals' perceptions about and sensitivity to nonverbal behaviors, for enhancing individuals' repertoires of nonverbal behaviors, and to the relative effects of components in nonverbal behavior training programs.

Details about the 64 studies are summarized in Tables 1 to 3. Table 1 lists reports of projects designed to increase teachers' perceptions and knowledge about nonverbal behaviors; Table 2 lists those dealing with other teacher and pupil outcomes (conducted in actual classrooms or scaled-down versions of these); and Table 3 lists those studies reporting the relative effectiveness of components of the training programs. The tables are not mutually exclusive since a number of studies deal with more than one of the variables used to cluster projects into a table.

For convenience, details about the studies appear under several headings in the tables. Information is provided about authors, experimental subjects, the research design, components of the training program, (inclusion of theory, demonstrations, modeling, discrimination training, practice, or feedback), and the outcome measures. It is appropriate to note that studies have used high and low inference measures which may be directly related to the objectives of a training program (e.g., frequency of nonverbal behaviors, voice delivery), to ancillary teacher variables not clearly related to the objectives of the training (e.g., assertiveness, clarity, warmth, attentiveness), and to pupil outcomes (e.g., attitude to the content or teacher, and achievement). Where authors provided sufficient details, it was possible to calculate effect sizes (ES) using procedures recommended by Glass (1977) and Glass, McGaw, and Smith (1981), and these values have been incorporated into the tables. Vote counting was also used to help with interpretations of the findings from studies.

In the ensuing sections, the discussion first deals with research on the enhancement of individuals' perceptiveness about nonverbal behaviors. Attention is then focused on the training studies in actual and scaled-down classrooms listed in Table 2, followed by a review of the research on the effectiveness of components of a training program. The chapter concludes with a brief statement about the essential elements of a nonverbal behavior training program and unresolved issues for further study.

EFFECTS OF TRAINING ON TEACHERS' AWARENESS OF NONVERBAL BEHAVIORS

Tables 1A, 1B, and 1C summarize details about 38 projects that have attempted to enhance teachers' awareness of nonverbal behaviors. As these tables indicate, during training the trainees were presented with some theories and/or details about nonverbal behaviors, read written materials, watched demonstrations and films, participated in discussions, and engaged in exercises to decode or to discriminate between various types of nonverbal behaviors. A minority of the projects contained periods for practice, usually consisting of 5 to 10-min encounters with peers and feedback sessions. The time devoted to training varied greatly across the studies, ranging from a minimum of 15 min to a maximum of 40 hr. A majority of the projects (25) were designed as pre-, posttest investigations but without random assignment of subjects. In 11 studies (see Table 1C) the pretest constituted the only method of "training" by which the subjects were sensitized to nonverbal behaviors. As Table 1C shows, an average effect size of 0.43 was calculated for ten of these. It is interesting to note that for the first six studies in Table 1C, where very short pretests, often consisting of two dozen still pictures, were used, only small gains were obtained: Average effect size was calculated as 0.10. On the other hand, when a relatively long test such as PONS (Rosenthal, Hall, DiMatteo, Rogers, & Archer, 1979) was used larger gains were obtained. For example, for the Rosenthal et al. (1979) and Klinzing, Kunkel, Schiefer, and Steiger (1984b) studies, the average effect size was 1.27. The PONS test uses a 47-min black-and-white film consisting of 220 two-second auditory and visual segments to be classified and consequently provides intensive practice in the decoding of nonverbal cues. This feature undoubtedly has a considerable effect even when there is no further nonverbal training.

The criteria used to assess whether teachers' awareness of and sensitivity to nonverbal behaviors had altered included their knowledge about nonverbal behavior (Shapiro, 1976), the meanings they attached to different nonverbal behaviors (e.g., Hansford, 1977), and their judgments of students' comprehension based on students nonverbal behaviors (e.g., Jecker, Maccoby, & Breitrose, 1965). Given these variations in criteria and the variations between the training programs, it is perhaps fortunate that the majority of studies (31) report that their training programs had a positive effect, whereas only 4 indicated negative effects. For 26 studies the findings were reported as statistically significant at the .09 level or less, and for 27 (see Tables 1A, 1B, and 1C), the average effect size was calculated as 0.71. This value was interpreted to indicate that the training programs had increased teachers' perceptiveness of nonverbal behaviors.

The various training components were not equally effective, however. A long detailed pretest has a greater sensitizing effect (Rosenthal et al., 1979) than a shorter one. Short indirect training sessions, such as the transcendental meditation as used by Guild (Table 1A), are less effective than short sessions directed specifically at nonverbal behaviors (e.g., Berkowitz, Table 1A) or than extended microteaching sessions (Hansford, 1977). Criterion measures may also be affected by features not associated with the training programs. For example, as Strother, Ayres, and Orlich (1971) found, they

TABLE 1A Studies on Training Nonverbal Perceptiveness with True Experimental Designs

Author/Context/Variable	Method	Treatment	Results
1. Davitz (1964 reported by Rosenthal et al., 1979) Tone of voice	Pretest–posttest control group design	Experimental group: Practice and feedback Control group: no training	Tone of voice: $p < 0.05$ Control group: pretest–posttest: ES $= 0.45$ [a] Experimental group: pretest–posttest: ES $= 0.78$ [a]
2. Jecker et al. (1965) 20 graduate students Ability of teachers to judge comprehension from nonverbal cues.	Pretest–posttest control group design Ratings of student comprehension while answering a question (about 84–100 clips)	Experimental group: 6–8 hours of discrimination training based on similar material as in the pre- and posttests. Control group: 6–8 hours of film demonstration of nonverbal communication	Accurate guesses: $p < 0.02$ (comparison of gains); ES $= 0.95$
3. Reich (1970) 40 undergraduate students Identification of emotions Accuracy in expressing emotions	Posttest-only control group design Identification of emotions from 32 clips, presented on audio- and videotapes by an actor Enacting 6 different emotions, rated by students	4½ hours of sensitivity training	Identification of emotions: ES $= -0.50$ ($p > 0.05$) Accuracy in expressing emotions ES $= 0.12$ ($p > 0.05$)
4. Strother et al. (1971) 10 elementary school teachers Ability to predict students' achievement score from nonverbal cues	Posttest-only comparison group design Teachers' judgement of student competency minus students' score in an examination	2 hours of group instruction for teachers and pupils	No sign. results: ES $=$ — [b]
5. Phillips (1975) 48 student teachers (elementary and middle school) Among others: Nonverbal sensitivity	Posttest-only non-equivalent control group design Profile of nonverbal sensitivity (PONS-test: Rosenthal et al., 1979)	Written information about non-verbal sensitivity, suggestions for observing and using nonverbal behaviors during student teaching PONS-test with feedback	Nonverbal sensitivity: ES $= 0.47$; (p not calculated)

(continued)

93

TABLE 1A (Continued)

Author/Context/Variable	Method	Treatment	Results
6. Hansford (1977) 74 teacher trainees Nonverbal perceptiveness (PONS)	Pretest-posttest comparison group design, 3 groups Profile of Nonverbal Sensitivity (full PONS test, Rosenthal et al. (1979)	Group 1: Regular seminar, group discussion Group 2: Peer-microteaching with video-feedback Group 3: Peer-microteaching with video-feedback and peer feedback 7 sessions, two hours each	Nonverbal sensitivity (PONS-test): Peer-microteaching with video- and group feedback significantly outperformed the other groups ($p<0.01$); ES = —[b]
7. Huntley (1978)	see Table 2B	see Table 2B	Ability to recognize nonverbal behavior: ES = -0.19; (ANOVA), $p>0.05$)
8. Berkowitz (reported by Rosenthal et al., 1979) 25 clinical staff members	Posttest-only-control group design Profile of Nonverbal Sensitivity, one week after training	90 min of training directly related to the PONS-test	Nonverbal sensitivity (PONS-test): $p<0.09$; ES = 0.58[a]
9. Guild (reported by Rosenthal et al., (1979) 30 meditators and 30 non-meditators Nonverbal sensitivity (PONS)	Pretest-posttest-comparison group design Profile of Nonverbal Sensitivity (full PONS test Rosenthal et al., 1979)	Transcendental meditation, resting	Nonverbal sensitivity (PONS-test): $p>0.05$[b]
10. Purdom (reported by Rosenthal et al., 1979) College students Nonverbal sensitivity (PONS)	Posttest-only control group design Profile of Nonverbal Sensitivity (full PONS test, Rosenthal et al., 1979)	Course work in nonverbal communication	Nonverbal sensitivity (PONS-test): $p>0.05$; ES = -0.04[a]
11. Klinzing et al. (1984a) 34 becoming secondary school teachers Nonverbal Sensitivity (PONS)	Pretest-posttest-control group design Profile of Nonverbal Sensitivity Among others: Profile of Nonverbal Sensitivity (full PONS test, Rosenthal et al., 1979)	Theory presentation, discrimination training, preliminary exercises, practice in a microteaching format, and feedback (28-30 hr)	Nonverbal sensitivity (PONS test): $p<0.06$; ES = 1.03

M ES = 0.33 (based on 8 studies)

[a] ES (effect size) calculated by Rosenthal et al. (1979)
[b] Not enough data reported to calculate ES.

TABLE 1B Studies on Nonverbal Perceptiveness Using Preexperimental Designs (Pre- and Posttest Design)

Author/Context/Variable	Method	Treatment	Results
1. Allport (1924) 12 young women Accuracy of reading faces	Pre-posttest design Pre- and posttests consisted of still pictures by Rudolph (1903)	Discrimination-training with similar material as in the pre- and posttests (studying a chart of facial expressions for 15 min)	Accuracy of reading faces: ES = 0.55 [a] (pre- and posttest); $p < 0.05$
2. Guilford (1929) 15 students of social psychology Accuracy of reading faces	Pre-posttest design Pre- and posttests consisted of 24 pictures (Rudolph, 1903)	Study of the anatomy of facial expressions and of analytical features of groups of expressions Discrimination training (identification of emotions from Rudolph's, 1903) pictures. 10 days ≅ 20 hr	Accuracy of reading faces: ES = 1.68 [a] (pre- and posttest); $p < 0.05$
3. Jenness (1932) Study 1 [b] University students Accuracy of reading faces	Replication of the study of Allport (1924) Pre-posttest design Still pictures by Rudolph (1903)	Discrimination training with similar material as in the pre- and posttests (studying a chart of facial expressions for 15 min)	Accuracy of reading faces: ES = 0.52 [a] (pre- and posttest); $p < 0.05$
4. Jenness (1932) Study 2 [b] University students Accuracy of reading faces	Pre-posttest design Still pictures by Rudolph (1903)	Discrimination training with similar material as in the -pre- and posttests (studying a chart of facial expressions for 45 min)	Accuracy of reading faces: ES = 0.98 [a] (pre-posttest); $p < 0.05$
5. Mittenecker (1960) Study 1 3 groups (N = 10 to 24) of adults Estimation of intelligence of persons shown on still pictures	Pre-posttest design Pre- and posttests consisted of 7 series of 3 pictures which had to be ranked according to the intelligence of the persons on the pictures	Group 1 (n = 24): Discrimination training based on similar materials as in pre- and posttests, plus feedback Group 2 (n = 14): Discrimination training without feedback Group 3 (n = 10): Feedback	Mistakes in ranking of 3 pictures (7 series according to the intelligence of the persons on the pictures): Group 1 pretest: $M = 19.17$ posttest: $M = 17.18$ $p < 0.05$ Group 2 pretest: $M = 18.00$ posttest: $M = 18.00$ $p > 0.05$ Group 3 pretest: $M = 18.40$ posttest: $M = 19.00$ $p > 0.05$

(continued)

TABLE 1B (Continued)

Author/Context/Variable	Method	Treatment	Results
6. Mittenecker (1960) Study 2 34 adults Estimation of self-confidence of persons shown on still pictures	Pre-posttest design: 8 series of 3 pictures which had to be ranked according to the self-confidence of the persons on the pictures	Discrimination training based on similar materials as pre- and post-tests plus feedback	Mistakes in ranking of 3 pictures (8 series): pretest: $M = 20.59$ posttest: $M = 19.12$ $p < 0.05$
7. Lanzetta and Kleck (1970)[b]		Feedback and punishment	ES = 0.00[a]; $p > 0.05$
8. Kohnle (1971)[b]		Discrimination training	ES = 1.14[a]; $p < 0.05$
9. Mohamed (1974)[b]		Encounter group	ES = 1.26[a]; $p < 0.05$
10. McCoid[b] 56 undergraduate students Sensitivity to nonverbal cues (PONS)	Pre-posttest design Pre- and posttest: Profile of Non-verbal Sensitivity (PONS; Rosenthal et al., 1979)		ES not calculated, $p > 0.05$
11. Fitzner (1982) Klinzing et al. (1983) Preliminary field test 11 becoming secondary school teachers Among others: Sensitivity to nonverbal cues (PONS test)	Pre-posttest design Participants were pre- and post-tested with the full PONS test (Rosenthal et al., 1979)	Theory presentation, preliminary exercises, practice and feedback (8 days; 35–40 hr)	Sensitivity to nonverbal cues (PONS test); (pre- and posttest); ES = 1.34; ($p < 0.05$)
12. Fitzner (1982) Klinzing et al. (1983) Study 1B 21 becoming secondary school teachers Among others: Sensitivity to nonverbal cues (PONS test)	Pre- and posttest design Participants were pre- and post-tested with the full PONS test (Rosenthal et al., 1979)	Theory presentation, discrimination training, preliminary exercises, practice, and feedback (8 days, 40 hr)	Sensitivity to nonverbal cues (PONS test) (pre- and posttest); $p < 0.05$; ES = 1.77

(continued)

TABLE 1B (Continued)

Author/Context/Variable	Method	Treatment	Results
13. Fitzner (1982) Klinzing et al. (1983) Study 2B 23 becoming secondary school teachers Among others: Sensitivity to nonverbal cues (PONS test)	Pre- and posttest design Participants were pre- and post-tested with the full PONS test (Rosenthal et al., 1979)	Theory presentation, discrimination training, preliminary exercises, practice, and feedback (8 days, 40 hr)	Sensitivity to nonverbal cues (PONS test) (pre- and posttest); $p < 0.05$; ES = 1.66
14. Fitzner (1982) Klinzing et al. (1983) Study 3 12 becoming secondary school teachers Among others: Sensitivity to nonverbal cues (PONS test)	Pre- and posttest design Participants were pre- and post-tested with the full PONS test (Rosenthal et al., 1979)	Theory presentation, discrimination training, preliminary exercises, practice, and feedback (8 days, 40 hr)	Sensitivity to nonverbal cues (PONS test) (pre- and posttest); $p < 0.05$; ES = 1.25
15. Fitzner (1982) Klinzing et al. (1983) Study 4 25 becoming secondary school teachers Among others: Sensitivity to nonverbal cues (PONS test)	Pre- and posttest design Participants were pre- and post-tested with the full PONS test (Rosenthal et al., 1979)	Theory presentation, discrimination training, preliminary exercises, practice, and feedback (25 hr, 1 semester)	Sensitivity to nonverbal cues (PONS test) (pre- and posttest); $p < 0.05$; ES = 1.49

[a] ES estimated by Rosenthal et al. (1979).
[b] Reported by Rosenthal et al. (1979).

M ES = 1.14
(based on 12 studies)

TABLE 1C Studies on Nonverbal Perceptiveness Assessing the Effects of Pretesting

Author/Context	Variable	Test	Results
1. Jenness (1932)[a] Study 3 University students	Accuracy of reading faces	Still pictures from Rudolph (1903); retest after 15 min	ES = −0.08[b], $p > 0.05$; (pre- and posttest)
2. Jenness (1983)[a] Study 4 University students	Accuracy of reading faces	Still pictures from Rudolph (1903); retest after 3 months	ES = −0.02[b], $p > 0.05$; (pre- and posttest)
3. Kline and Johanssen (1935) University students	Recognizing emotions from face and/or body	2 × 20 still pictures (body and/or face) "Retest" after 1 week	ES = 0.34[b], $p < 0.05$; (pre- and posttest)
4. Walton (1936)[a]	Accuracy in decoding facial expressions	Still photos	ES = 0.22[b], $p > 0.05$; (pre- and posttest)
5. Mittenecker (1960) Study 1 Adults (2 groups)	Estimation of intelligence of persons shown on pictures	21 still photos; retest after about 30–60 min	ES = —[c], $p > 0.05$; (pre- and posttest)
6. Miller et al. (1975)[a]	Decoding nonverbal behaviors	Motion pictures	ES = 0.00[a], $p > 0.05$; (pre- and posttest)
7-10. Rosenthal et al. (1979) 4 samples of high school, college, or university students in the USA and Australia	Nonverbal sensitivity (PONS)	220 motion pictures (full PONS-test); retest after about 6 weeks	ES = 1.48, $p < 0.05$; (pre- and posttest)

(continued)

TABLE 1C (Continued)

Author/Context	Variable	Test	Results
11. Klinzing et al. (1984b) University students (becoming secondary school teachers)	Nonverbal sensitivity (PONS)	Full PONS test (Rosenthal et al., 1979); retest after 1 week	ES = 1.05 ($p<0.01$) (experimental vs. control group)
12. Shapiro (1976) 60 subjects (elementary school personnel) Knowledge of nonverbal communication	Pre- and posttest-control group design Knowledge about nonverbal communication Training: self-contained module on nonverbal communication	36-item knowledge test	M ES = 0.43 (based on 10 studies) M ES (studies 1 to 6) = 0.10 Significant gains in knowledge of nonverbal communication (ANCOVA, $p<0.001$)

[a] Studies reported by Rosenthal et al. (1979).
[b] ES (effect size) calculated by Rosenthal et al. (1979).
[c] Not enough data reported to calculate ES.

may be influenced by teachers' knowledge of pupils' prior achievement scores on the curriculum. Lack of precision in a training program and failure to conceptualize clearly what may be communicated via nonverbal aspects of behavior may affect criterion measures also. These two features explain, in part, why the objectives of Reich's (1970) program were not attained, and they may account for diminished effectiveness in other programs (e.g., Huntley, 1978).

Notwithstanding the preceding reservations, the research overall indicates that teachers' awareness of, and sensitivity to nonverbal behaviors can be enhanced, especially by short periods of direct practice or extended periods of microteaching. It is encouraging to note that a comparable conclusion can be drawn from the results of research in psychology and counseling where individuals have been trained to become more sensitive to nonverbal behaviors.[3]

BEHAVIORAL AND OTHER CHANGES IN ACTUAL AND SCALED-DOWN CLASSROOMS

Tables 2A and 2B contain details about 33 projects in which researchers studied the impact of training programs on experienced and trainee teachers' repertoire of nonverbal behaviors. The training programs were designed to change the quality and the quantity of teachers' nonverbal behaviors, e.g., facial expressions, voice modulations, gestures, body movements, eye contacts, movement around classes, kneeling and sitting next to pupils. In some of the studies, the training program was designed to improve combinations of nonverbal behaviors, for example, those regarded as being associated with "enthusiasm," "animation," or "variation of stimuli." A majority of the studies were of a pre-, posttest design in either an actual classroom or in a scaled-down version, generally a microteaching situation which lasted for about 5 to 15 min using 4 to 9 students who were often peers. A number (15) of the studies were pre- or quasiexperimental designs. Like the studies listed in Tables 1A, 1B, 1C, the training programs of the studies in Tables 2A and 2B contained sessions for the presentation of theory, modeling, discrimination training, practice, and feedback.

Ratings of teacher behavior were frequently used and the criteria for the quality of the trained teachers' nonverbal behaviors included enthusiasm, speech quality, warmth, displayed energy in class, persuasiveness, and the attentiveness and displayed interest of students. In most cases these features were directly related to the objectives of the training program, e.g., stimulus

---

[3] Studies from psychology and counseling investigating the effects of training people to be more aware about nonverbal behaviors and of the messages these communicate include those by Delaney (1966), Hertweg (1966), Hoffman (1964), Mattis (1964), and Pinnas (1975).

TABLE 2A Training of (Expressive) Nonverbal Behaviors: Training Effects Assessed in Training Situations

Author(s)/Context	Method/Instrumentation	Treatment	Students/Teachers Attitudes to Training	Training Effects On		Payoff Evaluation
				Behaviors Directly Related to the Training Objectives	Variables Containing More Than the Behaviors Directly Related to the Training Objectives	Student/Audience Attitudes, Directly Observable Behaviors, and Achievement
Cooper & Stroud (1967) 145 student teachers (secondary school)	Pre-posttest design Student and supervisor ratings (7-point scale)	Theory presentation (60 min) Discrimination training and modeling (50 min) Practice: 2 micro-teaching cycles with feedback (90 min)	---	**Stimulus variation** Student rating: $p<0.001$ Supervisor rating: $p<0.001$ ES = 0.72s (student rating)	---	---
Berliner (1969)	See Table 3		---	$p>0.05$ ES = —[a]	---	---
Reich (1970)	See Table 1A		---	$p>0.05$ ES = 0.12	---	---
Pancrazio and Johnson (1971)	See Table 3		Positive reactions of the trainees to the training	$p>0.05$ ES = 1.15	---	---

(continued)

TABLE 2A (Continued)

| Author(s)/Context | Method/Instrumentation | Treatment | Training Effects On | | | Payoff Evaluation |
			Students/Teachers Attitudes to Training	Behaviors Directly Related to the Training Objectives	Variables Containing More Than the Behaviors Directly Related to the Training Objectives	Student/Audience Attitudes, Directly Observable Behaviors, and Achievement
Hodge (1972) 54 student teachers (secondary school)	Posttest-only-control group design Low-inference observation	Theory presentation (slide show 12 min) Discrimination training Practice: 1 microteach with feedback (peer-teaching)	Positive reactions of the trainees to the training	Total nonverbal behaviors: $p > 0.05$ ES = 0.48	----	Audience (peers) achievement: $p > 0.05$, ES = 0.24
Becker (1973) 18 student teachers (elementary school)	Pre-posttest design Peer ratings 5-point rating scale	Short theory presentation, modeling Practice: 1 microteach with feedback	Positive reactions of the trainees to the training	Among others: Silence and nonverbal cues: $p < 0.05$ ES = -0.87	----	----

TABLE 2A (Continued)

Author(s)/ Context	Method/ Instrumentation	Treatment	Training Effects On			Payoff Evaluation
			Students/Teachers Attitudes to Training	Behaviors Directly Related to the Training Objectives	Variables Containing More Than the Behaviors Directly Related to the Training Objectives	Student/Audience Attitudes, Directly Observable Behaviors, and Achievement
Pierce & Halinski (1974) 45 student teachers (secondary school) Among others: Stimulus variation Silence and non-verbal cues	Posttest-only comparison group design Achievement test	Group A: Training on traditional lesson planning Group B: Training in the use of behavioral objectives Group C: Training in the use of behavioral objectives and the 12 Stanford teaching skills. In addition, all groups received an 8-hour training in classroom observation, 3 hours of peer teaching, and 1 hour of teaching pupils	----	----	----	Pupil achievement $p > 0.05$ ES = −0.44

(continued)

103

TABLE 2A (Continued)

Author(s)/Context	Method/Instrumentation	Treatment	Training Effects On			Payoff Evaluation
			Students/Teachers Attitudes to Training	Behaviors Directly Related to the Training Objectives	Variables Containing More Than the Behaviors Directly Related to the Training Objectives	Student/Audience Attitudes, Directly Observable Behaviors, and Achievement
Langthaler & Wothke (1979) Study 1 12 student teachers (elementary school)	Pre-posttest design High-inference ratings by the participants Questionnaire	Practice: 4 microteaching cycles with feedback for 3 groups of teaching skills	Positive reactions of the participants to the training	Among others: head-, arm-, hand-, etc. movements: $p<0.05$ ES = 2.36	Energy: $p<0.05$ ES = 0.88	----
Langthaler & Wothke (1979) Study 2 44 student teachers (elementary school)	Pre-posttest non-equivalent control group design High inference ratings by the participants of the training Questionnaire	Practice: 4 microteaching cycles with feedback for 3 groups of teaching skills	Positive reactions of the participants to the training	Among others: head-, arm-, hand-, etc. movements: $p<0.05$ ES = 0.40	Energy: $p<0.05$ ES = 0.68	---
Fitzner (1982); Klinzing et al. (1983) Preliminary field test 11 student teachers (secondary school)	Pre-posttest design Observer ratings Questionnaire	Theory presentation (180 min) Discrimination training (15 min) Practice: 5 microteaching-type exercises with feedback	Positive reactions of the participants to the training	Voice delivery, eyes, eye contact, facial expressions, gestures, body movement/posture: $p<0.01$ MES = 1.32	Global ratings (composite score): Activity, warmth, interest, attention, assurance $p<0.01$ MES = 0.88 Retention test after 1 month vs. pre-test: $p<0.05$	---

TABLE 2A (Continued)

Author(s)/ Context	Method/ Instrumentation	Treatment	Training Effects On			Payoff Evaluation
			Students/Teachers Attitudes to Training	Behaviors Directly Related to the Training Objectives	Variables Containing More Than the Behaviors Directly Related to the Training Objectives	Student/Audience Attitudes, Directly Observable Behaviors, and Achievement
Fitzner (1982) Klinzing et al. (1983) (Study 1A) 21 student teachers (secondary school)	Pre-posttest design Observer ratings Questionnaire	Theory presentation (180 min)	---	Voice delivery, eyes, eye contact, gestures: $p<0.05$ eyes, body movement, facial expressions $n.s.$ $MES=0.27$	Global ratings (composite score): Activity, warmth, interest, attention, assurance $p<0.05$ $MES=0.68$	---
Fitzner (1982) Klinzing et al. (1983) Study 1B Continuation of study 1b (same student teachers)	Pre-posttest design Observer ratings Questionnaire	Theory presentation (180 min) Discrimination training and modeling (200 min) Practice: 4 microteaching-type exercises with feedback	Positive reactions of the participants to the training	Voice delivery, eyes, eye contact, facial expressions, gestures, body movement $p<0.01$ $MES=1.01$	Global ratings (composite score): Activity, warmth, interest, attention, assurance $p<0.05$ $MES=0.78$	---
Fitzner (1982) Klinzing et al. 1983 Study 2A 25 student teachers (secondary school) exp. gr.: $n=10$ contr. gr.: $n=13$	Posttest-only design Observer ratings	*Exp. gr.:* Theory presentation (60 min) +150 min of discrimination training *Contr. gr.:* Theory presentation (60 min)	---	Expressive nonverbal behavior: exp. vs. contr.: $p<0.05$ $MES=1.38$	Overall ratings (see Study 1) (composite score): exp. vs. contr.: $p<0.05$ $MES=1.62$	---

(continued)

105

TABLE 2A (Continued)

Author(s)/Context	Method/Instrumentation	Treatment	Students/Teachers Attitudes to Training	Behaviors Directly Related to the Training Objectives	Variables Containing More Than the Behaviors Directly Related to the Training Objectives	Payoff Evaluation: Student/Audience Attitudes, Directly Observable Behaviors, and Achievement
				Training Effects On		
Fitzner (1982) Klinzing et al. (1983) Study 2B: Continuation of study 2A	Pre-posttest design Observer ratings Questionnaire	Theory presentation (180 min) discrimination training (150 min) Practice: 5 micro-teaching-type exercises with feedback	Positive reactions of the trainees to the training	Expressive non-verbal behavior: $p<0.01$; M ES $=1.98$ Retention test after 2 months vs. pre-test: $p<0.05$	Overall ratings (see study 1) (composite score): $p<0.01$; M ES $=1.14$ Retention test after 2 months vs. pre-test: $p<0.05$	---
Fitzner (1982) Klinzing et al. (1983) Study 3 12 student teachers (secondary school)	Pre-posttest design Observer ratings Questionnaire	Theory presentation (180 min) discrimination training (150 min) Practice: 5 micro-teaching-type exercises with feedback	Positive reactions of the trainees to the training	Expressive non-verbal behavior: $p<0.05$ M ES $=1.29$	Overall ratings (see study 1) (composite score): $p<0.05$ M ES $=0.55$ Retention test after 3 months vs. pre-test: $p<0.05$	---
Fitzner (1982) Klinzing et al. (1983) Study 4 25 student teachers (secondary school)	Pre-posttest design Observer ratings Questionnaire	Theory presentation (180 min) discrimination training (50–90 min) model tapes (10 min) Practice:—	Positive reactions of the trainees to the training	Expressive non-verbal behavior: $p<0.01$ M ES $=1.21$	Overall ratings (see study 1) (composite score): $p<0.05$ M ES $=0.59$	---

TABLE 2A (Continued)

Author(s)/Context	Method/Instrumentation	Treatment	Training Effects On			Payoff Evaluation
			Students/Teachers Attitudes to Training	Behaviors Directly Related to the Training Objectives	Variables Containing More Than the Behaviors Directly Related to the Training Objectives	Student/Audience Attitudes, Directly Observable Behaviors, and Achievement
Klinzing et al. (1984a)	Pre-posttest control group design Ratings of trained observers Intuitive ratings Questionnaire	Theory presentation (70 min) discrimination training (90 min) modeling (10 min) Practice: 5 micro-teaching-type exercises with feedback	Positive reactions of the trainees to the training	Expressive non-verbal behavior: $p<0.01$ $M\,ES=0.83$	Ratings (assertiveness, persuasiveness, clarity, interest, verbal speech quality) (composite score): $M\,ES=0.48$ (p mostly <0.05)	----
				$M\,ES=0.92$ (based on 13 studies)	$M\,ES=0.75$ (based on 8 studies)	$M\,ES=0.10$ (based on 2 studies)

[a] Not enough data reported to calculate ES.

107

TABLE 2B Training of (Expressive) Nonverbal Behaviors: Training Effects Assessed in Real Classroom Situations

Author(s)/ Context	Method/ Instrumentation	Treatment	Training Effects On			Payoff Evaluation
			Students/Teachers Attitudes to Training	Behaviors Directly Related to the Training Objectives	Variables Containing More Than the Behaviors Directly Related to the Training Objectives	Student/Audience Attitudes, Directly Observable Behaviors, and Achievement
Young (1973) 6 inservice vocational teachers (high school) and their pupils	Posttest-only-control group design Emmer Enthusiasm Scale Pupil ratings Achievement test	Theory presentation, role playing (6 hr)	----	Teacher enthusiasm: $(ES = 1.14)$[b]	Pupil ratings of interest in instructional unit: exp. gr.: $M = 3.51$ contr. gr.: $M = 3.02$	Pupil achievement: $p < 0.05$ $ES = -0.93$
Raymond (1973) 20 preservice science teachers (secondary school)	Posttest-only control group design Low-inference observation Student rating of teacher effectiveness	Theory presentation, modeling (10 min) 1 microteaching cycle	----	Silence and non-verbal cues: $p < 0.10$ $ES = 0.77$	Teacher-initiated positive nonverbal interactions: $p < 0.05$ $ES = 1.11$	Student ratings of teacher effectiveness: $p < 0.10$ $ES = 0.44$
Dawson et al. (1975) Study 1 2 undergraduate students with pupils (patients in psychiatric ward)	Pre-posttest design Low-inference observation	Discrimination training (1 hr) practice	----	Positive posture/ posture pretest: $M = 0.53$ posttest: $M = 0.90$[b]	----	----

TABLE 2B (Continued)

| Author(s)/ Context | Method/ Instrumentation | Treatment | Training Effects On | | | Payoff Evaluation |
			Students/Teachers Attitudes to Training	Behaviors Directly Related to the Training Objectives	Variables Containing More Than the Behaviors Directly Related to the Training Objectives	Student/Audience Attitudes, Directly Observable Behaviors, and Achievement
Dawson et al. (1975) Study 2 3 undergraduate students with pupils (patients in psychiatric ward)	Pre-posttest-control group design Low inference observation of students and pupils	Discrimination training (1 hr) practice	----	Positive posture/ posture exp. gr.: $M = 0.91$ (posttest) contr. gr.: $M = 0.67$ (posttest)	----	Correct pupil answers per min. exp. gr: $M = 2.49$ (posttest) contr. gr.: $M = 1.05$ (posttest)[b]
Phillips (1975) 48 elementary and middle-school student teachers Nonverbal sensitivity Indirect/direct nonverbal behavior	Posttest-only non-equivalent-control group design Profile of Non-verbal Sensitivity (PONS) (Rosenthal et al., 1979) Classroom observation with IDER-system (French & Galloway, 1968)	Control group: Student teaching Experimental group: theory presentation: written informations and suggestions for practice and observation. Discrimination training (PONS) with feedback	----	Encouraging/ restrictive nonverbal behavior: $ES = 1.20$ $p < 0.05$	----	----
Ellett and Smith (1975)	See Table 3		----	$p < 0.05$ $ES = ----$[a]	----	----

(continued)

109

TABLE 2B (Continued)

Author(s)/ Context	Method/ Instrumentation	Treatment	Training Effects On			Payoff Evaluation
			Students/Teachers Attitudes to Training	Behaviors Directly Related to the Training Objectives	Variables Containing More Than the Behaviors Directly Related to the Training Objectives	Student/Audience Attitudes, Directly Observable Behaviors, and Achievement
Borg (1975) 25/15 inservice teachers (4th, 5th, 6th grade pupils)	Pre-posttest non-equivalent control group design	Theory presentation, discrimination training, modelling, 4 practice sessions, each for 3 teaching skills with feedback	---	Among others: voice modulation. Experimental group: pre-post: $p<0.01$ ES=0.76 Exp. vs. contr. gr.: $p>0.05$; ES=0.16	---	---
Becker et al. (1977) 30 teachers (adult education)	Pre-posttest-control group design	Theory presentation (60–120 min) modelling, 1 microteach with feedback	---	---	Engaged/interested: $p>0.05$ ES = -0.17	---

TABLE 2B (Continued)

Author(s)/Context	Method/Instrumentation	Treatment	Training Effects On			Payoff Evaluation
			Students/Teachers Attitudes to Training	Behaviors Directly Related to the Training Objectives	Variables Containing More Than the Behaviors Directly Related to the Training Objectives	Student/Audience Attitudes, Directly Observable Behaviors, and Achievement
Beisner (1977) 40 elementary school teachers	Pretest-posttest-non equivalent control group design. Self-analysis (16 items 5-point rating scales) based on Flanders (1970) Interaction Analysis (Galloway 1968, Scholl 1975)	Theory presentation: Theoretical knowledge necessary for the process. Practice/Feedback: Self-confrontation via TV (20 min) plus self-evaluation and supervision and 1 month time for implementation of the behaviors emphasized into the instructional process	---	Encouraging/restricting non-verbal behaviors (self-ratings) ES = 0.69 (ANOVA, $p < 0.05$)	---	---
Collins (1978) 20 perservice teachers	Pre-posttest-control group design Observer ratings	Group instruction, discrimination training 1 microteaching peer-teaching cycle with feedback, 1 microteaching cycle with feedback	---	Enthusiasm: $p < 0.001$ ES = 4.66 Follow-up: $p < 0.01$ ES = 2.99	---	---

(continued)

TABLE 2B (Continued)

Author(s)/Context	Method/Instrumentation	Treatment	Training Effects On			Payoff Evaluation
			Students/Teachers Attitudes to Training	Behaviors Directly Related to the Training Objectives	Variables Containing More Than the Behaviors Directly Related to the Training Objectives	Student/Audience Attitudes, Directly Observable Behaviors, and Achievement
Huntley (1978) 28 student teachers (elementary and secondary school)	Pretest- and post-test-control group design 10 min. observation with the IDER system (French & Galloway, 1968) Identification of nonverbal behaviors on two 5-min videotapes	Theory presentation: Introduction into nonverbal communication. Discrimination training: 35 min. classroom and videotape observation Practice/Feedback: 4 selected student teachers presented a microteach (3 sessions, 4 hours training	----	Nonverbal encouraging/restricting behaviors ES = −0.42 (ANOVA, $p > 0.05$) Ability to recognize nonverbal behavior ES = −0.19 (ANOVA, $p > 0.05$)	----	----

112

TABLE 2B (Continued)

Author(s)/Context	Method/Instrumentation	Treatment	Training Effects On			Payoff Evaluation
			Students/Teachers Attitudes to Training	Behaviors Directly Related to the Training Objectives	Variables Containing More Than the Behaviors Directly Related to the Training Objectives	Student/Audience Attitudes, Directly Observable Behaviors, and Achievement
Dunn (1978) 14 student teachers (home economics)	Posttest-only non equivalent control group design Three-20 min. intervals were observed with the FIAC (Flanders, 1970) and the IDER system (French & Galloway, 1968)	Theory presentation: not reported Discrimination training/Modelling: 4 hours instruction into the FIAC (Flanders, 1970) and IDER system (French & Galloway, 1968) Three films developed at Stanford University (Allen et al., 1969) 10 min each	----	Encouraging/restricting non-verbal behaviors ES = 0.16 (direction not reported) (ANOVA, $p = 0.76$)	----	----

(continued)

TABLE 2B (Continued)

Author(s)/Context	Method/Instrumentation	Treatment	Training Effects On			Payoff Evaluation
			Students/Teachers Attitudes to Training	Behaviors Directly Related to the Training Objectives	Variables Containing More Than the Behaviors Directly Related to the Training Objectives	Student/Audience Attitudes, Directly Observable Behaviors, and Achievement
Garrett (1979) Study 1 29 student teachers	Posttest-only non-equivalent control group design Pupil Observation Survey (POS, Veldman & Peck, 1963)	Theory presenta-tion: Information about nonverbal communication, supplemented by slide shows and discussion. Discrimination training: Observa-tion exercises. Practice/feedback: Short role playing (200-min training)	----	----	Pupil Observation Survey (nonverbal communication) ES = 0.24 (ANOVA, $p < 0.05$)	
Garrett (1979) Study 2 78 student teachers (High School)	Posttest-only con-trol group design Pupil Observation Survey (POS, Veldman & Peck, 1963)	Same as in Study 1	----		Pupil Observation Survey (nonverbal communication) ES = 0.23 ANOVA, $p < 0.05$	

TABLE 2B (Continued)

			Training Effects On			Payoff Evaluation
Author(s)/ Context	Method/ Instrumentation	Treatment	Students/Teachers Attitudes to Training	Behaviors Directly Related to the Training Objectives	Variables Containing More Than the Behaviors Directly Related to the Training Objectives	Student/Audience Attitudes, Directly Observable Behaviors, and Achievement
Bettencourt (1979) 17 inservice teachers with their pupils (4th, 5th, 6th grades)	Pre- and posttest-control group design Observer ratings Pupil ratings Achievement test	2 hours of group instruction, discrimination training (2 hours) 1 microteaching peer-teaching cycle with feedback, 1 microteaching cycle with feedback	----	Enthusiasm: $p<0.003$ M ES $=1.31$	----	Achievement: $p>0.05$ ES $= -0.20$ Attitudes toward teacher $p>0.05$ ES $=0.67; 0.89$ Attitudes toward content: $p>0.05$ ES $=0.30$
Fetter (1981) 28 health educators	Posttest-only control group design Observations in 5 min intervals in a regular classroom with the Focused Observation Instrument (Bradley et al. 1978) (Low inference, 14 categories	Theory presentation: Readings from the work of Galloway (1970) Discrimination training; Completion of a self rating form (1×) Practice/Feedback: One self-confrontation via TV with completion of a self-rating form	----	Positive nonverbal behaviors: M ES $= -0.02$ (t-tests, $p>0.05$ except "utilization of visuals")	---	----

(continued)

115

TABLE 2B (Continued)

Author(s)/ Context	Method/ Instrumentation	Treatment	Training Effects On			Payoff Evaluation
			Students/Teachers Attitudes to Training	Behaviors Directly Related to the Training Objectives	Variables Containing More Than the Behaviors Directly Related to the Training Objectives	Student/Audience Attitudes, Directly Observable Behaviors, and Achievement
Gillett & Gall (1981) 18 inservice teachers (grades 1–4)	Pre- and posttest-control group design Observer ratings Low-inference observation of pupils	See Collins (1978) & Bettencourt (1979)	----	Enthusiasm: $p < 0.02$ ES = 1.49	----	On-task behavior $p < 0.05$ ES = 1.94
Schum (1974)	See Table 3			$p < 0.05$ ES[a]		
				MES = 1.10 (based on 10 studies)	MES = 0.35 (based on 4 studies)	MES = −0.23 (achievement) based on 3 studies

[a] Not enough data reported to calculate ES.
[b] Not included in ES calculation because of small N.

variation for the study by Cooper and Stroud (1967), Table 2A. In others they were not, e.g., persuasiveness in the study by Klinzing et al. (1984a), Table 2A. Nevertheless these ancillary features were deemed to be important byproducts of the training programs. Additional criteria were used to assess the effects of the training programs. They included trained teachers' attitudes to the training programs and their students' attitude to the teacher, achievement, on-task behavior, and perceptions of the teacher's effectiveness. These last four features may be deemed to be a part of, what is called by some (Okey & Cieslar, 1973; Scriven, 1967), a "payoff evaluation."

Nineteen of the studies report significant gains (≤ 0.10 level) in outcome measures, and from 23 reports an overall effect size of 1.00 can be calculated. Only five projects conducted in scaled-down settings reported mixed or negative findings. The overall effect size for the scaled-down setting studies was 0.92. On the other hand, the value for projects in actual classrooms, which reported significant gains, was 1.1 (see Table 2B). It is appropriate to note that both preservice and inservice teachers perceived the training programs favorably and, on the basis of the effect sizes for the studies involving each group, the training programs can be considered to be equally effective for teachers with different amounts of experience.

If it is accepted that some of a teacher's nonverbal behaviors, e.g., smiles, eye contacts, and kneeling next to pupils, convey messages like "I'm interested in you" and "I want to help you," then when more of these are exhibited, it seems reasonable to expect that pupils will evince greater interest in curriculum units, display a more positive attitude toward the teacher, and regard the teacher as an effective instructor. This is not clearly the payoff in the training studies reviewed here. Several studies (e.g., those by Bettencourt, 1979; Raymond, 1973; Young, 1973) which obtained negative or nonsignificant findings, imply that effects referred to cannot be expected. With respect to another payoff, pupil achievement, the relevant projects (see Table 2B) yield an overall effect size of -0.23—a result that conflicts with the findings from the research referred to in the opening sections of this chapter. A few studies have noted some positive payoffs when the quality and quantity of teachers' nonverbal behaviors have been enhanced; Dawson, Dawson, and Forness (1975) report a higher frequency of correct answers by pupils, and Gillett and Gall (1981), more on-task pupil behavior.

There appear to be several reasons for the mixed or negative findings from some projects. First, a number of them (e.g., Becker, 1973; Hodge, 1972; Pancrazio & Johnson, 1971) contained relatively short training or treatment components and little or no opportunity to practice nonverbal behaviors. By contrast, with comparable studies which obtained positive results, it seems that a training component must span four or more hours and there must be two or more practice sessions. Second, excessive use of nonverbal behaviors can distract pupils from learning tasks and reduce their achievement gains. This appears to have occurred in Young's (1973) study where the experimental teachers, in contrast to those in the control, received very high ratings on their expression of nonverbal behaviors. Third, an unusual or novel curriculum which raises pupils' motivational levels may be more salient with respect to enhancing attitudes, achievement, or perceptions about the teacher's effectiveness than changes in the teacher's nonverbal behaviors. This feature appears to have operated in Bettencourt's (1979) study. Another factor which may reduce the salience of nonverbal behaviors is the teaching style. Nonverbal behaviors, according to the studies reviewed, have a greater effect where the teacher's style is didactic, whole-class teaching than when it fosters pupil discussion or pupil inquiry in concert with audiovisual materials.

It should be noted that in some of the studies on the associations between nonverbal behavior and students' attitudes and achievement which reported positive associations, the difference between experimental and control groups was artificially maximized, e.g., by restricting teacher movement, humor, friendliness and voice inflections. In most of the training studies listed in Tables 2A and 2B, on the other hand, the trained teachers were compared with ones who were behaving "naturally." An unresolved issue in the research is "What are the relative effects of enhanced, natural, and depressed levels of teacher nonverbal behavior?" An associated issue is that of optimal levels for the expression of nonverbal behaviors for effective instruction. It was already stated that very high levels can have deleterious effects.

TRAINING COMPONENTS AND THEIR RELATIVE EFFECTIVENESS

Eleven of the studies reviewed investigated the relative effectiveness of the components of the training programs, namely, theory presentation, modeling or discrimination training, practice, and feedback. Table 3 contains details of the projects including the components under investigation. The studies have a number of features in common with the studies discussed in the previous two sections. A pre-, posttest comparison group design was employed in the majority, a variety of criterion measures were used, and preservice and experienced teachers served as subjects. The limitations which apply to the studies have already been indicated in previous sections and will not be repeated here. The focus will be the training components.

The following conclusions about the training components have been derived from a detailed, careful examination of the studies. First, theory presentation alone, especially when it is offered in a lecture–discussion format is not very effective in enhancing the quality and quantity of nonverbal behavior (Fitzner, 1982). A comparable conclusion has been derived from reviews of studies dealing with training in verbal skills (Joyce & Showers, 1981). When a lecture presentation, however, is combined with periods of

TABLE 3 Studies on Training Elements and their Various Combinations

Author/Context	Method/Instrumentation	Treatment	Results
1. Schum (1974) 20 student teachers Communication using eyes, mouth, and general body gestures	Pre- and posttest comparison group design Low-inference observation of nonverbal behaviors during a 15-min period in student teaching	Experimental group: Theory presentation: not reported Discrimination training: Training in self-analysis Practice: 2×15-min of prepared lessons with videotape feedback and self-analysis Comparison group: 2×15-minutes of prepared lessons with videotape feedback only	ANOVA results (nonverbal behaviors (Main results): 1. Increase of total number of nonverbal responses in the experimental group from pre- to posttest, decrease in the comparison group ($p < 0.05$) 2. Significant increase of encouraging nonverbal behaviors in the experimental group, decrease in the comparison group ($p < 0.05$)
2. Berliner (1969) 89 student teachers (secondary school) Stimulus variation	Pre- and posttest comparison group design (5 groups) Pre- and posttests in a microteaching situation (with pupils) Low-inference observation	For all groups 1 hour of theory presentation, and one microteach between pre- and posttests For groups 2–4 discrimination training provided by a supervisor Group 1: 5 min positive videotaped model with comments Group 2: 5 min positive videotaped model Group 3: 5 min negative videotaped model Group 4: Both models (of groups 2 and 3) Group 5: Control group (without models	Stimulus variation: Data reported graphically or verbally only 1. Little (not sign.) between-group differences 2. Considerable gain for all groups from pre - to posttest in time spent in movements, no gain in total number of focusing acts, and time spent in gesturing, considerable drop in frequency of gestures

(continued)

TABLE 3 (Continued)

Author/Context	Method/Instrumentation	Treatment	Results
3. Pancrazio & Johnson (1971) (home economics, social studies) 74 student teachers Nonverbal behaviors related to pupil initiating and responding behaviors	Pre- and posttest comparison group design (3 groups) Pre- and posttests were conducted in a microteaching situation (videotaped) with pupils Low-inference observation	*Theory presentation:* Written instruction (for all groups) Group A: Videodemonstration plus discrimination training (40 min) Group B: Lecture–discussion based on still pictures plus discrimination training Group C: Practice in a microteaching situation (10–15 min) plus unsupervised self-confrontation via TV	Nonverbal behaviors: 1. No significant ($p > 0.05$) results from pre- to posttests 2. No sign. ($p > 0.05$) differences between groups 3. No sign. ($p > 0.05$) differences between home economics and social study teachers or sex of the students Pre- and posttest effect size for home economic student teachers $MES = 1.15$[a]
4. Hiscox & Van Mondfrans (1972), Study 1 48 student teachers Among others: Stimulus variations	Pre- and posttest comparison group design Pre- and posttests were conducted in a peer-microteaching situation. Ratings of the peers on 7-point rating scales and the Stanford Teacher Competence Appraisal Guide (STCAG)	Lectures on the skills to be accomplished with modeling the skills to be emphasized For each of the skills (evoking student-initiated questions, stimulus variation) one microteaching cycle Group 1: Videotape feedback Group 2: Audio feedback plus feed-back from the peers and a super-visor based on the ratings	Stimulus variation: Sign. ($p < 0.05$) ANOVA results were obtained for two of 7 items of the specific scales and 1 of 13 STCAG-scales favoring the audiotape treatment
5. Hiscox & Van Mondfrans (1972), Study 2 32 student teachers Among others: Nonverbal cues	Pre- and posttest-comparison group design Method as in Study 1	As in Study 1	Nonverbal cues: No significant ($p > 0.05$) ANOVA results between groups on all measures

TABLE 3 (Continued)

Author/Context	Method/Instrumentation	Treatment	Results
6. Ellett & Smith (1975) 40 teachers of all grade levels Among others: Nonverbal behaviors (Factor IV on the BEST-instrument)	Pre- and posttest comparison group design Teachers were videotaped and observed during 16 consecutive weeks at 2-week intervals for about 18 minutes on the BEST-instrument (20 items, five-point scales) in their classes	Experimental group: 7 times videotape feedback plus self-rating on the BEST-instrument Comparison group: 7 times videotaping and mostly self-confrontation via TV	Nonverbal behavior (Factor IV of the BEST-instrument): Experimental subjects modified their behavior significantly ($p < 0.05$) more than the subjects in the comparison group
7. Edwards (1975) 55 student teachers Among others: Nonverbal cues, stimulus variation	Posttest-only comparison group design Posttests conducted in a 15-min microteaching peerteaching situation, rated on a 10-item, nine-point rating scale	All trainees got self-instructional materials, videotapes illustrating the skills, and discrimination training, and taught three microteaching cycles (peer-teaching) with self-feedback In addition: Group 1: supervisory feedback Group 2: peer feedback	No significant differences ($p > 0.05$) in all skills trained
8. Brusling (1976) 48 student teachers (elementary school) Silence and nonverbal behaviors (facial expressions, pointing, head movements, gestures, locomotion)	Multifactorial design The following factors were manipulated: Modeling (cued, noncued, no model) Videotape replay (yes, no) Sequence of two models: (female-male vs. male-female) Sex of student teachers Data were collected in four consecutive microteaches (with pupils) and in 20 minutes of student teaching (3 months later) with a low-inference observation instrument	For all groups: 1-hr lecture accompanied by written material Four microteaches plus the different treatments (see method) assigned to the different groups of trainees (total duration of treatment approx. 2 hr)	RESULTS—TEST CONDITION I (training situation) Multivariate analysis of covariance 1. across lessons 2, 3, and 4 (lesson 1 as covariate) *Lesson 1:* Sign. effects ($p < 0.10$) were obtained for model presentation (for locomotion), self-confrontation via TV (for gestures), and interaction effect (model × self-confrontation × sex) for gestures *(continued)*

TABLE 3 (Continued)

Author/Context	Method/Instrumentation	Treatment	Results
			Lesson 3: Sign. effects ($p < 0.10$) were obtained for model presentation (locomotion) and self-confrontation (head movement) *Lesson 4:* Sign. effects were obtained for model presentation (locomotion) ($p < 0.05$) RESULTS—TEST CONDITION II (real classroom situation) 2. *Lesson 5:* Sign. effects ($p < 0.10$) were obtained for self-confrontation (facial expressions, head movement), for model presentation × self-confrontation (locomotion, pointing), for model presentation × sex (facial expressions), and for self-confrontation × sex (facial expressions) 3. Skill validity: No sign. relationship between nonverbal behaviors and the amount of pupil talk REMARKS: Positive reactions of the student teachers to the training

TABLE 3 (Continued)

Author/Context	Method/Instrumentation	Treatment	Results
9. Klinzing et al. (1984a)	See Table 2a		
10. Fitzner (1982); Klinzing et al. (1983) Study 1a	See Table 2a		
11. Fitzner (1982); Klinzing et al. (1983) Study 2a	See Table 2a		

ᵃ Not enough data reported to calculate ES for social studies student teachers.

discrimination training, significant increases in the uses of expressive non-verbal behaviors (gestures, eye contact, body movement, vocal delivery, and facial expressions) occur (Fitzner, 1982). It seems that the discrimination training should occur for about three hours or more.

Second, providing models of nonverbal behaviors without a follow-up does not lead to significant gains in the quality and quantity of trainees' nonverbal behaviors. Modeling has been conducted using videotapes (perceptual modeling), usually of short duration (about 5 min), and typescripts (symbolic modeling), and those projects that have attempted to ascertain their relative effects have done so without a great deal of success. It does seem that a short exposure to a videotape is insufficient to produce desired changes in nonverbal behaviors. When videotapes are used as a basis for extended discrimination training, however, there are positive gains. Also, when extended discrimination training is combined with videotape feedback, significant changes occur in trainee's nonverbal behaviors. So, a third conclusion is that extended discrimination training, based on videotapes or using a videotape feedback, can be a successful training strategy (e.g., Fitzner, 1982; Schum, 1974).

Fourth, extended practice with focused feedback, e.g., codings or ratings, by an observer or the teacher, of specific behaviors, can have positive training effects. This point of view has been gleaned from those studies (e.g., Ellett & Smith, 1975) where trainees were able to practice the relevant skills on four or more occasions and from comparable studies dealing with training in verbal skills (e.g., Gall, Saunders, Nielson, & Smith, 1974; Nuthall, 1976). But two caveats should be noted. First, teachers must know clearly what are the goals of the training program and what has to be demonstrated at the final assessment. When these features are not known, practice becomes less effective (cf. Wagner, 1973). Second, overdoing self-analysis feedback can have negative effects when it requires extra effort. This was evident in one project (Klinzing et al., 1984a) where the final performance for an experimental group which received a reduced amount of feedback (self-confrontation using video replay) was slightly greater than another experimental group which received 5 additional hours of self-confrontation video feedback. The reduction in time for the feedback was associated with a reduced pressure of work, a more relaxed atmosphere among the experimental group, and a better final performance.

CONCLUSION

1. Review and Reflections

Although there has been considerable variation between the projects with respect to their designs and the outcomes measured, by and large the research indicates that, provided two and preferably more of the components, theory presentation, modeling, discrimination training, practice, and feedback are included in a training program, the quality and quantity of teachers' nonverbal behavior can be enhanced. Short training, few opportunities to practice, and overwork due to excessive feedback can reduce the effectiveness of a program. Furthermore, extensive use of nonverbal behaviors can lower pupils' achievement but may have a slight positive effect on their attitudes to the teacher. Also, when pupils are involved in inquiry and discovery activities or in using novel curriculum materials, teachers' nonverbal behaviors are not as salient as in whole-class teaching characterized by lecture–discussion.

There are still unanswered questions. Several of these have been mentioned in the preceding paragraphs. For example, Is there an optimal level for the expression of nonverbal behaviors for effective instruction? If so, can teachers be trained to attain that level? What are the relative effects of enhanced, natural and depressed levels of teacher nonverbal behavior? Other issues have a direct bearing on the quality of the training programs. Given that successful training has been achieved using two and more of the training components specified earlier, do differences in the quality of the program's components significantly affect the outcomes? It seems appropriate now to study the effects of variations in the quality and the nature of training components. Finally, the research reviewed here needs to be set into the broader context of studies on teaching. The preceding findings must be integrated with the results from other studies, for example, those dealing with students' and teachers' verbal behaviors, teachers' decision-making and management skills, and, in particular, the roles of teachers' beliefs and intentions.

2. Guidelines for Teacher Education

The following guidelines are based on the reported studies and their results, on recommendations of other research reports (Joyce & Showers, 1981), on aspects of Bandura's (1977) social learning theory, and on the experiences of the authors in conducting training clinics for improving nonverbal communication in the classroom.

Courses on nonverbal communication should not aim at a context-free training of nonverbal behaviors. Rather, they should aim at developing or broadening teachers' repertory of nonverbal behavior and perception in order to promote their expressivity and their flexibility in coping with a variety of different situations and to improve their ability to convey messages to an audience effectively. This is to be done mainly by completing, commenting, framing, and illustrating the verbal message. At the same time, the courses are to help close the gap between intended and actually performed behavior or the gap between "knowing that" and "knowing how" (Gage, 1978). To achieve this complex objective, it seems appropriate to provide training for each nonverbal "channel" separately in a way that allows for a gradual step by step integration of the acquired skill into the subsequent skill area.

For example, when starting with voice delivery and continuing with facial expressions, gaze, eye contact, gestures, posture, body movement, and use of space, the focus of training is on one channel at a time, but the behaviors trained are continuously integrated into the subsequent training.

The first step is an *introductory session* dealing with the basic concepts of nonverbal aspects of communication and with various research approaches. It is important that this component presents information about contexts and situations in which the different nonverbal signals are used appropriately and functionally. It should be designed to acquaint teachers with the training objectives and their rationale and specifically with what must be demonstrated at the end of the training. It is very important for the teachers to understand precisely what they are doing at any given time during the training procedures. Knowing exactly what they are doing and why they are doing it will lessen the possibility of later organizational problems and may motivate them toward self-improvement after completing the course. Following the initial session, each different nonverbal channel should be presented, including the following training components: theory presentation, demonstration of the behaviors to be accomplished (printed material, video- or audio-tape) combined with discrimination training, and practice in specially designed training situations and in the real classroom with precise focused feedback.

Theory Presentation. The objective of this training component (20–30 min) is the understanding of the structure, meaning, functions, and effects of specific nonverbal signs and signals. This includes: information about personality or expressing of emotions and interpersonal attitudes, while speaking or listening, and making use of their regulatory effects.

Emphasis should be given to the regular links with verbal structures and the enhancement of the clarity and unambiguity of verbal material by completing, commenting, qualifying, or illustrating the verbal message. It is also important to stress the function of nonverbal behavior as a device for emphasis, structure, and organization of the verbal information to aid understanding.

Demonstration of Behaviors to be Accomplished, Discrimination Training. Directly following and strongly related to the theory presentation is the next training component: demonstration of the behaviors to be accomplished combined with intensive discrimination training. The objective of this training component is to facilitate the identification of essential features of the respective nonverbal "channel" and the accuracy of observation. This is to serve two purposes: Acquisition of symbolic representation of the demonstrated nonverbal behaviors which serves as a guide for an appropriate performance (Bandura, 1977), and provision of a focus as a device for corrective feedback in the practice sessions. Still pictures, audiotapes, films and/or videotapes are recommended for intensive practice (at least 2–3 hr) in decoding emotions and into personal attitudes and in identifying nonverbal features that provide for emphasis, structure, and organization of the verbal information. Observational systems (like the ones discussed by Woolfolk & Brooks, 1983) and ratings (like the nonverbal scales developed by Collins, 1978) supplemented by examples of specific behaviors can be helpful in training the participants to observe reliably.

Practice and Feedback. The symbolic representations acquired as a result of these components must then be converted into appropriate actions and refined on the basis of informative, focused feedback. Since real classroom situations are too complex and fleeting to allow training in acquiring the target skills, it becomes necessary to provide specially designed scaled-down training situations. Short lectures (news, reports, tales) can be organized easily and quickly in small groups of peers or pupils, if possible with the opportunity for correcting and improving the behavior in a reteach. After at least one or two cycles (teach–reteach), the teachers in most cases are ready to experiment with and to implement the behaviors in the real classroom. Here, they can "coach" each other (Joyce & Showers, 1982) or be helped by an instructor in employing the behaviors appropriately and effectively.

One important part of the practice in the scaled-down training encounters as well as in the real classroom is an informative feedback (Fuller & Manning, 1973), consisting of video playback with a focus like the use of direct observation, ratings, and feedback discussion in a peer group or with an instructor. As a first step, in the scaled-down encounters concentration should center directly on the target skills. Later in the real classroom, additional emphasis should be placed on the consequences of using those skills appropriately and effectively in various situations. The results of the studies reviewed promise that a training of this kind increases the probability that expressive nonverbal behaviors will be acquired with a high proficiency and have a direct influence on teacher classroom performance.

The focus in these guidelines has been on *training* individuals in non-verbal expressiveness. To ensure, however, that teachers' nonverbal behaviors continue to develop throughout their professional career, it seems highly desirable to incorporate elements of the preceding guidelines (e.g., collaborative coaching, direct observation of their own classes, provision of informative feedback, and collaborative discussions) into ongoing inservice education activities like those advocated by Joyce and Showers (1982). By doing this, the examination and development of nonverbal behaviors will not be isolated from the context in which they occur (cf. Doyle, 1977).

REFERENCES

Allport, F. H. (1924). *Social psychology*. Boston, MA: Houghton Mifflin

Bandura, A. (1977). *Social learning theory*. Englewood Cliffs, NJ: Prentice-Hall.

Becker, G. E. (1973). *Optimierung schulischer Gruppenprozesse durch situatives Lehrtraining. [Improving classrom group processes via situational teacher training].* Heidelberg, West Germany: Quelle & Meyer.

Becker, G. E., Clemens-Lodde, B., Flöser, A., Hahn, W., Jaus-Mager, J., & Köhl, K. (1977). *Modellversuch: Entwicklung und Evaluation von Trainingseinheiten zum situativen Lehrtraining für Dozenten und Ausbilder in der beruflichen Erwachsenenbildung. Abschlussbericht.* [Pilot project: development and evaluation in training components for a situational teacher training, designed for teachers in the adult vocational education. Final report.] Heidelberg, West Germany: Forschungszentrum für Rehabilitation und Prävention.

Beisner, L. R. (1977). *Self-analysis procedures as related to teacher perception of verbal and nonverbal behaviors.* Unpublished doctoral dissertation, Ball State University. Muncie, IN. (University Microfilms International, Ann Arbor, MI, No. 78-3912)

Berliner, D. C. (1969). *Microteaching and the technical skills approach to teacher training* (Tech. Rep. No. 8). Stanford, CA: Stanford Center for Research and Development in Teaching, School of Education, Stanford University.

Bettencourt, E. M. (1979). *Effects of training teachers in enthusiasm on student achievement and attitudes.* Unpublished doctoral dissertation, University of Oregon. (University Microfilm International 792 7226)

Birdswhistell, R. (1970). *Kinesics and context: Essay on body motion communication.* Philadelphia: University of Pennsylvania Press.

Borg, W. R. (1975). Protocol materials as related to teacher performance and pupil achievement. *The Journal of Educational Research, 69,* 23-29.

Bradley, B. T., Field, J. F., & Gillespie, W. L. (1978). *Focused observation and feedback designed for analysis of teacher behavior.* East Lansing, MI: Michigan State University.

Brophy, J. E., & Evertson, C. M. (1974a). *Process-product correlations in the Texas teacher effectiveness study: Final report.* Austin, TX: The University of Texas at Austin.

Brophy, J. E., & Evertson, C. M. (1974b). *The Texas teacher effectiveness project: Presentation of nonlinear relationships and summary discussion.* Austin, TX: The University of Texas at Austin.

Brusling, C. (1976). Die Auswirkungen von Modellvorführungen mit unterstützenden Hinweisen und Selbstkonfrontation in einem Microteaching-Arrangement, ausgerichtet auf die Entwicklung nichtverbalen Verhaltens. In W. Zifreund (Ed.), *Training des Lehrverhaltens und Interaktionsanalyse* [The effects of cueing during the demonstration of models and self-confrontation in a microteaching setting on the development of nonverbal behavior. In W. Zifreund (Ed.), The training of teaching behaviors and interaction analysis.] Weinheim, West Germany & Basel, Switzerland: Beltz.

Collins, M. L. (1978). *The effects of training for enthusiasm on the enthusiasm displayed by preservice elementary teachers.* Paper presented at the Annual Meeting of the American Educational Research Association, Toronto.

Conners, C. K., & Eisenberg, L. (1966). *The effect of teacher behavior on verbal intelligence in Operation Headstart children.* Baltimore, MD: John Hopkins University School of Medicine. ERIC Document Reproduction Service No. ED 010 782).

Cooper, J. M., & Stroud, T. (1967). The Stanford summer micro-teaching clinic, 1966. In D. W. Allen (Ed.), *Microteaching: A description*. Stanford, CA: Stanford University.

Davitz, J. R. (1964). *The communication of emotional meaning*. New York: McGraw Hill.

Dawson, P. J., Dawson, K. E., & Forness, S. R. (1975). Effect of video feedback on teacher-behavior. *The Journal of Educational Research, 68,* 197–201.

Delaney, D. (1966). *A study of the effectiveness of sensitivity training on the perception of nonverbal communications in counselor education*. Unpublished doctoral dissertation, Arizona State University.

Dittman, A. T., & Llewellyn, L. G. (1968). Relationship between vocalisations and head nods as listener responses. *Journal of Personality and Social Psychology, 9,* 79–84.

Doyle, W. (1977). The uses of nonverbal behaviors: Toward an ecological model of classrooms. *Merrill-Palmer Quarterly, 23,* 179–192.

Driscoll, J. B. (1979). The effects of a teacher's eye contact, gestures, and voice intonation on student retention of factual material. *Dissertation Abstracts International, 39* (9-B), 455 f.

Dunn, J. D. (1978). *The effects of instruction in interaction analysis and microteaching on the verbal and nonverbal teaching behaviors of selected home economics student teachers*. Unpublished doctoral dissertation. The University of Alabama. (University Microfilm International, Ann Arbor, MI, No. 7819171)

Edwards, C. H. (1975). Changing teacher behavior through self-instruction and supervised microteaching in a competency based program. *The Journal of Educational Research 68*(8), 219–222.

Ehrensberger, R. (1945). An experimental study of the relative effectiveness of certain forms of emphasis in public speaking. *Speech monographs, 12,* 94–111.

Ekman, P., & Friesen, W. V. (1972). Hand movements. *Journal of Communication, 22,* 353–374.

Ellett, L. E., & Smith, E. P. (1975). Improving performance of classroom teachers through videotaping and self-evaluation. *AV Communication Review, 23*(3), 277–288.

Fetter, M. P. (1981). *The utilization of systematized self-analysis of nonverbal teaching behavior in school health education settings*. Unpublished doctoral dissertation. Syracuse University. (University Microfilms International, Ann Arbor, MI, No. 8123900)

Fitzner, T. (1982). Das Training von expressivem nichtverbalem Lehrverhalten [The training of expressive nonverbal teaching behavior]. *Unterrichtswissenschaft, 4,* 329–349.

Flanders, N. A. (1970). *Analyzing teaching behavior*. Reading, MA: Addison-Wesley.

Fortune, J. C. (1967). *The generality of presenting behaviors in teaching pre-school children*. Memphis, TN: Memphis State University. (ERIC Document Reproduction Service No. ED 016285).

French, R. L., & Galloway, C. M. (1968). *A description of teacher behavior: Verbal and nonverbal*. Washington DC: U.S. Department of Health, Education, & Welfare, Office of Education (ERIC Document Reproduction Service No. ED 028 134)

Fuller, F. F., & Manning, B. A. (1973). Self-confrontation reviewed: A conceptualization for video playback in teacher education. *Review of Educational Research, 43*(4), 469–528.

Gage, N. L. (1978). *The scientific basis of the art of teaching.* New York: Teachers College Press.

Gall, M. D., Saunders, W., Nielson, E., & Smith, G. (1974). *The effects of variations in microteaching on prospective teacher's acquisition of questioning skills.* Paper presented at the Annual Meeting of the American Educational Research Association, Chicago, IL.

Galloway, C. M. (1968). Nonverbal communication. *Theory into Practice, 7,* 173–174.

Garrett, B. A. (1979). *Pupil perceptions of selected Mississippi State University student teacher participants in a nonverbal communication training program as measured by the pupil observation survey.* Unpublished doctoral dissertation, Mississippi State University. (University Microfilm International, Ann Arbor, MI, No. 7927086)

Gillett, M., & Gall, M. (1981). *The effect of teacher enthusiasm on the at-task behavior of students in elementary grades.* Paper presented at the Annual Meeting of the American Educational Research Association, Los Angeles, CA.

Glass, G. V. (1977). Integrating findings: The meta-analysis of research. In L. S. Shulman (Ed.), *Review of Research in Education, 5,* 352–379.

Glass, G. V., McGaw, B., Smith, M. L. (1981). *Meta-analysis in social research.* Beverly Hills & London: Sage.

Goffman, E. (1963). *Behavior in public places.* London: Collier-MacMillan.

Guilford, J. P. (1929). An experiment in learning to read facial expression. *Journal of Abnormal and Social Psychology 24,* 191–202.

Hall, E. T. (1966). *The hidden dimension.* New York: Doubleday.

Hansford, B. C. (1977). Microteaching, feedback, dogmatism, and nonverbal perceptiveness. *The Journal of Psychology, 95,* 231–235.

Hertweg, R. (1966). *Semantic differential ratings of counselor nonverbal communication.* Unpublished doctoral dissertation, Arizona State University.

Hiscox, S. B., & Van Mondfrans, A. P. (1972). *Feedback conditions and the type of teaching skill in microteaching.* Paper presented at the Annual Meeting of the American Educational Research Association.

Hodge, R. L. (1972). *An empirical study of the acquisition of nonverbal teaching behaviors by secondary teacher candidates in a teaching laboratory.* Unpublished doctoral dissertation, The University of Texas at Austin. (University Microfilms 73-7571)

Hoffman, M. (1964). *The effects of training on the judgment of nonverbal behavior. An experimental study.* Doctoral Dissertation, Harvard University.

Huntley, S. V. (1978). *A study of the effects of nonverbal behavior awareness training on the perception and performance of student teachers in elementary and secondary education.* Unpublished doctoral dissertation, The University of Toledo, OH. (University Microfilms International, Ann Arbor, No. 79-14845)

Jecker, J. D., Maccoby, N., & Breitrose, H. S. (1965). Improving accuracy in interpreting nonverbal cues of comprehension. *Psychology in the Schools, 2,* 239–244.

Jenness, A. (1932). The effects of coaching subjects in the recognition of facial expressions. *Journal of General Psychology, 7,* 163–178.

Joyce, B. R., & Showers, B. (1981). *Teacher training research: Working hypotheses for program design and directions for further studies.* Paper presented at the Annual Meeting of the American Educational Research Association, Los Angeles, CA.

Joyce, B., & Showers, B. (1982). The coaching of teaching, *Educational Leadership, 40,* 4–10.

Kaufman, P. (1976). The effects of nonverbal behavior on performance and attitudes in a college classroom. *Dissertation Abstracts International, 37* (1-A), 235.

Kline, L. W., & Johannsen, D. E. (1935). Comparative role of the face and of the face-body-hands as aids in identifying emotions. *Journal of Abnormal and Social Psychology, 29,* 415–426.

Klinzing, H. G., Fitzner, T., Klinzing-Eurich, G. (1983). *Effects of a training program on expressive nonverbal behavior.* Paper presented at the Annual Meeting of the American Educational Research Association, Montreal. (ERIC Document Reproduction Service No. Ed 233 999)

Klinzing, H. G., Kunkel, K., Schiefer, H., & Steiger, S. (1984a). *The effects of nonverbal expressive behavior training on teacher clarity, interest, assertiveness, and persuasiveness during microteaching.* Paper presented at the Annual Meeting of the American Educational Research Association, New Orleans, LA.

Klinzing, H. G., Kunkel, K., Schiefer, H., & Steiger, S. (1984b). *Effects of pretesting on the PONS (Profile of Nonverbal Sensitivity) and its psychosocial correlates.* Paper presented at the Ninth Annual Conference of the Association for Teacher Education in Europe, Linz, Austria.

Kohnle, S. R. (1971). Conflicting verbal and nonverbal communication in therapy. Doctoral dissertation. University of Washington.

Land, M. L. (1980). *Joint effects of teacher structure and teacher enthusiasm on student achievement.* Paper presented at the Annual Meeting of the Southwest Educational Research Association, San Antonio, TX. (ERIC Document Reproduction Service No. ED 182 310)

Langthaler, W., & Wothke, W. (1979). *Effektivitätsuntersuchung eines Microteaching-Kurses an Verhaltensproben* [Effects of a microteaching training program on teaching behavior.]. *Psychologie in Erziehung und Unterricht, 26,* 276–283.

Lanzetta, J. T., & Kleck, R. E. (1970). Encoding and decoding of nonverbal affect in humans. *Journal of Personality and Social Psychology, 16,* 12–19.

Mattis, S. (1964). *Minor studies in communication of emotion.* In J. Davitz (Ed.), *The communication of emotional meaning.* New York: McGraw Hill.

Miller, R. E., Giannini, A. J., & Levine, J. M. (1975). *Nonverbal communication in man with a cooperative conditioning task.* Western Psychiatric Institute.

Mittenecker, E. (1960). Die Variation von Lern- und Verstärkungsbedingungen bei der eindrucksmässigen Beurteilung von Persönlichkeitsmerkmalen. In *Bericht über den 22. Kongress der Deutschen Gesellschaft für Psychologie.* [The variation of learning and reinforcement conditions in the rating of personality characteristics. In *Report on the 22nd convention of the German Association of Psychology*]. Göttingen, West Germany: Hogrefe.

Nuthall, G. (1976). Ein Vergleich des Nutzens von Microteaching mit zwei Schülertypen-Zehnjährigen Schülern und Studienkollegen, die die Schülerrolle übernehmen. In W. Zifreund (Ed.), *Training des Lehrverhaltens und Interaktions-*

analyse [A comparison of the use of microteaching with two types of pupils— 10 year-old pupils and peers acting as pupils. In W. Zifreund (ed.). *Training of teaching behaviors and interaction analysis.*] Weinheim, West Germany, and Basel, Switzerland: Beltz.

Okey, J. R., & Cieslar, J. L. (1973). Designs for the evaluation of teacher training materials. *AV Communication Review, 3,* 299–310.

Pancrazio, S. B., & Johnson, W. D. (1971). *Comparison of three teacher training approaches in nonverbal behaviors which encourage classroom interaction.* Paper presented at the Annual Meeting of the American Educational Research Association, New York (ERIC Document Reproduction Number ED 049 198).

Phillips, F. O. (1975). *Nonverbal sensitivity and nonverbal behavior of preservice teachers in student teaching.* Doctoral Dissertation, University of Georgia, Athens. (University Microfilms, Ann Arbor, MI, 76 6442)

Pierce, W., & Halinski, R. (1974). An evaluation of microteaching training techniques using pupil outcomes as the evaluation criterion. *Contemporary Education, 46,* 45–50.

Pinnas, R. M. (1975). *The effect of microcounseling on attentiveness and sensitivity to nonverbal cues.* Unpublished doctoral dissertation, The University of Miami, FL.

Raymond, A. (1973). The acquisition of nonverbal behaviors by preservice science teachers and their application during student teaching. *Journal of Research in Science Teaching, 10,* 13–24.

Reich, L. H. (1970). *Non-verbal communication of emotions: A study of the relationship between training, expression, and recognition of emotion.* Doctoral dissertation, Arizona State University (University Microfilms, Ann Arbor, MI 70-24, 409)

Rosenshine, B. (1968). *Behavioral predictors of effectiveness in explaining social studies material.* Doctoral dissertation, Stanford University, CA. (University Microfilms, Ann Arbor, MI)

Rosenthal, R., Hall, J. A., DiMatteo, M. R., Rogers, P. L., & Archer, D. (1979). *Sensitivity to nonverbal communication: The PONS test.* Baltimore & London: The John Hopkins University Press.

Rudolph, H. (1903). *Der Ausdruck der Gemütsbewegungen des Menschen. Atlas. [The expression of human emotions. An atlas.]* Dresden, Germany: Küthmann.

Scheflen, A. E. (1976). *Körpersprache und soziale Ordnung [Body language and social order.]* Stuttgart, West Germany: Klett.

Scholl, R. L. (1975). *Nonverbal behavior categories.* Miami University, FL. (mimeographed)

Schum, W. C. (1974). The effects of training student teachers in self-analysis of nonverbal response patterns. Paper presented at the Annual Meeting of the American Educational Research Association, Chicago.

Scriven, M. (1967). The methodology of evaluation. In: B. O. Smith (Ed.), *Perspectives of curriculum evaluation.* Chicago, IL: Rand McNally.

Shapiro, J. N. (1976). *Modular instruction in nonverbal communication.* Doctoral Dissertation, The Ohio State University, (University Microfilms, Ann Arbor, MI 77-2501)

Smith, H. A. (1979). Nonverbal communication in teaching. *Review of Educational Research, 49*(4), 631–672.

Sommer, R. (1969). *Personal space.* Englewood Cliffs, NJ: Prentice Hall.

Strother, D. B., Ayres, H. J., & Orlich, D. C. (1971). *The effects of instruction in nonverbal communication on elementary school teacher competency and student achievement: Final Report.* Pullman, WA: Washington State University. (ERIC ED 056 005)

Veldman, D. J., & Peck, R. F. (1963). Student teacher characteristics from the pupils' viewpoint. *Journal of Educational Psychology, 54*(6), 346–355.

Walton, W. E. (1936). Emphatic responses in children. *Psychological Monographs, 48,* 40–67.

Wagner, A. C. (1973). Changing teaching behavior: A comparison of microteaching and cognitive discrimination training. *Journal of Educational Psychology, 64,* 299–305.

Williams, R. G., & Ware, J. E. (1976). Validity of student ratings of instruction under different incentive conditions: A further study of the Dr. Fox effect. *Journal of Educational Psychology, 68,* 48–56.

Williams, R. G., & Ware, J. E. (1977). An extended visit with Dr. Fox: Validity of student satisfaction with instruction ratings after repeated exposures to a lecturer. *American Educational Research Journal, 14*(4), 449–457.

Woolbert, C. H. (1920). Effects of various modes of public reading. *Journal of Applied Psychology, 4,* 162–185.

Woolfolk, A. E., & Brooks, D. M. (1983). Nonverbal communication in teaching. In E. W. Gordon (Ed.), *Review of Research in Education,* (Vol. 10). Washington, DC: American Educational Research Association.

Young, E. M. (1973). *Effect of teacher enthusiasm on vocational business education student achievement.* Unpublished doctoral dissertation, University of Missouri, Columbia (University Microfilms 74-18676)

7

Individual and Institutional Influences on the Development of Teacher Perspectives

Kenneth M. Zeichner
University of Wisconsin-Madison

Lortie (1973) concludes, in his examination of "the riddle of teacher sociali-zation," that there are several credible explanations of the socialization process available and that the socialization of teachers is "undoubtedly a complex process not readily captured by a simple, one-factor frame of ref-erence" (p. 488). When one examines the empirical literature on teacher socialization, including that work which has been completed since 1973, Lortie's analysis is strongly confirmed. There is clearly a lack of consensus in the literature with regard to the potency and influence of various socializ-ing agents and mechanisms that affect the development of teacher perspec-tives over a career.

Amid this debate over the relative contribution of specific people and contextual factors to the socialization of teachers, there is also disagreement over the degree to which the development of occupational perspectives by teachers is influenced by individual or institutional factors. On the one hand, some have argued that individual teacher characteristics, disposi-tions, and capabilities are more influential in determining the course of teacher socialization than are the various institutional characteristics associ-ated with teacher education and schooling. Other studies have emphasized the potency of institutional influences and have ignored the role of individ-ual and biographical factors. A third position, exemplified by the work of Lacey (1977) and Pollard (1982) in England and by Tabachnick and Zeich-ner (1984) and Zeichner and Tabachnick (1985) in the United States, has considered the *interaction* of individual and institutional factors and has emphasized the role of both individual intent and institutional constraint in the development of teacher perspectives.

In addition to the lack of consensus over the most potent socializing agents and mechanisms and the existence of different points of view regarding the relative contribution of individual and institutional influences, there is also much disagreement about the degree of stability or change in the perspectives of individual teachers throughout their formal training and careers. When are teaching perspectives first formed, and how do they change and develop (if at all) during formal training and inservice school experience? Here some studies have documented a great deal of discontinuity between anticipatory socialization, formal training, and inservice school experience, and have shown dramatic changes in the perspective of teachers at different points in time. Studies also exist which demonstrate a great deal of stability in perpectives across time.

Finally, there is also much disagreement about the nature of teaching perspectives themselves, both at an individual and occupational level. These differences are concerned with the degree of internal consistency in the perspectives of individual teachers and with the degree of homogeneity in perspectives in the occupation as a whole. Some studies have emphasized the internally consistent nature of individual teachers' perspectives and the uniformity of perspectives in the occupation as a whole. Other studies have emphasized the contradictions embedded in the perspectives of individual teachers and the heterogeneous "teacher cultures" existent in various "segments" of the occupational group.

This chapter will review the empirical evidence which currently exists with regard to each of these issues of controversy: (a) the nature of teacher perspectives; (b) the influence of specific socializing agents and mechanisms on the development of teacher perspectives; (c) the relative contribution of individual intent and institutional constraint to the development of teacher perspectives; and (d) the degree of stability in individual teachers' perspectives from the advent of formal training through the early years of a teacher's career. Because most of the extant research has focused on the socialization of student teachers or beginning teachers, this chapter will not consider the development of teacher perspectives beyond the initial transition to teaching.

Following an analysis of different points of view on the nature of individual and occupational perspectives themselves, consideration will be given to alternative explanations regarding the development of teacher perspectives: (a) prior to formal training; (b) during preservice teacher education; and (c) during the early years of school experience. In doing so, the issue of stability or change in perspectives across these three points in time will also be addressed. Pollard's (1982) conceptual model, describing three layers of social contextualization (interactive, institutional, and cultural) will be employed as a heuristic device for analyzing the individual and institutional influences on the development of teacher perspectives subsequent to formal training. Finally, following this analysis of the influence of specific socializing agents and mechanisms and the stability or change in perspectives across time, the relative contribution of individual intent and institutional constraint will be considered. Empirical evidence will be reviewed related to contrasting points of view on this issue, and an argument will be offered in support of an interactive model of teacher socialization. Throughout the analysis, an attempt will be made to identify the strength of the empirical evidence supporting particular points of view and to suggest areas where there is a particular need for further empirical work to be initiated.

THE NATURE OF TEACHER PERSPECTIVES

Becker, Geer, Hughes, and Strauss (1961), in their study of the socialization of medical students, define *perspectives* as "a coordinated series of ideas and actions a person uses in dealing with some problematic situation" (p. 34). According to this view, perspectives differ from attitudes since they involve actions and not merely dispositions to act. Also, perspectives are defined in relation to specific problematic situations and do not necessarily represent generalized beliefs or ideologies (see Sharp & Green, 1975). The construct of perspectives has been widely utilized in studies of teacher socialization.[1]

Although the classification of individual teachers' perspectives into dichotomous categories such as "progressive/traditional," "formal/informal," and "custodial/humanistic" has been criticized for many years (see Anderson, 1959; Travers, 1971) as overly reductionist, this practice still dominates the literature on teacher socialization. According to this view, the various dimensions of individual teachers' perspectives are internally consistent and the categories themselves (e.g., progressive/traditional) are mutually exclusive. Along with this practice, it has been commonly assumed that most teachers share a uniform teaching culture and that the degree of diversity in teaching perspectives in the occupation as a whole is very small.

Several criticisms have been raised in the literature regarding the validity of both of these views. First, Hammersley, (1977a) urged researchers to be cautious of assuming that there is necesarily a logical consistency between the various components of individual teachers' perspectives and that there are no similarities among teachers who hold different perspectives on some dimensions.

The diversity of teaching forms is of course rather more complex than is represented in such dichotomies. Furthermore, exisiting typologies

---

[1] See Hammersley (1977a); Berlak and Berlak (1981); and Tabachnick and Zeichner (1984) for examples of specific dimensions which have been investigated within the rubric of teaching perspectives.

often both overlap and conflict with one another as well as compounding what on analyses turn out to be distinct dimensions. The assumptions which are seen as going together often do so neither logically nor empirically. (Hammersley, 1977a, p. 15)

There is recent evidence from several empirical studies (e.g., Barr & Duffy, 1978; Sharp & Green, 1975; Bussis, Chittenden, & Amarel, 1976; Berlak & Berlak, 1981; Tabachnick & Zeichner, 1984) that bipolar unidimensional characterizations of perspectives have greatly oversimplified differences within and among teachers. First, with regard to the mutual exclusivity of categories of perspectives and the assumption of homogeneity within categories, Berlak and Berlak (1981) conclude:

> Despite their ambiguities, the labels formal/informal as commonly used in the schools we visited, do in some general way distinguish two types of teachers. . . . However, it is only in dealing with the extremes that this division does not present insurmountable problems. . . . There is clearly a wide range of patterns that teachers and kids commonly associated with informal, and a range they associated with formal. (p. 199)

Similarly, Tabachnick and Zeichner (1984) have documented significant overlap between and significant variance within the categories of "progressive" and "traditional" in their study of the development of teaching perspectives during student teaching. Finally, Gray and Satterly (1981) go a step further and question the use of tripartite classifications when they conclude that the differences between teachers within "styles" (in Bennett's, 1976, study) were far greater than the differences between the "styles" themselves.

The typical assumption of internal consistency among the various dimensions of individual teachers' perspectives has also been challenged by recent research. For example, the studies of Barr and Duffy (1978), Berlak and Berlak (1981), and Tabachnick and Zeichner (1984) have all documented (with regard to the perspectives of specific teachers) that individual dimensions of perspectives do not always fit researchers' conceptions of what goes logically together and that the individual dimensions themselves frequently change as teachers are faced with changing circumstances.

Berlak and Berlak (1981) argue that it is not surprising to find these contradictions and inconsistencies within the perspectives of individual teachers, since contradictions are embedded in the society and institutions in which teachers work.

> Teachers take on or assume some of the social attitudes, values, and beliefs of the multiple groups or communities to which they belong or with whom they come into contact over the course of their lifetimes. . . .

The diversity of these various experiences and ideas within the "generalized other" often results in multiple and conflicting beliefs about evaluations of most schooling acts, within as well as among teachers. (Berlak & Berlak, 1981, p. 100)

It has also been conventional to assume a high degree of homogeneity in perspectives in the occupation as a whole. According to this view, teachers are socialized into a uniform "teacher culture." Feiman-Nemser and Floden (1986) conclude that this assumption of cultural uniformity in the occupation is untenable.

Teachers differ in age, experience, social and cultural background, gender, marital status, subject matter, wisdom, and ability. The schools in which they work also differ in many ways, as do the groups of students they teach. All these differences may lead to differences in teaching culture. (Feiman-Nemser & Floden, 1986)

This conclusion is supported by several empirical studies where diverse teaching cultures were discovered even within single schools (e.g., Gracey, 1972; Metz, 1978; Carew & Lightfoot, 1979). This existence of diverse teaching cultures has important implications for the study of the development of teacher perspectives, for once one accepts this view, it logically follows that teachers are faced with conflicting pressures to act in different ways and the internalization of a particular set of norms becomes problematic. Berlak and Berlak's (1981) notion of "dilemmas" attempts to capture these contradictions and inconsistencies at both the institutional and individual level. Whatever conclusions one reaches with regard to the developmental issues to be discussed subsequently, the nature of perspectives themselves, the dynamic "product" of this developmental process, needs to be viewed in more complex and subtle ways than has typically been the case.

PRETRAINING INFLUENCES

Teachers teach as they were taught during their many years as students. Their professional preparation comes late in their own schooling and is too little and too thin to separate them from what their experience has taught them that teaching is. Their professional preparation and subsequent practice merely reinforce their own perceptions. Teachers fail to transcend the conventional wisdom of their own profession and continue to teach as they were taught. (Goodlad, 1982, pp. 19–20)

There are many like Goodlad who argue that experiences predating formal training are more profoundly influential in the making of a teacher than the efficacy of either preservice training or socialization in the workplace during a career. The apparent persistence of particular forms of pedagogy (see Sirotnik, 1983) is explained by the failure of reform initiatives and the overt curriculum of teacher education to overcome the effects of this anticipatory socialization. Feiman-Nemser (1983) summarizes the arguments related to the three most prevalent explanations of the influence of pretraining experiences on the development of teacher perspectives. First, Stephens (1967) proposes an "evolutionary" theory to account for the development of teacher perspectives and emphasizes the role of "spontaneous pedagogical tendencies" in explaining why teachers act as they do. According to this view:

> Human beings have survived because of their deeply ingrained habits of correcting one another, telling each other what they know, pointing out the moral, and supplying the answer. These tendencies have been acquired over the centuries and are lived out in families and classrooms. Thus children not only learn what they are told by parents and teachers, they also learn to be teachers. (Feiman-Nemser, 1983, p. 152)

A second position outlined by Feiman-Nemser (1983) is the "psychoanalytic" explanation found in the work of Wright (1959) and Wright and Tuska (1967, 1968). These studies suggest that teacher perspectives are affected to a considerable extent by the quality of relationships as a child with important adults (e.g., mother, father, teachers) and that becoming a teacher is to some extent a process (sometimes unconscious and sometimes deliberate) of trying to become like the significant others in one's childhood. According to this view, early relationships with significant others are the prototypes of subsequent relationships throughout life and the kinds of teachers that education students become are governed by the effects this childhood heritage has on their personalities (Wright & Tuska, 1967). These studies offer empirical data in support of this "childhood romance theory of teacher development," including several statements written by teachers which illustrate the significance of a conscious identification with a teacher during childhood (see Wright, 1959). According to this view, the "reality shock" which is apparently experienced by many beginning teachers is explained by the failure of training to overcome these early fantasies about teaching and teachers (Wright & Tuska, 1968).

A third viewpoint on the role of pretraining experience on the development of teacher perspectives emphasizes the influence of the thousands of hours spent as a pupil in what Lortie (1975) refers to as an "apprenticeship of observation." According to this view, teacher socialization occurs largely through the internalization of teaching models during the time spent as a pupil in close contact with teachers. According to Lortie (1975), the activation of this latent culture during formal training and later school experience is a major influence in shaping teachers' conceptions of the teaching role and role performance. Formal training at the university is viewed as having little impact in altering the cumulative effects of this anticipatory socialization. Lortie (1975) even questions the use of the term socialization to describe entry into the teaching role:

> The connotations of the term socialization seem somewhat askew when applied to this kind of induction, since they imply greater receptivity to a preexisting culture than seems to prevail. Teachers are largely self-made. The internalization of common knowledge plays only a limited part in their movement to work responsibility. (p. 85)

Lortie's argument is based, in part, on several studies where teachers attested to the tangential role of their formal training and where they frequently referred to the continuing influence of their earlier mentors (see Lortie, 1975). Generally, however, there is little empirical evidence which directly supports Lortie's position or the other two points of view. Most of the empirical evidence in support of the influence of pretraining experiences on the development of teacher perspectives is indirect in nature and demonstrates a continuity in perspectives during formal training without supporting a particular theoretical explanation. Studies conducted by Petty and Hogben (1980) and Hogben and Lawson (1983) in Australia, by Maddox (1968) and Mardle and Walker (1980) in England, and by Zeichner and Grant (1981) and Tabachnick and Zeichner (1984) in the United States clearly indicate that biography exerts a powerful influence on the development of teacher perspectives, but much work remains to be done to clarify the particular nature of this influence.

THE IMPACT OF PRESERVICE TEACHER EDUCATION

Feiman-Nemser (1983) argues that it is impossible to understand the impact of the preservice preparation of teachers on teacher development without knowing more about what this preparation is like. Sarason, Davidson, and Blatt's (1962) characterization of preservice preparation as "an unstudied problem" remains as true today as it was 20 years ago, despite the literally hundreds of studies which have been conducted on the impact of education courses and field experiences on teacher development. Generally, these studies have not provided much information about the substance of preservice preparation beyond descriptions of course titles and credit distributions (see Zeichner, 1985), and they have provided even less information about how the knowledge and skills communicated to prospective teachers during training are received and then incorporated into the perspectives of teachers (e.g., see Zeichner, 1984; Feiman-Nemser & Floden, 1986).

There are two major elements in the professional education component of a preservice preparation program: (a) the educational methods and foundations courses; (b) the field experiences which are typically carried out in K–12 classrooms. First, with regard to the influence of the formal knowledge distributed in education courses on the development of teacher perspectives, there is much evidence that pedagogical methods and content knowledge introduced to students in campus courses has little influence on the subsequent actions of students in classrooms even during initial training (e.g., Hodges, 1982; Grant, 1981; Katz & Raths, 1982). There is also evidence that when attempts are made to systematically train prospective teachers in the performance of specific teaching skills through the use of procedures such as microteaching, that the continued use of the skill by prospective teachers outside of the laboratory is highly dependent on whether the ecological conditions in classrooms are conducive to the use of the skills. Copeland's (1980) work suggests that the impact of formal courses in education cannot be assessed apart from consideration of these ecological conditions.

These and similar studies are all concerned in one way or another with the impact of the overt curriculum of initial preparation on the development of teacher perspectives. Dale (1977a, 1977b) and Bartholomew (1976) argue, on the other hand, that the chief impact of initial preparation comes not through the formal knowledge and skills imparted to teachers, but through the *hidden curriculum* of teacher preparation programs. For example, Dale (1977a, 1977b) conducted a content analysis of typical English courses in the philosophical, sociological, and psychological foundations of education and concluded that initial training fosters a cognitive style of "liberal individualism" which predisposes prospective teachers to see the world in particular ways, to become conscious of it having particular properties and possibilities, and to reject or never recognize other properties and possibilities. Dale (1977a) specifically argues that this cognitive style

> directs teachers to seek the source of pupils' problems and the solution
> of these problems in the individuals concerned as well as providing a
> context for them to see their own failures and satisfactions as individual
> matters. (p. 51)

On the other hand, according to Dale, this cognitive style does not lead teachers to question the nature and the values of the system in which they practice or to seek the solutions to problems confronting them in social relations and institutions rather than in individuals. Haberman (1981) has offered an analysis of the hegemony of "the psychological way of knowing" in United States teacher education which essentially supports Dale's thesis.

Bartholomew (1976) analyzes other aspects of the hidden curriculum of preservice preparation (the pedagogical practices and social relations and social organization of programs) and concludes that, despite the fact that teacher education programs encourage students to use liberal phrases and to affirm liberal slogans in places other than the university, the facts of socialization *within* the university (e.g., the separation of theory and practice) encourage the development of "objectivist" conceptions of knowledge, fragmented views of curriculum, and a view of learners as passive recipients of officially approved knowledge. According to Bartholomew (1976) and others such as Giroux (1980), Ginsburg (1984), and Popkewitz (in press), the real impact of preservice preparation lies in these images of teacher, learner, knowledge, curriculum, and professional which are subtly communicated to prospective teachers through the covert processes of the hidden curriculum of teacher education programs. Thus, despite the overwhelming evidence related to the low impact of the formal curriculum of teacher education, one must be cautious in generalizing these findings to the impact of the preservice experiences as a whole. Generally, arguments related to the impact of the hidden curriculum in preservice preparation have been offered on logical and theoretical grounds with very little substantiating empirical evidence. With the exception of Ginsburg's (1984) study of the development of perspectives toward professionalism, we do not have very strong empirical evidence which confirms that students actually incorporate elements into their perspectives in ways consistent with the theoretical arguments.

The second aspect of preservice preparation which has received much attention in the literature in relation to the development of teacher perspectives is the field-experience component. Here those who have analyzed the empirical literature have consistently characterized the knowledge base related to the socializing impact of these experiences as weak and ambiguous (e.g., Zeichner, 1980, 1984; McIntyre, 1983; Griffin, Barnes, Hughes, O'Neal, Edwards, & Defino, 1983). Today, despite the existence of numerous individual studies which have demonstrated specific effects of field experiences on the development of individual teachers under particular conditions, there continues to be a great deal of debate about the role these experiences play in the development of teacher perspectives and about the relative contribution of various people and factors within these experiences to the socialization process. Zeichner (1980), for example, describes two "myths" related to the impact of these experiences which have survived despite the existence of hundreds of individual studies. Generally, studies related to the role of field experiences in the development of teacher perspectives have not attended to the quality or substance of these experiences and have not identified the particular kinds of field programs and components within programs (e.g., characteristics of placement sites) which are related to the development of particular kinds of perspectives by individual students who differ from each other. Field experiences seem to have different effects upon the development of perspectives depending upon the nature of a program and the characters and dispositions of individual students, but we currently know very little about these effects beyond the conflicting scenarios which have been constructed from analyses of central tendencies.

In summary, the question of impact of preservice preparation on the development of teacher perspectives has several dimensions. Studies of the influence of the formal curriculum of programs suggest that preservice programs are not very powerful interventions. On the other hand, studies of the influence of the hidden curriculum of programs suggest without much documentation, that the impact of preservice training may be far greater than has often been thought. Finally, studies of field experiences indicate that these experiences have differential effects on teacher development but do not illuminate the particular characteristics of programs or individuals which are related to specific effects. This whole area is clearly one where a great deal of empirical work remains to be done.

THE IMPACT OF SCHOOL EXPERIENCE

> The practical activity of teachers does not exist in a vacuum. The strategies employed by teachers arise in the context of a school organization which provides the prevailing circumstances taken into account by teachers in their routine activity. The school organization provides dilemmas and imperatives, possibilities and opportunities, and it is these which explain the existence of particular strategies in the classroom. (Denscombe, 1980, p. 290)

Pollard (1982) has developed a conceptual model describing three layers of social contextualization which is heuristic in understanding the influence of the workplace of the school on the development of teacher perspectives. According Pollard, teacher perspectives (or "coping strategies") represent active and creative responses by teachers to the constraints, opportunities, and dilemmas posed by the immediate contexts of the classroom and school, and it is through these immediate determinants of teacher perspectives that the wider structure of society, the state and mode of production have their impact.

At the *interactive* level within the classroom, Pollard (1982) describes several different kinds of influence on the pragmatic perspectives of teachers. Two of these influences: (a) the socializing role of pupils, and (b) the influence of the ecology of the classroom will be considered here. Lortie (1975) argues that the psychic rewards of teaching come largely from pupils. Jackson (1968) suggests that teachers most often look to their pupils for validation of their efforts rather than to colleagues or administrators. There is substantial evidence that pupils' responses reinforce the teachers' behavior which evoke them and that pupils play an important role in influencing teacher perspectives (Hammersley, 1977b).

This position on the significant role of pupils in occupational socialization is supported both on logical grounds and by empirical research. Haller (1967) and Doyle (1979) argue that the important role of pupils in teacher socialization is understandable given the typical isolation of teachers from their colleagues and supervisors and given the transitory and invisible nature of the learning process.

> This invisibility of the learning process has important consequences for the teacher, for it means that there is no single objective and immediate method by which he can unequivocally assess his performance. Instead, most teachers rely on observations of their students, oftentimes watching for highly transitory reactions in pupil behavior which they believe indicates that learning has occurred. (Haller, 1967, p. 318)

These and other "logical" explanations of the importance of pupils in the occupational socialization of teachers are consistent with bidirectional models of childhood socialization (e.g., Dreitzel, 1973) and are supported by a substantial number of empirical studies on classroom influence (e.g., Fiedler, 1975; Noble & Nolan, 1976; Brophy & Evertson, 1981). According to Doyle (1979), "The influence of students ranges from the general teaching methods and patterns of language that teachers use in classrooms to the type and frequency of teacher questions and feedback given to individual students" (p. 139). Furthermore, the individual characteristics of both teachers and students seem to affect the ways in which pupils influence teacher perspectives. For example, according to Doyle (1979), "Research has shown that high-achieving students appear to have the greatest amount of influence on teachers, especially when the teacher is high in measures of cognitive complexity" (p. 139).

As a result of these studies, there is little question that classroom influence is reciprocal in nature and that teachers' perceptions of pupils' characteristics, expectations, and behaviors influence the development of teacher perspectives. The Wisconsin studies of teacher socialization (Zeichner & Tabachnick, 1985) reinforce this conclusion and document the powerful role of pupil responses in influencing the teaching perspectives of beginning teachers. Despite this general knowledge, we currently have very little understanding of how the specific characteristics of teachers and pupils mediate the development of particular kinds of perspectives.

Doyle (1979), after demonstrating through a review of research that pupils are significant socializing agents, goes on to argue that student effects are just one facet of the larger question of the effects of classrooms on teachers. Doyle (1977, 1979), Copeland (1980), and others have emphasized the role of the ecology of the classroom in shaping teachers' perspectives. Doyle and Ponder (1975) define the ecological system of the classroom as "that network of interconnected processes and events which impinges upon behavior in the teaching environment" (p. 183). Doyle (1977) has identified five distinctive features of classrooms that he claims are crucial in shaping the work of teachers: multidimensionality, simultaneity, immediacy, unpredictability, and history. Others such as Dreeben (1973), Westbury (1973), Sharp & Green (1975), Dale (1977a, 1977b), and Denscombe (1980, 1982) all discuss various factors related to the material conditions and the social organization of the classroom and how they affect teachers' perspectives. Among these teacher–pupil ratios, limited material resources, and time. According to Doyle (1979):

> Classrooms are crowded with people, activity and interruptions; many events take place at the same time, and there is little time for the teacher to reflect before acting or even to anticipate the course of events. In addition classroom groups meet regularly over an extended period of time so that rules that evolve for the behavior of teachers and students and decisions at one point have consequences for action in the future. . . . If teachers met their students one at a time and at the students' initiative, the setting for teaching would contain few of these elements. (p. 139)

According to this view of classrooms as ecological environments, learning to teach involves "learning the texture of the classroom and the sets of behaviors congruent with the environmental demands of that setting" (Doyle, 1977, p. 51). It is felt that the environmental demands posed by current classroom arrangements establish limits on the range of teacher behaviors that can be successful in particular settings and that "successful" teachers must learn a set of coping strategies which are appropriate to particular settings. These ecological classroom conditions, however, not only act as constraints on the actions of teachers, but they also exert positive pressures to act in certain ways. According to Hammersley (1977), these social forces "both constrain and facilitate action. . . . The social context and its interpretation by individual teachers make certain actions possible and block or make difficult other lines of action which in a different setting might be possible" (p. 7). Although there seems to be little doubt at present that the characteristics of the classroom as a workplace need to be closely examined in any attempt to understand the development of teacher perspectives, the analysis cannot remain at the level of the classroom alone, because these ecological conditions are themselves products of policy decisions and political actions at levels beyond the classroom.

At the *institutional* level of analysis (Pollard, 1982), socializing influences related to the characteristics of schools as workplaces come into focus. Fenstermacher (1980) has argued that teachers' experiences with the institutional characteristics of schools are the most potent determinants of their perspectives toward teaching. In a similar vein, Dreeben (1970, 1973) has written extensively about how certain organizational properties of schools have implications for the character of teachers' work. Dreeben's thesis is that certain structural properties of schools such as their internal spatial arrangement (e.g., egg crate vs. open plan); modes of affiliation (e.g., hired vs. conscripted); and authority relations (e.g., between teachers and administrators) shape the character of teachers' work activities and that teacher perspectives can be construed as adaptive responses to the problems and dilemmas posed by this work context. There are many others of various theoretical persuasions (e.g., Larkin, 1973; Denscombe, 1980; Freedman, Jackson, & Boles, 1983; Gitlin, 1983; Zeichner & Tabachnick, 1985) who have described how particular institutional characteristics of schools by themselves or as mediators of influence from the social, economic, and political context of schooling affect the character of teachers' work.

Despite all of these attempts to conceptualize school structure and to examine the perspectives of teachers in relation to specific institutional characteristics, Schlechty (1976) has concluded that "there currently exists no adequate description or formulation of the structural characteristics of schools" (p. 83). What we have, according to Schlechty, is a variety of different lenses for viewing these structural characteristics which reflects the variety of sociological paradigms and theoretical frameworks which have been employed in the study of schools as organizations.

Pollard (1982), drawing upon the seminal work of Bachrach and Baratz (1962) on political decision making, proposes the construct of "institutional bias" as a heuristic for analyzing school-level influences on the work of teachers. According to Pollard, "institutional bias" represents a stability of understanding within particular schools which reflect the social values and educational ideas of those with the most influence within a school. This institutional bias derives inputs from teacher cultures existent within a school, from administrator perspectives, from parents, material and legal constraints, etc., and presents individual teachers with particular problematics, despite oftentimes conflicting expectations which are exerted upon teachers within individual schools through both formal and informal channels. The influence of two specific elements of institutional bias on the development of teacher perspectives will be described in the present chapter: (a) inputs from colleagues; and (b) the influence of those with formal sanctioning power over teachers.

First, with regard to the influence of colleagues and "teacher cultures" on the development of teacher perspectives, Eddy (1969) argues that even in the isolation of their own classrooms "new teachers entering the school soon learn that they are not alone, but part of a group of colleagues who attempt to guide and help them in many ways" (p. 101). Eddy feels that experienced colleagues are a constant source of help and guidance for beginning teachers and that through them neophytes develop world views of educational categories and processes consistent with that of other teachers in their schools.

> Like new workers in all settings, they are largely dependent on their more experienced colleagues to teach them the procedures for coping with the demands made upon them by their supervisors and subordinates...for the provision of education tools, for establishing work routines, for preparing classroom displays, and for preparing plans and filling out student records. (Eddy, 1969, p. 106)

In a similar vein, Waller (1932) argues:

> The significant people for a school teacher are other teachers and by comparison with good standing in that fraternity, the good opinion of students is a small thing and of little price. A landmark in one's assimilation into the profession is that moment when he decides that only teachers are important. (p. 389)

Although there is substantial evidence that beginning teachers view their experienced colleagues as highly influential in the process of learning to teach (e.g., Grant & Zeichner, 1981; Howey, 1983), and some evidence which suggests that norms within the teacher peer group exert a powerful influence on teacher perspectives (e.g., Hoy, 1968), there is also evidence which suggests that the influence of "teacher cultures" is mediated by certain characteristics of beginning teachers (e.g., McArthur, 1978) and that formal attempts by teachers to influence the work of their colleagues occur only under particular conditions (e.g., McPherson, 1972; Newberry, 1977). The literature suggests that most of the influence of colleagues on the development of teacher perspectives, with the possible exception of those relatively few schools where norms of collegiality predominate (e.g., Little, 1982), probably occurs informally in a manner similar to Newberry's (1977) description of the processes of influence in a study of first-year teachers:

> Focused conversation between beginning and experienced teachers on teaching practices was minimal, and the opportunity to observe other teachers at work was nonexistent. The beginning teachers' limited knowledge of other teachers' practices was based on information gained indirectly. They acquired this information informally as they visited and interacted with teachers outside actual classroom teaching situations. They heard comments in the staff room and looked at materials brought in by experienced teachers. They also heard comments and saw materials around the duplicating machine. Looking through open classroom doors or visiting other teachers' classrooms before or after school also

informed beginners about the kind of work in which other teachers were currently engaged and the materials and techniques they used. (p. 14)

There is little question that the influence of colleagues needs to be taken into account in attempts to understand the origin of teacher perspectives despite the existence of an ethos of privacy and individualism within many schools (Denscombe, 1980). Given that teachers work under similar conditions, collegial influence is probably closely tied to the common circumstances that teachers face in the structural characteristics of schools and the ecological conditions of classrooms. It is also very clear, as studies by Carew and Lightfoot (1979) and Metz (1978) have shown, that several diverse "teacher cultures" often exist even in a single school and that teachers may often face conflicting attempts by colleagues to influence them.

Edgar and Warren (1969) challenge this view of the strong socializing role of colleagues and argue that colleagues per se and the contextual effects of the workplace are less important in explaining the perspectives of teachers than are the attitudes of significant evaluators, those having power over teachers in terms of their ability to apply organizational sanctions. However, despite the existence of this one study which indicated that beginning teachers' perspectives toward autonomy in the teacher role were influenced by the perspectives of significant evaluators, the empirical literature does not generally confirm the view that teachers' superordinates contribute substantially to the development of teacher perspectives. On the contrary, there is overwhelming evidence that teachers receive very little direct assistance and advice from their superiors (see Zeichner, 1983) and that teachers can frequently insulate themselves from the directives and sanctions of significant evaluators when they choose to do so (Zeichner & Tabachnick, 1985). This is not to say that the classroom is an impregnable sanctuary where teachers are free from administrative influence. The literature does suggest, however, that it is more through the structural imperatives of the job than through the influence of individual administrators that teaching perspectives are developed and maintained overtime. It appears that individual administrator influence on teacher perspectives is exerted primarily through selection and recruitment rather than through socialization on the job.

At the *cultural* level of analysis (Pollard, 1982), an attempt is made to link the perspectives of individual teachers and the microlevel of the classroom and school to ideologies, practices, and material conditions at the macrolevel of society (e.g., inequalities in wealth and power). Here there have been two main types of analyses. First, those such as Wise (1979), Apple (1983), and Gitlin (1983) have explored how practices and policy initiatives outside of the school affect the material resources available to teachers and the character of the teacher's work. According to this view, teacher perspectives represent active and creative responses by teachers to constraints, dilemmas, and opportunities which are determined externally at a societal level and mediated through institutional structures and processes. Here studies have amply documented how such factors in the culture as a whole such as the bureaucratization of work, the deskilling of labor, and cultural stereotypes of women (see Feiman-Nemser & Floden, 1986) have affected the circumstances of teachers' work, although the linkages to the perspectives of individual teachers have not been as well-documented as the influence on the institutional context of teaching.

A second type of analysis of the relationship between cultural forms and teacher perspectives has attempted to link the perspectives of individual teachers to forms of meaning and rationality which are dominant in the society as a whole. Dale's (1977a, 1977b) arguments related to the development of a cognitive style of "liberal individualism," Giroux's (1980) analysis of the development of a "technocratic rationality," and Popkewitz's (in press) thesis regarding the influence of the professionalization of knowledge and the ideology of professionalism are all examples of attempts to demonstrate an effect of "cultural codes" on the development and nurturance of individual perspectives. As was pointed out earlier, however, there is very little, if any, empirical evidence available which substantiates these claims and which document that individual teachers actively incorporate forms of meaning and modes of rationality into their perspectives in ways consistent with the macrolevel theories.

Generally, the cultural-level analysis has received the least amount of attention of the three levels in relation to the development of teacher perspectives. Although many of the analyses at a macrolevel are very persuasive and although some definite influences have been amply documented regarding the link between the cultural and the institutional contexts, there is much work that remains to be done regarding the influence of "cultural codes" and the material conditions of society on the socialization of teachers.

STABILITY AND CHANGE IN THE DEVELOPMENT OF TEACHING PERSPECTIVES

Zeichner and Tabachnick (1981) outline three scenarios, drawn from an analysis of the empirical literature, regarding the issue of stability and change in the development of teaching perspectives. According to this analysis, the commonly accepted view holds that teachers, willingly or unwillingly, are cajoled and molded into shapes acceptable within their schools, shapes contrary to the perspectives that teachers allegedly developed during their training. Numerous studies of both elementary and secondary teachers in several countries have shown that beginning teachers experience statistically significant shifts in attitudes and perspectives during their first year.

For example, teachers have been shown to shift in an authoritarian direction in their attitudes toward pupils (e.g., Liguana, 1970) and pupil control (e.g., Hoy, 1968); to shift their attitudes toward the teacher role (e.g., Edgar & Warren, 1969); and to generally shift from more "progressive" to "traditional" teaching perspectives (e.g., Hanson & Herrington, 1976) during this first year. Lacey (1977) summarizes the impression given by much of this research as follows:

> The major findings of this research underline the importance of discontinuity between training and the reality of teaching. The attitudes of beginning teachers undergo dramatic change as they establish themselves in the profession away from the liberal ideas of their student days toward the traditional patterns in many schools. (p. 48)

Two different kinds of challenges have been raised in the literature regarding this view which emphasizes discontinuity in the development of teaching perspectives. First, Bartholomew (1976), Giroux (1980), and Tabachnick, Popkewitz, and Zeichner (1979–1980) have questioned the commonly accepted view that the socializing influence of the training colleges is more liberalizing than the socializing influence of the workplace. According to this view, the universities and schools exert similar pressures on the development of teaching perspectives, and the university, contrary to its liberal rhetoric, legitimates and reinforces existing school practices.

A second challenge exemplified by the work of Lortie (1975), Mardle and Walker (1980), and Denscombe (1982) emphasizes the role of anticipatory socialization and the basic continuity of classroom experience (as a pupil and as a teacher) in influencing the development of perspectives. For example, Mardle and Walker (1980) conclude:

> Indeed preservice experience may be more profoundly influential than either the efficacy of training or the colleague control of later years. . . . Teachers do not become resocialized during their course of training nor in the reality of the classroom, since in essence this is a reality which they never actually left. (p. 99)

Despite the existence of much empirical evidence which would support a view emphasizing discontinuity and change in the development of teaching perspectives, there is also empirical research, consistent with the arguments raised in the two challenges, which has documented a great deal of stability in perspectives between the end of preservice training and the end of the first year. Studies conducted by Petty and Hogben (1980), Power (1981), and Zeichner and Tabachnick (1985) all challenge the thesis of discontinuity and offer different explanations for the lack of changes in perspectives. According to the advocates of both of the challenges to the dominant scenario, the "progressive" to "traditional" shift in perspectives which has been documented in numerous studies of the socialization of beginning teachers is not a true shift in perspectives at all, but instead represents the removal of a veneer which students temporarily adopt in response to what they see as the progressive ideology of the university. Once prospective teachers leave training and the liberal *rhetoric* of the university, their perspectives, which remained latent throughout their professional training, are reaffirmed. Shipman's (1967) and Lacey's (1977), and Tabachnick and Zeichner's (1984) documentation of the use of "impression management" by prospective teachers during their training support this explanation regarding the essential stability in the development of perspectives in the face of the alleged shifts.

It should be noted that in both groups of studies, those that demonstrate changes and those which do not, some teacher experience significant shifts in attitudes and perspectives while others do not. Furthermore, among those whose perspectives apparently shift, the changes are often in different directions. These conclusions regarding change or stability in the development of teaching perspectives between the completion of training and the end of the first year have been based in almost all cases on analyses of central tendencies in groups of teachers studied. Also, few researchers in either camp have conducted analyses of observed training. With few exceptions, these studies have relied exclusively on teacher self-reports of their behavior or on attitude surveys for their data.

In the final analysis when attention is focused on the socialization of individual beginning teachers, neither group of studies is very helpful in illuminating how specific beginning teachers are socialized into particular settings. Although most commentators on teacher induction have concluded that the resolution of the issue of stability or change in the development of perspectives during the transition period is highly context dependent (e.g., Applegate, Flora, Johnston, Lasley, Mager, Newman, & Ryan, 1977); Tisher, 1982), the studies almost never provide specific information about the personal characteristics and life histories of individual teachers or information about the nature of the settings in which they work. Consequently, this research for the most part has not illuminated the particular individual characteristics and contextual factors which are related to change or stability in particular cases. (See Zeichner, 1983, for a discussion of some of these factors.)

Finally, there has been very little attention given to the development of teaching perspectives beyond the first year(s) of teaching. Despite the existence of several credible theories regarding stages that teachers pass through over the course of a career (e.g., see Fuller, 1969; Katz, 1972; Burden, 1979; Christiansen, Burke, Fessler, & Hagstrom, 1983), we know relatively little about stability or change in the development of teaching perspectives and about the personal and contextual factors that affect the course of teacher development after the transition period. Research which focuses on the development of teaching perspectives at different points in teachers' careers would greatly enhance our understanding of the degree of continuity or discontinuity in teacher development throughout a career.

THE ROLE OF INDIVIDUAL INTENT AND INSTITUTIONAL CONSTRAINT IN THE DEVELOPMENT OF TEACHER PERSPECTIVES

The problem of the development of teacher perspectives is one instance of the larger sociological question of the relationship between individuals and institutions or between action and structure (Giddens, 1979). Brim (1966) outlines two fundamental interests in the study of this problem.

> One interest is in how individuals adjust to society and how in spite of the influence of society they manage to be creative and to transform the social order into which they have been born. The other interest is in how society socializes the individual—how it transforms the raw material of biological man into a person suitable to perform the activities of society. (pp. 3–4)

Historically, the study of the development of teacher perspectives has followed the latter of these traditions. Following Brim's (1966, p. 5) advice that "the inquiry at all times is concerned with how society changes the natural man, not how man changes his society," most studies of teacher socialization have portrayed teachers as relatively *passive* entities always giving way to institutional forces; have not made the internalization of institutional norms problematic; and have emphasized a consensus view of institutions which minimizes the influence of conflicting institutional pressures on teachers (Lacey, 1977).

Although a variety of factors at the classroom, institutional, and cultural levels and factors within teachers' biographies have been shown to be related to the development of teaching perspectives, teachers have not been viewed as active participants in determining the course of their development. On the one hand, teachers are viewed as "prisoners of the past" (of anticipatory socialization during childhood or preservice training); and on the other hand, they are seen as prisoners of the present (of pressures emanating from the workplace or the society).

There is ample evidence that neither of these views is very helpful in understanding the development of teaching perspectives; that conformity (to the past or present) is not the only outcome of socialization; and that even when conformity does occur, it occurs in different degrees, in different forms, and has different meanings for different individual teachers within

different institutional contexts. A growing number of studies of occupa-
tional socialization in general (e.g., Olesen & Whittaker, 1968; Bucher &
Stelling, 1977); of teacher socialization (e.g., Lacey, 1977; Zeichner &
Tabachnick, 1985); and of adult development (e.g., see Sprinthall & Thies-
Sprinthall, 1983) have demonstrated that the strong degree of determinism
which pervades the literature on teacher socialization may be misguided.

One example of these emerging positions on teacher socialization as
an *interactive* process is Lacey's (1977) conceptual model which is based on
the view of a constant interplay between choice and constraint in the process
of learning to teach. Lacey (1977) challenges Becker's (1964) view of "situational adjustment" (i.e., the individual turns him- or herself into the kind of
person the situation demands) as the only possible outcome of occupational
socialization and proposes the construct of *social strategy* as a heuristic
device for understanding how and to what degree teachers conform to institutional pressures. Lacey defines a *social strategy* as a purposeful and active
selection of actions and ideas by teachers and the working out of their inter-
relationships in specific contexts. He then identifies three different strategies that he claims are employed by teachers in the face of institutional
constraints.

First, *internalized adjustment* refers to a strategy where individuals
comply with an authority figure's definition of a situation and believe these
constraints to be for the best. This strategy indicates those situations where
an individual willingly develops into the kind of person the situation demands and where socialization entails both behavioral conformity and
value commitment.

On the other hand, *strategic compliance* refers to those instances
where individuals comply with the constraints posed by a situation, but retain private reservations about doing so. This strategy implies that individuals do not always act in ways consistent with their underlying beliefs, and
identifies those situations where conformity is essentially an adaptive response without the corresponding value basis on which the behavior presumably rests. Finally, the strategy of *strategic redefinition* refers to those
situations where successful attempts to change are made by individuals who
do not possess the formal power to do so. These individuals attempt to
widen the range of acceptable behaviors in a situation and to introduce new
and creative elements into a social setting.

Zeichner and Tabachnick (1985) have elaborated Lacey's (1977) interactive model by broadening the definition of "strategic redefinition" to include both those attempts which are successful and those which are not and
by adding a temporal dimension to the model to enable longitudinal studies
of teacher development. Lacey (1977), Tabachnick and Zeichner (1984), and
Zeichner and Tabachnick (1985), in documenting examples of both strategic
compliance and strategic redefinition in the development of teaching per-

spectives, have provided some support for an interactive view of the sociali-zation process. Although these studies have been recently criticized for underestimating the effects of anticipatory socialization (Feiman-Nemser & Floden, 1986) and for overemphasizing the degree to which the mere pres-ence of strategic compliance and strategic redefinition in a few cases poses a challenge to the dominant view of institutional determinism (Jordell, 1984), they do raise questions concerning the degree to which teachers readily and completely acquiesce to institutional demands which warrant further ex-ploration.

Another line of empirical evidence which supports an interactive view of the development of teaching perspectives is that research which has viewed teacher development as an instance of adult development. Sprinthall and Thies-Sprinthall (1983) and Oja (1980) summarize an impressive body of empirical data based on stage theories of cognitive development which demonstrates how the characteristics and purposes of individuals mediate institutional influences in determining the actions of teachers. This rapidly growing body of research, together with numerous studies of socialization into occupations other than teaching (e.g., Olesen & Whittaker, 1968), are consistent with the findings of Lacey (1977) and Zeichner and Tabachnick (1985). All of these strands of evidence justify a reexamination of the high degree of institutional determinism which has characterized explanations of the development of teaching perspectives. Although the development of teacher perspectives clearly entails more than simple expressions of the ideas, characteristics, and capabilities that teachers bring to the workplace (all of the external forces discussed earlier exert some influence), the strength and direction of teacher development is also clearly influenced to some degree by the purposes and intentions of individual teachers who do not simply acquiesce to the forces around them.

CONCLUSION

The purpose of this chapter has been to assess the strength of the empirical evidence supporting different positions with regard to: (a) the nature of teacher perspectives at both an individual and an occupational level; (b) the influence of various socializing agents and mechanisms on the development of perspectives; (c) the degree to which the development of teaching per-spectives is influenced by individual intent and institutional constraint; and (d) the degree of stability or change in the development of teaching perspec-tives during the transition from training to the workplace. In doing so, evi-dence related to the socializing influence of early childhood experiences, preservice training and workplace characteristics at the classroom, school, and societal levels was addressed.

First, two views on the nature of teaching perspectives at both an individual and occupational level were considered. The dominant point of view assumes internal consistency among the various dimensions of individual teachers' perspectives and a high degree of homogeneity in perspectives in the occupation as a whole. It was argued that this view of the nature of teacher perspectives unjustifiably oversimplifies differences within and among teachers and that the assumption of occupational uniformity underestimates the degree of diversity in "teaching cultures" which has been documented even within single schools.

The assessment of the socializing influence of various individual, institutional, and cultural factors confirmed Lortie's (1973) assessment that the empirical evidence supports a variety of explanations for the development of teaching perspectives. First, with regard to the role of early childhood experience in teacher socialization, it was concluded that although research has confirmed the significance of pretraining influences in a general way, this support is largely indirect and does not substantiate any particular theoretical explanation. It was argued that much work remains to be done to clarify the particular nature of these pretraining influences.

When the evidence was examined with regard to the influence of preservice training on the development of perspectives, it was concluded that the dominant view of preservice training as a weak intervention fails to consider the effects of the hidden curriculum of teacher education programs and that the effects of preservice training may in fact be greater than has often been thought to be the case. It was further concluded that most of the arguments related to the impact of the hidden curriculum of teacher training have not been substantiated to date by empirical evidence and that studies need to be initiated which consider whether in fact prospective teachers incorporate elements into their teaching perspectives in ways consistent with the theoretical arguments. Finally, with regard to the influence of field experiences in preservice training, it was concluded that these experiences have different effects upon the development of teaching perspectives depending upon the nature of individual and program characteristics, but that research has not illuminated the particular factors (both individual and social) which are related to the development of particular kinds of teaching perspectives during field experiences.

The analysis of workplace influences at three different levels revealed that there is some evidence in the literature supporting the view that pupils, the ecology of the classroom, colleagues, and institutional characteristics of schools all play significant roles in the development of teaching perspectives. The specific nature of these influences was described (e.g., the informal and contradictory nature of colleague influence) together with areas where more research is particularly needed (e.g., how individual characteristics of pupils and teachers mediate pupil influences on teacher perspectives). It was also concluded that research has not generally confirmed Edgar and Warren's (1969) claim that "significant evaluators" play a substantial role in the development of perspectives. Finally, it was concluded that although some evidence has been accumulated related to the influence of various factors in the culture as a whole (e.g., stereotypes of women) on the conditions of teachers' work, the links between these cultural factors and the perspectives of individual teachers have not been firmly established. It was argued that the cultural level of analysis has received very little attention to date and that much empirical work remains to be done regarding the influence of "cultural codes" and the material conditions of society on the socialization of individual teachers.

When the questions of stability or change in the development of teaching perspectives was considered, it was concluded that the resolution of this issue in the case of specific teachers is highly context dependent. It was argued that the extant research has generally failed to illuminate the particular individual characteristics and contextual factors which are related to stability or change in specific cases; nor has it addressed the issue of stability or change in the development of teaching perspectives beyond the first year(s) of teaching. Longitudinal studies which consider the ways in which specific individual and contextual characteristics influence the development of teaching perspectives at different points in teachers' careers are needed.

Evidence was also considered regarding the degree to which individual intent and institutional constraint influence the development of teaching perspectives. Recent research on occupational socialization, teacher socialization, and adult development was cited which challenges the strong degree of institutional determinism that pervades the literature and arguments were offered for the adoption of a more *interactive* view of teacher development.

Finally, it becomes increasingly clear as a result of the analysis of the evidence related to all of these issues, that there is no one explanation which can account for the development of teaching perspectives and the degree of change or stability in these perspectives over a career. Although various generalizations can now be formulated on the basis of the available empirical literature regarding central tendencies in the development of teaching perspectives, the development of perspectives by individual teachers is greatly influenced by the predispositions, characteristics, and capabilities of teachers who differ from one another and the characteristics of the settings in which they work, settings that pose different constraints and opportunities for action. Research on the development of teaching perspectives must clearly pay more attention in the future to the uniqueness as well as the commonality in teacher development. The dominant practice of describing only central tendencies in the development of teaching perspectives cannot illuminate the diversity that unquestionably characterizes the socialization of teachers and the occupational group. A greater understanding of the socializing conditions of particular schools and of the ways in which individual teachers develop particular kinds of teaching perspectives is a key to understanding the most likely roads to strengthening and improving both teacher education and the quality of school programs.

REFERENCES

Anderson, R. (1959). Learning in discussions: A resume of the authoritarian-democratic studies. *Harvard Educational Review,* 201–215.

Apple, M. (1983). Curricular form and the logic of technical control: The building of the possessive individual. In M. Apple & L. Weis (Eds.), *Ideology and practice in education.* Philadelphia, PA: Temple University Press.

Applegate, J., Flora, R., Johnston, J., Lasley, T., Mager, G., Newman, K., & Ryan, K. (1977). *The first-year teacher study.* Columbus, OH: Ohio State University. (ERIC Document Reproduction Service No. ED 135 766)

Bachrach, P., & Baratz, M. (1962). Two faces of power. *American Political Science Review, 56,* 947–952.

Barr, R., & Duffy, G. (1978). *Teachers' conceptions of reading: The evolution of a research study* (Research Series No. 17). East Lansing, MI: Institute for Research on Teaching.

Bartholomew, J. (1976). Schooling teachers: The myth of the liberal college. In G. Whitty & J. M. Young (Eds.), *Explorations in the politics of school knowledge.* Driffield, England: Nafferton Books.

Becker, H. (1964). Personal change in adult life. *Sociometry, 27,* 40–53.

Becker, H., Geer, B., Hughes, E., & Strauss, A. (1961). *Boys in white.* Chicago, IL: University of Chicago Press.

Bennett, N. (1976). *Teaching styles of pupil progress.* London: Open Books.

Berger, P., & Luchmann, T. (1967). *The social construction of reality.* New York: Doubleday.

Berlak, A., & Berlak, H. (1981). *Dilemmas of schooling: Teaching and social change.* London: Methuen.

Brim, O. (1966). Socialization through the life cycle. In O. Brim & S. Wheeler, (Eds.), *Socialization after childhood: Two essays.* New York: Wiley.

Brophy, J., & Evertson, C. (1981). *Student characteristics and teaching.* New York: Longman.

Bucher, R., & Stelling, J. (1977). *Becoming professional.* Beverly Hills, CA: Sage.

Burden, P. (1979). Teachers' perceptions of the characteristics and influences on their personal and professional development. *Dissertation Abstracts International, 40,* 5404-A. (University Microfilms No. 8008776)

Bussis, A., Chittenden, E., & Amarel, M. (1976). *Beyond surface curriculum.* Boulder, CO: Westview Press.

Carew, J., & Lightfoot, S. L. (1979). *Beyond bias: Perspectives on classrooms.* Cambridge, MA: Harvard University Press.

Christiansen, J., Burke, P., Fessler, R., & Hagstrom, D. (1983). *Stages of teachers' careers: Implications for staff development.* Washington, DC: ERIC Clearinghouse on Teacher Education.

Copeland, W. (1980). Student teachers and cooperating teachers: An ecological relationship. *Theory and Practice, 18,* 194–199.

Dale, R. (1977a). Implications of the rediscovery of the hidden curriculum for the sociology of teaching. In D. Gleason (Ed.), *Identity and structure: Issues in the sociology of education.* Driffield, England: Nafferton Books.

Dale, R. (1977b). *The structural context of teaching.* Milton Keynes, England: The Open University Press.

Denscombe, M. (1980). The work context of teaching: An analytic framework for the study of teachers in classrooms. *British Journal of Sociology and Education, 1,* 279–292.

Denscombe, M. (1982). The hidden pedagogy and its implications for teacher training. *British Journal of Sociology of Education, 3,* 249–265.

Doyle, W. (1977). Learning the classroom environment: An ecological analysis. *Journal of Teacher Education, 28,* 51–55.

Doyle, W. (1979). Classroom effects. *Theory into Practice, 18,* 138–144.

Doyle, W., & Ponder, G. (1975). Classroom ecology: Some concerns about a neglected dimension of research on teaching. *Contemporary Education, 46,* 183–188.

Dreeben, R. (1970). *The nature of teaching: Schools and the work of teachers.* Glenview, IL: Scott, Foresman.

Dreeben, R. (1973). The school as a workplace. In R. Travers (Ed.), *Second handbook of research on teaching.* Chicago, IL: Rand McNally.

Dreitzel, H. P. (1973). *Childhood and socialization.* New York: Macmillan.

Eddy, E. (1969). *Becoming a teacher.* New York: Teachers College Press.

Edgar, D., & Warren, R. (1969). Power and autonomy in teacher socialization. *Sociology of Education, 42,* 386–399.

Feiman-Nemser, S. (1983). Learning to teach. In L. Shulman & G. Sykes (Eds.), *Handbook of teaching and policy.* New York: Longman.

Feiman-Nemser, S., & Floden, R. (1986). The cultures of teaching. In M. Wittrock (Ed.), *The third handbook of research on teaching.* Chicago: IL: Rand McNally.

Fenstermacher, G. (1980). What needs to be known about what teachers need to know? In G. Hall, S. Hord, & G. Brown (Eds.), *Exploring issues in teacher education: Questions for future research.* Austin, TX: University of Texas Research and Development Center for Teacher Education.

Fiedler, M. (1975). Bidirectionality of influence in classroom interaction. *Journal of Educational Psychology, 67,* 735–744.

Freedman, S., Jackson, J., & Boles, K. (1983). Teaching: An imperiled profession. In L. Shulman & G. Sykes (Eds.), *Handbook of teaching and policy.* New York: Longman.

Fuller, F. (1969). Concerns of teachers: A developmental conceptualization. *American Educational Research Journal, 6,* 207–226.

Giddens, A. (1979). *Central problems in social theory: Action, structure and contradiction in social analysis.* Berkeley, CA: University of California Press.

Ginsburg, M. (1984, April). *Reproduction and contradictions in preservice teachers' encounters with professionalism.* A paper presented at the annual meeting of American Educational Research Association, New Orleans, LA.

Giroux, H. (1980). Teacher education and the ideology of social control. *Journal of Education, 162,* 5–27.

Gitlin, A. (1983). School structure and teachers' work. In M. Apple & L. Weis (Eds.), *Ideology and practice in education*. Philadelphia, PA: Temple University Press.

Goodlad, J. (1982). Let's get on with the reconstruction. *Phi Delta Kappan, 63,* 19–20.

Gracey, H. (1972). *Curriculum or craftsmanship*. Chicago: IL: University of Chicago Press.

Grant, C. (1981). Education that is multicultural and teacher preparation: An examination from the perspectives of preservice students. *Journal of Educational Research, 75,* 95–101.

Grant, C., & Zeichner, K. (1981). Inservice support for first-year teachers: The state of the scene. *Journal of Research and Development in Education, 14,* 99–111.

Gray, J., & Satterly, D. (1981). Formal or informal? A reassessment of the British evidence. *British Journal of Educational Psychology, 51,* 187–196.

Griffin, G., Barnes, S., Hughes, R., O'Neal, S., Edwards, S., & Defino, M. (1983). *Clinical preservice teacher education: Final report of a descriptive study.* Austin, TX: University of Texas Research and Development Center for Teacher Education.

Haberman, M. (1981). *The legacy of teacher education, 1980–2000.* Hunt lecture presented at the annual meeting of AACTE, Houston, TX.

Haller, E. (1967). Pupils' influences in teacher socialization: A socio-linguistic study. *Sociology of Education, 40,* 316–333.

Hammersley, M. (1977a). *Teacher perspectives.* Milton Keynes, England: The Open University Press.

Hammersley, M. (1977b). *The social location of teacher perspectives.* Milton Keynes, England: The Open University Press.

Hanson, D., & Herrington, M. (1976). *From college to classroom: The probationary years.* London: Routledge & Kegan Paul.

Hodges, C. (1982). Implementing methods: If you can't blame the cooperating teacher, whom can you blame? *Journal of Teacher Education, 33,* 25–29.

Hogben, D., & Lawson, M. (1983). Attitudes of secondary school teacher trainees and their practice teaching supervisors. *Journal of Education for Teaching, 9,* 249–263.

Howey, K. (1983). Teacher education: An overview. In K. Howey & W. Gardner (Eds.), *Teacher education: A look ahead.* New York: Longman.

Hoy, W. (1968). The influence of experience on the beginning teacher. *Journal of Educational Research, 66,* 89–93.

Jackson, P. (1968). *Life in classrooms.* New York: Holt, Rinehart, & Winston.

Jordell, K. (1984, April). *Teacher socialization: Toward solving the riddle?* A paper presented at the annual meeting of American Educational Research Association, New Orleans, LA.

Katz, L. (1972). Developmental stages of pre-school teachers. *Elementary School Journal, 73,* 50–54.

Katz, L., & Raths, J. (1982). The best of intentions for the education of teachers. *Action in Teacher Education, 4,* 8–16.

Lacey, C. (1977). *The socialization of teachers.* London: Methuen.

Larkin, R. (1973). Contextual influences on teacher leadership styles. *Sociology of Education, 46,* 471–479.

Liguana, J. (1970). *What happens to the attitudes of beginning teachers?* Danville, IL: Interstate Printers.

Little, J. W. (1982). Norms of collegiality and experimentation: Workplace conditions of school success. *American Educational Research Journal, 19,* 325–340.

Lortie, D. (1973). Observations of teaching as work. In R. Travers (Ed.), *Second handbook of research on teaching.* Chicago: IL: Rand McNally.

Lortie, D. (1975). *School teacher: A sociological study.* Chicago, IL: University of Chicago Press.

Maddox, H. (1968). A descriptive study of teaching practice. *Educational Review, 20,* 177–190.

Mardle, G., & Walker, M. (1980). Strategies and structure: Critical notes on teacher socialization. In P. Woods (Ed.), *Teacher strategies.* London: Croom Helm.

McArthur, J. (1978). What does teaching do to teachers? *Educational Administration Quarterly, 14,* 89–103.

McIntyre, D. J. (1983). *Field experiences in teacher education.* Washington, DC: Foundation for Excellence in Teacher Education and the ERIC Clearinghouse in Teacher Education.

McPherson, G. (1972). *Small town teacher.* Cambridge, MA: Harvard University Press.

Metz, M. (1978). *Classrooms and corridors.* Berkeley, CA: University of California Press.

Newberry, J. (1977, April). *The first year of experience: Influences on beginning teachers.* A paper presented at the annual meeting of American Educational Research Association, New York City. (ERIC Document Reproduction Service No. ED 137 299)

Noble, C., & Nolan, J. (1976). Effect of student verbal behavior on classroom teacher behavior. *Journal of Educational Psychology, 68,* 342–346.

Oja, S. N. (1980). Adult development is implicit in staff development. *Journal of Staff Development, 1,* 7–56.

Olesen, V., & Whittaker, E. (1968). *The silent dialogue.* San Francisco, CA: Jossey-Bass.

Petty, M., & Hogben, D. (1980). Explorations of semantic space with beginning teachers: A study of socialization into teaching. *British Journal of Teacher Education, 6,* 51–61.

Pollard, A. (1982). A model of classroom coping strategies. *British Journal of Sociology of Education, 3,* 19–37.

Popkewitz, T. (in press). Ideology and social formation in teacher education. *Teaching and Teacher Education.*

Power, P. (1981). Aspects of the transition from education student to beginning teacher. *Australian Journal of Education, 25,* 288–296.

Sarason, S., Davidson, K., & Blatt, B. (1962). *The preparation of teachers: An unstudied problem.* New York: Wiley.

Schlechty, P. (1976). *Teaching and social behavior: Toward an organizational theory of instruction.* Boston, MA: Allyn & Bacon.

Sharp, R., & Green, A. (1975). *Education and social control.* London: Routledge & Kegan Paul.

Shipman, M. (1967). Theory and practice in the education of teachers. *Educational Research, 9,* 208–212.

Sirotnik, K. (1983). What you see is what you get: Consistency, persistency and mediocrity in classrooms. *Harvard Educational Review, 53,* 16–31.

Sprinthall, N., & Thies-Sprinthall, L. (1983). The teacher as an adult learner: A cognitive-developmental view. In G. Griffin (Ed.), *Staff development: The eighty-second yearbook of NSSE* (Part II). Chicago: IL: University of Chicago Press.

Stephens, J. (1967). *The processes of schooling.* New York: Holt, Rinehart, & Winston.

Tabachnick, B. R., Popkewitz, T., & Zeichner, K. (1979–1980). Teacher education and the professional perspectives of student teachers. *Interchange, 10,* 12–29.

Tabachnick, B. R., & Zeichner, K. (1984). The impact of the student teaching experience on the development of teacher perspectives. *Journal of Teacher Education, 35,* 6, 28–36.

Tisher, R. (1982, March). *Teacher induction: An international perspective on research and programs.* A paper presented at the annual meeting of American Educational Research Association, New York City.

Travers, R. (1971). Some further reflections on the nature of a theory of instruction. In I. Westbury & A. Bellack (Eds.), *Research into classroom processes.* New York: Teachers College Press.

Waller, W. (1932). *The sociology of teaching.* New York: Wiley.

Westbury, I. (1973). Conventional classrooms, "open" classrooms, and the technology of teaching. *Journal of Curriculum Studies, 5.*

Wise, A. (1979). *Legislated learning: The bureaucratization of the American classroom.* Berkeley: University of California Press.

Wright, B. (1959). Identification and becoming a teacher. *Elementary School Journal,* 361–373.

Wright, B., & Tuska, S. (1967). The childhood romance theory of teacher development. *School Review, 25,* 123–154.

Wright, B., & Tuska, S. (1968). From dream to life in the psychology of becoming a teacher. *School Review, 26,* 183–193.

Zeichner, K. (1980). Myths and realities: Field experiences in preservice teacher education. *Journal of Teacher Education, 31,* 45–55.

Zeichner, K. (1983). Individual and institutional factors related to the socialization of beginning teachers. In G. Griffin & H. Hukill (Eds.), *First years of teaching: What are the pertinent issues?* Austin, TX: University of Texas Research and Development Center for Teacher Education.

Zeichner, K. (1984, January). *The ecology of field experience: Toward an understanding of the role of field experiences in teacher development.* A paper presented at the annual meeting of Association of Teacher Educators, New Orleans, LA.

Zeichner, K. (1985). Preparation for elementary school teaching. In P. Burke & R. Heideman (Eds.), *Teacher competence: Issues in career-long teacher education.* Springfield, IL: Charles Thomas.

Zeichner, K., & Grant, C. (1981). Biography and social structure in the socialization of student teachers. *Journal of Education for Teaching, 1,* 198–314.

Zeichner, K., & Tabachnick, B. R. (1981). Are the effects of university teacher education washed out by school experience? *Journal of Teacher Education, 32,* 7–11.

Zeichner, K., & Tabachnick, B. R. (1985). The development of teacher perspectives: Social strategies and institutional control in the socialization of beginning teachers. *Journal of Education for Teaching, 11,* 1, 1–25.

8
Effects of Early Field Experiences

Hersholt C. Waxman
University of Houston

Herbert J. Walberg
University of Illinois at Chicago

> It is not to disparage teacher training that we remark upon the fact that teachers still learn to teach by teaching. The teacher gets something from experience which is not included in his "professional" courses, an elusive something which it is difficult to put between the covers of a book or to work up into a lecture. That elusive something is social insight. What the teacher gets from experiences is an understanding of the social situation of the classroom, and an adaptation of his/her personality to the needs of that milieu. That is why experienced teachers are wiser than novices. That is what we must try to include it in the regimen of those who aspire to be teachers. (Waller, 1932, p. 1)

> What students appear to learn during field-based experiences is often in conflict with the expressed intentions of those in both the schools and universities and indicates that these experiences are often miseducative rather than helpful. (Zeichner, 1980, p. 51)

The two quotations illustrate the diversity of opinion regarding research on the effects of early field experiencees, that is, field experiences for prospective teachers prior to student teaching. Many educators and researchers have made similar statements about the ambiguity of teacher education research. One of the major concerns among teacher educators is that practices are often based on unexamined assumptions (Tabachnick, Popkewitz, & Zeichner, 1980). Little empirical data support practices in preservice training (Howey, 1977). In his indictment of teacher education, Koerner (1963), for example, reflects the existing ambiguity of research evidence:

I would again emphasize that most arguments about teacher education no more lend themselves to "proof" than do debates about other educational problems. All the important questions one can ask about educating teachers must be answered on essentially suasive grounds; very few "data" exist on the best way to prepare people to teach in public schools or to administer them. Engineers are fond of referring to the degree of knowledge in technical fields at any given time as "the state of the art." In teacher education, the state of the art is infantile. An examination of the evidence available on the effectiveness of preparing teachers one way as against another leaves one in a familiar cul-de-sac, the only way out of which is through one's reasoned convictions. (pp. 3–4)

Zeichner's (1980) recent review of the research on preservice field-based experiences similarly reflects the equivocality of the research evidence:

Although it is difficult to draw any clear implications from the research on field-based experiences, two conclusions emerge from the existing data. First, from a review of the literature it can be concluded that field-based experiences are neither all beneficial in their effects as the abundant testimonials and the increased emphasis on these experiences would lead us to believe; nor are they merely vehicles for adapting new personnel into existing patterns as many critics would have us believe. Instead, field-based experiences seem to entail a complicated set of both positive and negative consequences that are often subtle in nature. (p. 46)

The contradictions and conflicting interpretations of the research as well as the shortage of experimental and longitudinal studies in this area constitute a serious national concern, especially in light of proposed reductions in the number of pedagogy courses offered in teacher education programs and increase the number of field experiences for prospective teachers in several states. On the other hand, some educators challenge the widespread belief that field experiences help prospective teachers become more effective teachers. While they maintain that they may give future teachers a taste of reality, they also claim that they can foster bad habits and narrow vision. As Nemser (1983) puts it, "What helps to solve an immediate problem may not be good teaching. A deceptive sense of success, equated with keeping order and discipline, is liable to close off avenues for further learning" (p. 156). The present chapter examines these conflicting perspectives and evaluates the research evidence on the effects of early field experiences.

OVERVIEW OF EARLY FIELD EXPERIENCES

Field experiences for preservice teachers are required by the National Council for the Accreditation of Teacher Education (NCATE, 1979 and the National Association of State Directors of Teacher Education (Utah State

Board of Education, 1979). In addition to student teaching, most states specify that teacher certification candidates should have other field experiences in various school settings. Early field experiences often consist of preservice teachers serving as a teachers' aide or assistant (Henry, 1982). In these experiences, preservice teachers typically observe classrooms, tutor individual students or small groups of students, or plan and/or teach a lesson to the class. Such early field experiences are assumed to help teacher education students make career decisions, assist them in role acquisition, and provide opportunities for practicing specific teaching techniques.

In a survey of 270 teacher education institutions, Webb (1981) found that 99% indicated that they offered early field experiences for prospective teachers. These experiences generally included activities such as observation, tutoring, working with small groups, and assisting with noninstructional tasks. Cronin (1983) explains how this "practicum" experience before student teaching "implements the 'gradual immersion' theory of teacher education, which suggests that the initial shock is less if one wades into the adult classroom role step by step—first as a spectator, then as a helper, then as an apprentice teacher, then as a new teacher on one's own" (p. 182). Cronin (1983) continues to explain how this sequence "helps weed out the 'not so sure' prospects" (p. 182).

In recent years there has been a significant trend toward increasing the number of clinical field experiences in preservice programs (Becher & Ade, 1982; Robinson & Mosrie 1979). As the introductory quote of Waller illustrates, many educators maintain that teacher education programs can only be effective if prospective teachers have extended early field experiences. As Becher and Ade (1982) contend, it is "assumed that the best opportunities for the improvement of preservice teacher education and the corresponding development of quality education for children, are provided as students work in the field practicing skills and developing competencies" (p. 24).

Illinois, Ohio, and other states, for example, have mandated additional field-based experiences, whereas other states such as New York and Oklahoma have initiated an intern year during which where prospective teachers must complete a carefully supervised internship in order to become a teacher. As Morris and Curtis (1983) put it, "Most states continue to recognize the importance of these experiences, either by statute or through program approval standards, as prerequisites for initial certification" (p. 5). Furthermore, several teacher training institutions like the University of Kansas also emphasize the importance of extended training by requiring all prospective teachers to go through 5-year teacher-education programs. These extended training programs often include more early field experiences, however, the situation may vary greatly depending on the individual institution.

Although many educators have proposed to extend preservice preparation (see for example, Denemark & Nutter, 1980; Smith, 1980), there are some concerns that extended field experiences and more pedagogy courses will not improve the quality of teaching in our nations' schools. Sykes (1983), for example, indicates that adding "more college and university course work would increase the initial costs of becoming a teacher beyond what the market might bear and fails to answer students' demands for more practical experience" (p. 105). Cronin (1983) similarly maintains that "the cost will discourage the economically disadvantaged and many minority candidates in particular from teaching careers" (p. 184). Tabachnick et al (1980) are also critical of extending field experiences because they contend that "proposals which 'solve' problems of teacher education by scheduling more student time in classrooms rest upon the apparently untenable assumption that more time spent in that way will automatically make better teachers" (p. 28).

Sykes (1983) addresses some other concerns with the proposals for extending preservice preparation:

> Extending teacher preparation is a plausible notion in light of the miniscule amount of time currently devoted to this enterprise, but it raises suspicions about the payoff in terms of improved teaching. California, for example, requires for a permanent teaching credential a fifth year of study beyond the bachelor's degree to obtain a teaching certificate. Other states such as New York require a Master's degree to convert a five-year provisional certificate to a permanent one. In practice such requirements have merely impelled teachers to take the most convenient courses at the local community college to obtain their certificate. The upshot has not been to strengthen pre-service education to any significant degree, as a hodge podge of too often trivial courses strung out over several years hardly improves the quality of instruction. (p. 107)

As previously discussed, several states have initiated an intern year for beginning teachers where they are supervised and evaluated on the job prior to receiving full certification. Other states are proposing to eliminate pedagogy courses and increase the number of early field experiences for prospective teachers.

SUPERVISION OF EARLY FIELD EXPERIENCES

One problem of the previously mentioned approaches, however, rests on the quality of supervision provided to these beginning teachers. As Cronin (1983) puts it, "Longer student teaching periods and internships may help improve the initial preparation of teachers, especially for the most challenging assignments—inner cities, changing neighborhoods, mobile families, etc. However, increasing the quality of time 'in training' will never substitute for the quality and appropriateness of supervision by both university personnel and experienced teachers in an effective school" (p. 190). Sykes

(1983) similarly adds that "at present neither university faculty nor experienced teachers have the incentives, the resources, or the expertise to effectively supervise beginning teachers" (p. 107).

Supervisors of early field experiences receive very little preparation or training (Puckett, 1982; Research Committee of National Field Directors' Forum, 1982). For example, 41% of the teacher education institutions that responded to a recent survey indicated that they neither required nor provided any preparation or training for supervising teachers who worked with preservice teachers in early field experiences (Puckett, 1982). Similarly, a study by the Research Committee of the Field Directors' Forum (1982) found that supervision of preservice teachers in early field experiences was very limited and generally only focused on individual students who experienced difficulties.

Black's (1980) study on the practices of compensating supervising teachers in the 50 states indicated that states generally do not provide funding for field-based experiences in teacher education programs. Such concerns led Morris and Curtis (1983, pp. 4–5) to conclude that provisions should be made for: (a) the appropriate preparation of teachers who work with teacher education students; (b) payments to teachers working with students in early field experiences and to supervisors of student teachers; and (c) uniform preparation throughout the state and periodic monitoring of all field-based experiences. Some validity seems apparent in these recommendations but, contrary to such optimistic suggestions for the improvement of teacher education, it should also be noted that there are very few research studies which have actually indicated that "better supervised" early field experiences improve the training or work success of prospective teachers. However, Applegate and Lasley (1982) concluded that teacher educators need to carefully train cooperating teachers to work with prospective teachers during field experiences. In this study, cooperating teachers indicated that there were six general problems in working with field experience students: (a) students were unprepared; (b) there was no active involvement with the university or college; (c) the students and university supervisor lacked professionalism; (d) there was a lack of commitment to teaching by the students; (e) students lacked initiative and enthusiasm; and (f) students lacked organization and management abilities. These factors need to be closely examined in other research studies, and additional research should also investigate the effects of training cooperative teachers on the field experiences of prospective teachers.

RESEARCH ON EARLY FIELD EXPERIENCES

Notwithstanding the difficulty of field research in natural settings, a number of studies with moderate technical adequacy have accumulated in teacher education. In his overview of research in teacher education, Turner (1975, pp. 87–89) presents a schema for organizing information about teacher education that includes seven important relationships: (a) selection and work success; (b) training and work success; (c) placement and work success; (d) selection and work success; (e) training and work success; (f) selection and training; and (g) moderating relationships. The emphasis of the present study, however, is to review the research on one of these basic relationships—that between training and work success. Although the construct of "teacher work success" is quite broad, Turner (1975) operationalizes this construct to include three classes of criterion variables:

1. Student attainment. The societal objectives of schooling focus on three types of student attainment: (a) intellectual and psychomotor achievement associated with learning subject matter and acquiring a variety of practical, artistic, and athletic skills; (b) socialization, including increasing independence, good personal work habits, interpersonal skills, defensible values, and personal character; and (c) mental health, including feelings about self and ability to handle personal frustrations and anxieties.
2. Professional judgment. The teacher's professional image or stature, as judged by school and college supervisors, peers, and school administrators, is an important dimension of teacher success since virtually all teachers are employed in some kind of institutional setting or formal work organization.
3. Student judgment. Student ratings of teachers and student reports about teaching form an important criterion of teacher success because students are the consumers of instruction, and because the image or reputation teachers have among students may have substantial impact on student response to instruction and on parental willingness to support the schools. (pp. 89–90)

Since these criteria are different and are not necessarily positively related to each other, two key problems arise that must be addressed in teacher education research:

It is to determine the means by which, and those points up to which, one set of criterion variables, such as student attainment, can be increased without inducing a decrease in another set of criterion variables, such as student attitude toward teachers or instruction, or teacher ability to function in school work settings.

A second problem in optimizing teacher success attributable to teacher preparation is that the success criteria occur after preparation. Thus to make relevant judgments about probable teacher success during preparation requires demonstrating that a criterion employed during the preparatory program is a correlate of a later criterion intrinsic to teacher work success. (Turner, 1979, pp. 90–91)

As Turner (1975) indicates, teacher education research should be based on a model in which the independent variable (or training) simultaneously determines several outcomes which affect each other. Unfortunately, this multivariate design is not reflected in the research conducted in teacher education.

Following Turner's (1975) operationalization of work success, the next sections of this chapter review the research on early field experiences on (a) student attainment, (b) professional judgment, and (c) student judgment.

EFFECTS OF EARLY FIELD EXPERIENCES ON STUDENT ATTAINMENT

This section analyzes research on the effect of early field experiences on the prospective teacher's academic performance, learning of skills, socialization into the culture of schools, and mental health.

As with most of the research on early field experiences, there are ambiguous findings regarding the research on the effects of field experiences on the prospective teacher's academic performance. Hedberg (1979) and Ingle and Robinson (1965), for example, found no difference in the achievement of prospective teachers who participated in field experiences and those who did not. Ingle and Zaret (1968) uncovered a similar result when they compared the degree of involvement in field experiences to course achievement. They found no difference between prospective teachers who merely observed versus those who served as tutors in their school settings. However, Denton (1982) disclosed that early field experiences positively influence subsequent course achievement. Sandefur (1970) also concluded that prospective teachers who had early field experiences obtained higher grades in student teaching and showed greater gains on the Professional Education section of the National Teachers Examination than a control group which did not receive these field experiences.

Numerous studies examined the influence of early field experiences on the learning of specific teaching skills. Veldman, Menaker, and Newlove (1970), for example, found that prospective teachers in early field experiences improved their verbal fluency and coherence significantly more than prospective teachers who did not have these field experiences. Sandefur (1970) also concluded that prospective teachers who had early field experiences were more democratic, understanding, stimulating, original, alert, responsible, systematic, and confident than prospective teachers who did not have field experiences. On the other hand, Scherer (1979) and Sunal (1980) did not find that prospective teachers with early field experiences were rated any higher on teaching skills than those prospective teachers who had not undergone such experiences. Subsequently, some educators such as Howey (1983) maintain that several skills such as the development and refinement of essential interpersonal communication skills, collaborative planning, problem-solving strategies, and documentation, measurement, and evaluation skills are probably better learned in focused laboratory sessions than in early field experiences. Needless to say, this still remains an empirical question which needs to be investigated.

Research on the effects of early field experiences on the prospective teacher's attitudes has often been contradictory. As previously discussed, several educators maintain that such experiences socialize the beginning teacher into the real world of school. For example, in their national study of teacher education programs, Joyce, Yarger, and Howey (1977) found that the majority of respondents in their survey indicated that field experiences were necessary and useful components of teacher preparation programs. Other studies which have specifically examined the impact of early field experiences on the attitudes and mental health of prospective teachers have also concluded such experiences to be favorable (Benton & Osborn, 1979; Marso, 1971; Scherer, 1979; Veldman et al., 1970). In their review of research on teacher education, Peck and Tucker (1973) describe many studies that found early field experiences beneficial for prospective teachers. Veldman et al., for example, determined that prospective teachers who had early field experiences were more interested in a teaching career and more satisfied with their teaching style and supervising professor than prospective teachers who did not have field experiences. Summarizing the results from many of these studies, Becher and Ade (1982) list some of the more successful effects of field experiences:

1. Improving general teaching behavior and performance;
2. Increasing professional orientations, attitudes, and commitment;
3. Increasing the preservice teacher's ability to determine readiness levels, clarify objectives, and motivate and evaluate students;
4. Reducing (racial) prejudice;
5. Facilitating understanding and acceptance of "disadvantaged" children;
6. Increasing personal orientations (i.e., becoming more self-actualized);
7. Increasing the use of indirect methods of teaching; and
8. Developing a preference for a democratic teaching style. (p. 24)

On the other hand, a number of studies indicate that field experiences are not helpful for the prospective teacher. Gibson (1976), Hoy and Rees (1977), Iannaccone (1963), Tabachnick (1980), and Tabachnick et al. (1980), for example, concluded that early field experiences contribute to the development of merely utilitarian teaching perspectives (i.e., a focus on *how* things are done in the classroom rather than considering *why* things are done). Becher and Ade (1982) also summarize some of the research that uncovered undesirable effects of field experiences:

Specifically, preservice teachers became more authoritarian, more rigid, more controlling, more restrictive, and more impersonal. In addition, they became less pupil-centered, less accepting, less "humanistic," and more "custodial" in their approach to teaching. They also showed an increase in the proportion of time spent stating facts and their own opinions and a decrease in time spent on student ideas and responses. (p. 24)

In other words, some research has found that early field experiences have negative effects on teaching behaviors as well as encourage acquiescence and conformity to existing school practices.

More specifically, several research studies focusing on teacher-role socialization have found that initial field experiences produce at least two types of psychological conflict (Walberg, 1970). Several studies suggest that the personality needs of prospective teachers (i.e., to establish rapport with children) conflict with the bureaucratic institutional role of the teacher. Such personality role conflict may result in less satisfaction and effectiveness in the beginning teacher (Walberg, 1970). This conflict may apparently deflate the professional self-image during the initial field experiences. Walberg (1968) and Walberg, Metzner, Todd, and Henry (1968), for example, discovered that self-ratings in the professional role of teacher declined significantly after practice teaching. The changes over time implied self-depreciation on intellectual mastery, lower expectations of pupil behavior and aspiration of self in the role of teacher, and less rapport with children in the class.

Studies utilizing the Minnesota Teacher Attitude Inventory have also shown a tendency of prospective teachers lowering their positive attitudes toward teaching during their first field experience (Getzels & Jackson, 1963; Rabinowitz & Rosenbaum, 1960). Horowitz (1968) found that prospective teachers' attitudes change from a personal to an institutional orientation. A recent quantitative synthesis of research studies supports this earlier research. Colosimo (1981) analyzed 24 studies of the effects of student teaching and concluded prospective teachers' attitudes generally shift from a humane to custodial attitude. In other words, this research indicates that the prospective teacher's needs to be humane and nurturant to students may conflict with the needs to establish order and discipline in the classroom.

A second type of psychological conflict may occur when the prospective teacher receives early training and experience in one type of school context or culture, usually a middle-class suburban or university laboratory school, but confronts students from another context (e.g., inner-city school) at some later point in his/her professional socialization. As Howey (1983) points out, "Current programs of preservice are typically not designed so that the novice can do extended practice teaching in different school sites or with different types of students" (p. 18). Several studies have concluded that schools in different cultures have different effects on factors such as self-concept and teaching attitudes of the prospective teacher (Walberg, 1968; Walberg et al., 1968).

A recent quantitative research synthesis of 38 studies found that on average, preteaching experiences have a small but significant effect on teaching attitudes and self-concept (Samson, Borger, Weinstein, and Walberg, 1983). The study-weighted overall mean-effect size for the 38 studies was .23 and the standard deviation was .61. The significant overall effect size indicates that the mean attitude score for students participating in early field experiences was at the 59th percentile relative to a mean of the 50th percentile for those not participating in such experiences. This indicates that early field experiences generally promote prospective teachers' self-concept and constructive teaching attitudes.

It should be pointed out, however, that there was a considerable spread of effects and 47% was negative. Furthermore, studies which were judged to not adequately control for mortality of subjects achieved expectedly higher effect sizes than more carefully designed studies, and studies which appeared to be more generalizable to other situations yielded more smaller estimates of effect. Thus, the conclusions from this research remain equivocal, because relatively few rigorous field trials of early field experiences have been reported.

EFFECTS OF EARLY FIELD EXPERIENCES
ON SUBSEQUENT PERFORMANCE

This section analyzes some of the research concerning the effect of early field experiences on the prospective teacher's subsequent performances. The research in this area is quite limited. Schalock (1979), for example, found very few studies that investigated the effect of simplified teaching conditions (e.g., the teaching of lessons in a supervised classroom or the assumption of full responsibility as a teacher for a limited period of time) on subsequent teaching performance.

However, the teacher preparation program at Oregon College of Education has conducted a number of studies on the effect of simplified teaching conditions (for example, 2- to 5-day full responsibility teaching experience prior to student teaching) on performance in student teaching (Gengler, 1977; Albritton, 1977; Girod, 1977). These studies found consistently low correlations between such short, intensive supervised teaching performance and student teaching performance. Another interesting result of these findings is that the characteristics of the instructional setting did not effect the performance of prospective teachers in these early field experiences. Sandefur (1970), on the other hand, found that prospective teachers who had early field experiences were more democratic, confident, and responsive during their student teaching performance than a control group of prospective teachers who had not participated in those experiences.

This is an important area that needs to be further investigated. Although several studies suggest that performance as a student teacher predicts performance as a full-time teacher (see, for example, Schalock, 1979), there should be randomized and longitudinal studies which examine the effect of early field experiences on subsequent performance as a classroom teacher.

EFFECTS OF EARLY FIELD EXPERIENCES ON STUDENT JUDGMENTS

One of the traditional problems hindering early field experiences has been the lack of valid and accurate information that prospective teachers could use in order to facilitate their professional growth. Many prospective teachers are unaware of their effectiveness in early field experiences, and they also lack information about the nature of their interactions with individual students. Several studies have found that teachers can make appropriate changes in their classroom style based on feedback about their classroom behavior (Ebmeier & Good, 1979; Good & Brophy, 1974; Stallings, 1980; Gage, Runkel, & Chatterjee, 1960; Good & Grouws, 1979; Moore, Schaut, & Fritzges, 1978). Through feedback, teachers can become aware of how their classroom functions and thus bring about changes they desire (Brophy, 1979).

As previously discussed, many early field experiences do not incorporate supervised observation and extensive feedback to prospective teachers. Supervising prospective teachers is a very costly operation for teacher education programs, especially since most states do not specifically allocate funds for field-based experiences. One alternative to the direct supervision of prospective teachers by university personnel is the use of student judgment, or student self-report instruments. These instruments can be administered to an entire class or just the individual students with whom the prospective teacher interacted during the early field experiences. They can be used to obtain feedback and have several advantages: (a) they are relatively inexpensive to administer; (b) they can be administered at a convenient or relevant time during the class; (c) they can be standardized; (d) they can be designed to maintain anonymity; (e) they are the product of observing the prospective teacher on many occasions under normal conditions; and (f) they can pick up a wealth of data in a very short time (Waxman, 1983). Such instruments can assess, for example, students' perceptions of the prospective teacher's instructional skills and strategies, learning environment, and attitudes toward teaching.

Student responses from self-report instruments have been found to be realistic and reliable measures of their classroom environment. Peck, Blattstein, and Fox (1978), Peck, Olsson, and Green (1978), Stallings, Needels, and Stayrook (1979), and Steele, House, and Kerrins (1971), for example, have shown that students' judgments about their teachers' behaviors agree significantly with the judgments of experienced classroom observers. Rosenshine (1971) also reports that the use of student ratings as predictors of the general effectiveness of teachers have yielded slightly stronger results than observer ratings. Studies which compared teachers', students', and classroom observers' reports of classroom processes have likewise found that students and classroom observers were in general agreement, although students' and observers' reports did not correspond very closely to teachers' reports (Ehman, 1970; Hook & Rosenshine, 1979; Steele et al., 1971).

Student perceptions have been very useful in helping educators understand classroom processes (Gage, 1972; Walberg, 1976). Students' ratings and evaluations have also been found to be effective feedback to classroom teachers (Talmage & Eash, 1979; Gage, 1972; McDonald, 1979). Several studies conclude that teachers adapt their behavior to students' feedback (Gage et al., 1960; Tuckman & Oliver, 1968). Furthermore, Tuckman and Oliver (1968), for example, found that students' feedback improved student teacher's instruction, whereas the supervisor's feedback had a negative effect.

Such results suggest that student feedback is a viable and effective mechanism for providing teachers with the information they about their classroom behavior. This feedback is intended to create what Heider (1958) would call an "imbalance" in teachers' perceptions of their own behaviors. This imbalance exists whenever teachers find out that their attitudes or perceptions of their teaching differ from that of their students. Teachers in such a state of imbalance are motivated to do something about their behavior in order to restore themselves to a balanced condition (Gage, 1972). A similar notion is that self-awareness increases teachers' control of their actions and the possibility that they will modify them. Walberg and Moos (1980) call this a "self-initiated analysis," and they likewise contend that information from students can be used to facilitate and enact change.

Little research on early field experiences, however, has utilized students' judgment to evaluate prospective teachers. A few studies utilizing students' perceptions have been used to evaluate the effectiveness of student teachers, but systematic feedback from students might usefully be incorporated in many teacher education programs (Fuller & Bown, 1975).

EVALUATING THE RESEARCH IN TEACHER EDUCATION

The current research and development activities of teacher preparation programs present a bleak scene. Program procedures, policies, and practices appear to be generally unrelated to research data, but based instead upon concepts, perceptions, and "common sense." The research that is performed is often poorly designed and controlled. (Watts, 1982, p. 49)

As educators often point out, the research in teacher education is characterized by a chronic inconsistency of results. Although NCATE standards for accreditation explicitly state that institutions producing teachers need to systematically evaluate students who are in preservice teacher education programs, there is very little sophistication in the evaluation design and research approaches used (Adams & Craig, 1981, 1983). Few evaluations, for example, would meet minimal standards for experimental design and measurement validity (Cook & Campbell, 1979).

The most prevalent evaluation approach has generally been a one-shot questionnaire sent to graduates of teacher education programs. In a survey designed to determine the state-of-the-practice in teacher education evaluation, for example, Adams and Craig (1981) analyzed the frequency of data collection procedures for approximately 400 teacher education institutions. They concluded that questionnaires were the most utilized form of collecting evaluation data in preservice programs. However, personal interviews, direct classroom observation, media-aided work sample observations, standardized tests, professional competence measures, and personal characteristics and attitude measures were also used to a lesser degree on preservice evaluations. They also found that smaller teacher education institutions tended to use more direct classroom observations and media-aided work sample observations than larger institutions. Institutional size may promote bureaucracy and impersonal and distal approaches.

The use of surveys alone is an inadequate indicator of program effectiveness. As Hall (1981) puts it, "Survey questionnaires with course happiness coefficients are very weak data to use in refining programs" (p. 70). Teacher education institutions should investigate moving toward "common core" instruments that can be used to make comparisons across teacher education programs (Schalock, 1979). In a similar vein, teacher education programs could establish a systematic evaluation system that provides relevant, meaningful data that can be used to aid program decision making (Craig & Adams, 1981). Research and development cooperatives might also be organized among teacher education institutions (Cooper, 1983; Watts, 1982).

Teacher education programs generally set standards or criteria at several screening points: program entry, student teaching, and certification (Schalock, 1979). Schalock (1979) lists several potential predictors of teaching effectiveness that could be readily measured during the prospective teacher's preparation prior to student teaching:

1. Knowledge related to teaching, including content to be taught.
2. Skills related to teaching.
3. Performance of teaching functions under simplified teaching conditions
    a. under simulated classroom conditions (e.g., peer teaching; response to filmed classroom events)

  b. under simplified classroom conditions (e.g., small groups in a
     classroom; microteaching)
  c. under the conditions of short-term conditions (e.g., two to five
     days).
4. Behavior of pupils taught under simplified conditions (e.g., time on
   task; frequency of disruptions).
5. Achievement of pupils taught under simplified conditions (e.g.,
   attainment of learning outcomes desired from a lesson or across two
   to five days of instruction). (p. 401)

Future research in teacher education should focus on these variables
as well as on how they predict performance in student teaching and subsequent performance as a classroom teacher. As Zeichner (1980) points out,
"It is only through closer study of field-based experiences (including their
contradictions) and through the development of policies and programs
based on more accurate knowledge of program impact that the actual consequences of field-based experiences will begin to approach our hopes for
them" (p. 52).

PROSPECTS

Campus-based preservice teacher preparation programs are in a crisis
stage. Unless action is taken to resolve their deficiencies, these programs
may be removed from college campuses and the preparation of school-
teachers reduced to some form of apprenticeship training. (Watts, 1982,
p. 53)

Teacher education institutions are facing several crises today. In addition to
being blamed for the incompetence of classroom teachers, the withdrawal
of qualified candidates from the teaching profession, and ill-prepared prospective teachers, they are now being told to eliminate some of their pedagogy courses and expand their field experiences and apprenticeship training.
Furthermore, they should be concerned about proposals to transfer teacher
education programs from higher education institutions to public schools
(Lyons, 1979; Schlechty & Vance, 1983). Finally, there is also the serious
concern that more prestigious research-oriented universities will eliminate
teacher education, because they will find it difficult to attract students in
their programs who meet the general university standards required of all
students (Schlechty & Vance, 1983). Consequently, teacher education would
continue to lose status in our society.
   As noted throughout this chapter, a number of sweeping statements
about the quality of research on teacher education have been made by re-
viewers in the mainstream as well as those outside the field. Research work-

ers and educators must retain both openmindedness and skepticism about the research on early field experiences, because there is a limited knowledge base regarding the effectiveness of our teacher education practices. More empirical studies and research syntheses are needed to help us understand the impact of early field experiences for prospective teachers.

Teacher education institutions need information on how a variety of educational factors interact with early field experiences and subsequently on how they affect prospective teachers. As Zeichner (1980) points out, most studies do not examine what actually takes place during early field experiences. Are some components of field experiences more beneficial for prospective teachers than others? Are there differences between "supervised" and "unsupervised" field experiences? How does the school context affect the preservice teacher? What is the influence of the cooperating teacher, the classroom environment, and/or the principal on the field experience? More longitudinal research is also needed. Longitudinal studies should investigate the effects of early field experiences on the subsequent teaching performance and attitudes of prospective teachers.

Little importance can be attached to many of the aberrant generalizations and findings reported from isolated studies, unless they are replicated in future research. Many of the studies described in this chapter have been conducted over 10 years ago. These as well as the more recent studies need to be replicated to determine their generalizability over time and institution. Teacher educators must concern themselves with producing more and better research, and teacher education institutions should systematically incorporate research/evaluation components in their programs of early field experience so that they could monitor and improve policies, practices, and their effects.

REFERENCES

Adams, R. D., & Craig, J. R. (1981). A survey of undergraduate teacher education evaluation practices. In S. M. Hord & R. D. Adams (Eds.), *Teacher education program evaluation, 1981: Theory and practice,* Austin, TX: Research and Development Center for Teacher Education.

Adams, R. D., & Craig, J. R. (1983). A status report of teacher education program evaluation. *Journal of Teacher Education, 34*(2), 33–36.

Albritton, R. (1977, November). *The OCE/TR search for predictors of success in teaching: Findings for first year teachers.* Paper presented at the first Oregon Conference on Research in Teacher Education, Corvallis: Oregon State University.

Applegate, J. H., & Lasley, T. J. (1982). Cooperating teachers' problems with preservice field experiences. *Journal of Teacher Education, 33*(2), 15–18.

Ayers, J. B. (1981). Design characteristics for meaningful teacher education evaluation. In S. M. Hord & R. D. Adams (Eds.), *Teacher education program evalu-*

ation, 1981: Theory and practice, Austin, TX: Research and Development Center for Teacher Education.

Becher, R. M., & Ade, W. E. (1982). The relationship of field placement characteristics and students' potential field performance abilities to clinical experience performance ratings. *Journal of Teacher Education, 33*(2), 24–30.

Benton, S. E., & Osborn, J. (1979). Early field based experiences in an education curriculum. *The Southern Journal of Educational Research, 13,* 119–125.

Black, D. (1980). *Cooperating teacher remuneration: Where are we?* Reston, VA: Association of Teacher Educators.

Brophy, J. E. (1979, April). *Using observation to improve your teaching.* (Occasional Paper No. 21). East Lansing, MI: Michigan State University, Institute for Research on Teaching.

Colosimo, M. S. (1981). *The effects of practice or beginning teaching on the self-concepts and attitudes of teachers—A quantitative synthesis.* Unpublished doctoral dissertation, University of Chicago, IL.

Cook, T. D., & Campbell, D. T. (1979). *Quasi-experimentation.* Chicago, IL: Rand McNally.

Cooper, J. M. (1983). Basic elements in teacher education program evaluation: Implications for future research and development. In K. R. Howey & W. E. Gardner (Eds.), *The education of teachers: A look ahead,* New York: Longman.

Craig, J. R., & Adams, R. D. (1981). User-oriented evaluation. In S. M. Hord & R. D. Adams (Eds.), *Teacher education program evaluation, 1981: Theory and practice.* Austin, TX: Research and Development Center for Teacher Education.

Cronin, J. M. (1983). State regulation of teacher preparation. In L. S. Shulman & G. Sykes (Eds.), *Handbook of teaching and policy,* New York: Longman.

Denemark, G., & Nutter, N. (1980). *The case for extended programs of initial teacher preparation.* Washington, DC: ERIC Clearinghouse on Teacher Education.

Denton, J. J. (1982). Early field experiences influence performance in subsequent coursework. *Journal of Teacher Education, 33*(2), 9–23.

Ebmeier, H., & Good, T. L. (1979). The effects of instructing teachers about good teaching on the mathematics achievement of fourth-grade students. *American Educational Research Journal, 16,* 1–16.

Ehman, L. A. (1970). *A comparison of three sources of classroom data: Teachers, students, and systematic observation.* Paper presented at the annual meeting of the American Educational Research Association, Minneapolis, MN.

Fuller, F. F., & Bown, O. (1975). Becoming a teacher. In K. Ryan (Ed.), *Teacher education,* Chicago, IL: National Society for the Study of Education.

Gage, N. L. (1972). *Teacher effectiveness and teacher education.* Palo Alto, CA: Pacific.

Gage, N. L., Runkel, P., & Chatterjee, B. (1960). *Equilibrium theory and behavior change: An experiment in feedback from pupils to teacher.* Urbana, IL: University of Illinois, Bureau of Educational Research.

Gengler, C. (1977, November). *The Oregon College of Education-Teaching Research for predictors of success in teaching: Findings for student teachers.* Paper presented at the first Oregon Conference on Research in Teacher Education, Corvallis: Oregon State University.

Getzels, J., & Jackson, P. (1963). The teacher's personality and characteristics. In N. Gage (Ed.), *Handbook of research on teaching*, Chicago, IL: Rand McNally.

Gibson, R. (1976). The effect of school practice: The development of student perspectives. *British Journal of Teacher Education, 2,* 241–250.

Girod, J. (1977, November). *Teaching performance under simplified conditions as a predictor of performance under more complex conditions.* Paper presented at the first Oregon Conference on Research in Teacher Education, Corvailis: Oregon State University.

Good, T. L., & Brophy, J. E. (1974). Changing teacher and student behavior: An empirical investigation. *Journal of Educational Psychology, 66,* 390–405.

Good, T. L., & Grouws, D. A. (1979). The Missouri Mathematics Effectiveness Project: An experimental study in fourth-grade classrooms, *Journal of Educational Psychology, 71,* 355–362.

Hall, G. E. (1981). What is the future of teacher education program evaluation? In S. M. Hord & R. D. Adams (Eds.), *Teacher education program evaluation, 1981: Theory and practice.* Austin, TX: Research and Development Center for Teacher Education.

Hedberg, J. D. (1979). The effects of field experience on achievement in educational psychology. *Journal of Teacher Education, 30,* 75–76.

Heider, F. (1958). *The psychology of interpersonal relationships.* New York: Holt, Rinehart, & Winston.

Henry, M. A. (1982). Testing out the field. In D. E. Orlosky (Ed.), *Introduction to education.* Columbus, OH: Merrill.

Hook, C., & Rosenshine, B. (1979). Accuracy of teacher reports of their classroom behavior. *Review of Educational Research, 49,* 1–12.

Horowitz, M. (1968). The effects of teaching experiences on attitudes of student teachers. *Journal of Teacher Education, 19,* 317–324.

Howey, K. R. (1977). Preservice teacher education: Lost in the shuffle? *Journal of Teacher Education, 28,* 26–28.

Howey, K. R. (1983). Teacher education: An overview. In K. R. Howey & W. E. Gardner (Eds.), *The education of teachers: A look ahead,* New York: Longman.

Hoy, W., & Rees, R. (1977). The bureaucratic socialization of student teachers. *Journal of Teacher Education, 28,* 23–26.

Iannaccone, L. (1963). Student teaching: A transitional stage in the making of a teacher. *Theory into Practice, 2,* 73–81.

Ingle, R. B., & Robinson, E. W. (1965). An examination of the value of classroom observation for prospective teachers. *Journal of Teacher Education, 16,* 456–460.

Ingle, R. B., & Zaret, E. A. (1968). A comparison of classroom observations and tutorial experiences in the preparation of secondary school teachers. *Educational Leadership, 2,* 164–168.

Joyce, B. R., Yarger, S. J., & Howey, K. R. (1977). *Preservice teacher education.* Palo Alto, CA: Booksend Laboratory.

Koerner, J. D. (1963). *The miseducation of American teachers.* New York: McGraw-Hill.

Lyons, G. (1979, September). Why teachers can't teach. *Texas Monthly,* pp. 123–

129, 208–220.

Marso, R. N. (1971). Project interaction: A pilot study in a phase of teacher preparation. *Journal of Teacher Education, 22,* 194–198.

McDonald, J. B. (1979). Planning for the evaluation of teaching. In W. R. Duckett (Ed.), *Planning for the evaluation of teaching,* Bloomington, IN: Phi Delta Kappa.

Moore, J. W., Schaut, J., & Fritzges, C. (1978). Evaluation of the effects of feedback associated with a problem-solving approach to instruction on teacher and student behavior. *Journal of Educational Psychology, 70,* 200–208.

Morris, J. E., & Curtis, K. F. (1983). Legal issues relating to field-based experiences in teacher education. *Journal of Teacher Education, 1983, 34*(2), 2–5.

National Council for the Accreditation of Teacher Education. (1979). *Standards for the accreditation of teacher education.* Washington, DC: Author.

Nemser, S. F. (1983). Learning to teach. In L. S. Shulman & G. Sykes (Eds.), *Handbook of teaching and policy,* New York: Longman.

Peck, R. F., Blattstein, A., & Fox, R. (1978, August). *Student evaluation of teaching: A multivariate validation study.* Paper presented at the annual meeting of the American Psychological Association, Toronto, Canada.

Peck, R. F., Olsson, N. G., & Green, J. L. (1978, April). *The consistency of individual teaching behavior.* Paper presented at the annual meeting of the American Educational Research Association, Toronto, Canada.

Peck, R. F., & Tucker, J. A. (1973). Research on teacher education. In R. M. W. Travers (Ed.), *Second handbook of research on teaching.* Chicago, IL: Rand McNally.

Puckett, E. H. (1982). *A national survey of field experiences in elementary teacher preparation programs.* Unpublished manuscript, Provo: Brigham Young University.

Rabinowitz, E., & Rosenbaum, I. (1960). Teaching experience and teachers' attitudes. *Elementary School Journal, 60,* 313–319.

Research Committee of the National Field Directors Forum. (1982, February). The director of student teaching/field experience, *ERIC Reports.*

Robinson, A. A., & Mosrie, D. (1979). Florida's new teacher certification law. *Phi Delta Kappan, 61,* 263–264.

Rosenshine, B. (1971). *Teaching behaviors and student achievement.* London: National Foundation for Educational Research in England and Wales.

Samson, G. E., Borger, J. D., Weinstein, T., & Walberg, H.J. (1983, April). *Effects of early field experiences for preservice teachers on self-concept and attitudes toward teaching—A quantitative synthesis.* Paper presented at the annual meeting of the American Educational Research Association, Montreal, Canada.

Sandefur, J. T. (1970). Kansas State Teachers College experimental study of professional education for secondary teachers. *Journal of Teacher Education, 21,* 386–395.

Schalock, D. (1979). Research on teacher selection. In D. Berliner (Ed.), *Review of research in education* (Vol. 7). Washington, DC: American Educational Research Association.

Scherer, C. (1979). Effects of early field experiences on student teachers' self-concepts and performance. *Journal of Experimental Education, 47,* 208–214.

Schlechty, P. C., & Vance, V. S. (1983). Recruitment, selection, and retention: The shape of the teaching force. *The Elementary School Journal, 83,* 469–487.

Smith, B. O. (1980). Pedagogical education: How about reform? *Phi Delta Kappan, 62,* 87–91.

Stallings, J. (1980). Allocated academic learning time revisited, or beyond time on task. *Educational Research,* 1980, *9*(11), 11–16.

Stallings, J., Needels, M., & Stayrook, N. (1979). *How to change the process of teaching basic reading skills in secondary school Phase II & Phase III,* Menlo Park, CA: SRI International.

Steele, J. M., House, E. R., & Kerrins, T. (1971). An instrument for assessing instructional climate through low-inference student judgments. *American Educational Research Journal, 8,* 447–466.

Sunal, D. W. (1980). Effects of field experiences during elementary methods courses on preservice teacher behavior. *Journal of Research in Science Teaching, 17,* 17–23.

Sykes, G. (1983). Public policy and the problem of teacher quality: The need for screens and magnets. In L. S. Shulman & G. Sykes (Eds.), *Handbook of teaching and policy,* New York: Longman.

Tabachnick, B. R. (1980). Intern-teacher roles: Illusion, disillusion, and reality. *Journal of Education, 162,* 122–137.

Tabachnick, B. R., Popkewitz, T. S., & Zeichner, K. M. (1980). Teacher education and the professional perspectives of student teachers. *Interchange, 10,* 12–29.

Talmage, H., & Eash, M. J. (1979). Curriculum, instruction, and materials. In P. L. Peterson & H. J. Walberg (Eds.), *Research on teaching: Concepts, findings, and implications.* Berkeley, CA: McCutchan.

Tuckman, B. W., & Oliver, W. S. (1968). Effectiveness of feedback to teachers as a function of source. *Journal of Educational Psychology, 59,* 297–301.

Turner, R. L. (1975). An overview of research in teacher education. In K. Ryan (Ed.), *Teacher education,* Chicago, IL: National Society for the Study of Education.

Utah State Board of Education (1979). *Standards for state approval of teacher education.* Salt Lake City, Utah: Author.

Veldman, D. J., Menaker, S. L., & Newlove, B. (1970). *The Porter Project: Teacher aides in a secondary school. A preliminary report.* Austin, TX: The Research and Development Center for Teacher Education.

Walberg, H. J. (1968). Personality—Role conflict and self-concept in urban practice teachers. *School Review, 52,* 41–49.

Walberg, H. J. (1970). Professional role discontinuities in educational careers. *Review of Educational Research, 40,* 409–420.

Walberg, H. J. (1976). Psychology of learning environments: Behavioral, structural, or perceptual? In L. S. Shulman (Ed.), *Review of Educational Research* (Vol. 4). Itasca, IL: Peacock.

Walberg, H. J., Metzner, S., Todd, R. M., & Henry, P. (1968). Effects of tutoring and practice teaching on self-concept and attitudes in educational students. *Journal of Teacher Education, 19,* 283–291.

Walberg, H. J., & Moos, R. H. (1980). Assessing educational environments. *New Directions for Testing and Measurement, 7,* 63–76.

Waller, W. (1932). *The sociology of teaching.* New York: Wiley.

Watts, D. (1982). Can campus-based preservice teacher education survive? Part III. *Journal of Teacher Education, 33*(3), 48–52.

Waxman, H. C. (1983, April). *Evaluating schools and classrooms with student perception data.* Paper presented at the annual meeting of the American Educational Research Association, Montreal, Canada.

Webb, C. (1981). Theoretical and empirical bases for early field experiences in teacher education. In C. Webb, N. Gehrke, P. Ishler, & A. Mendoza (Eds.), *Exploratory field experiences in teacher education,* Provo, UT: Utah State University.

Zeichner, K. M. (1980). Myths and realities: Field-based experiences in pre-service teacher education. *Journal of Teacher Education, 31,* 46–55.

9

Teacher Development: Implications for Teacher Education

Paul R. Burden
Kansas State University

Knowledge of the characteristics of teachers is important to teacher education for three reasons: providing a foundation upon which teacher educators can diagnose needs and abilities; offering a guide for ways to support teachers; and helping select teacher developmental objectives that focus on short-term or long-term personal growth (McNergney & Carrier, 1981, p. 120). Knowledge of teachers' personal and professional developmental changes can help teacher educators understand the needs and abilities of teachers at different points in their careers and can serve as a basis for planning interventions to promote developmental growth.

TEACHERS' CAREER DEVELOPMENT

Development generally refers to the phenomenon of change in form over time. This change usually is from relatively simple to complex forms; it often proceeds through stages, and transitions between stages frequently are viewed as relatively irreversible. The forces behind the changes are believed to be maturational factors within the individual as well as interactional factors between personal characteristics and environmental stimulation (Charlesworth, 1972). The terms phase and stage are very similar. A phase is any stage in a series of changes, as in development. A stage is a period in a process of development.

While adult development is not a fully articulated concept, an increasing amount of information has been generated about phases of adult life and adult developmental characteristics. Those who select teaching as a

185

career exhibit these phases and developmental characteristics as do all other adults. In addition, teachers express different professional skills, knowledge, behaviors, attitudes, and concerns during their careers. Taken together, this information can help teacher educators understand the needs and abilities of teachers as they advance through their careers.

Adult Development

As individuals move through life from youth to old age, changes constantly take place within them as well as within the settings in which they live and work. To understand teacher development, it is important to understand the interaction of physiological, psychological, and social aspects of human development.

Baltes and Goulet (1970) and Chickering (1976) divided adult development theorists into two basic groups: (a) developmental *age* theorists, who examine sections of the age span, and (b) developmental *stage* theorists, who examine various psychological processes related to age. Actually, the distinction between age and stage theorists is not totally discrete. Rather, age is the major variable for some theorists while stages in the structure of thinking is the major variable for others.

Developmental Ages. In reviewing adult development literature, Bents and Howey (1981) stated that age theorists are interested in determining if there are concerns, problems, and tasks that are common to most or all adults at various times in their lives. Chickering (1976) noted that some researchers take chronological age as a major variable and search for general orientations, problems, developmental tasks, personal concerns, or other characteristics associated with particular age or time periods. These researchers are also concerned with explaining why certain concerns, problems, and tasks might loom more prominentaly at one time of life than another, and how these affect adult behavior. Age theorists discuss adult development in such terms as life periods, passages, stages of life, and periods of transition.

Recent reviews of literature have attempted to identify different types of developmental age theorists. Oja (1980) noted that age-related developmental task models are suggested by: (a) "life-age" theorists such as Gould, Levinson, and Sheehy who consider roles, tasks, and coping behaviors needed at certain times of life, and (b) "life-cycle" theorists such as Erikson, Neugarten, and Havinghurst who emphasize the experiences adults encounter through various ages and cycles of life.

Age-linked developmental periods have been proposed by many theorists. Levinson, Darrow, Klein, Levinson, and McKee (1978) identified *periods of transition* in the lives of men and described the timing of typical life events. Gould (1972, 1978) detailed a similar set of *stages of life*. Sheehy (1976) popularized these concepts of age-linked behavior as she described *passages* in adults' lives.

A general pattern of adult development that Levinson, Gould, and Sheehy describe begins with the transition in the late teens and early twenties from adolescence to adulthood. The mid-twenties is a period of provisional adulthood where first commitments to work, marriage, and family, and to other adult responsibilities are lived out. These initial commitments are reexamined and their meaning questioned in another transitional period in the late twenties and early thirties. At that time, long-range implications of continuing with the current work, spouse, community, and life style become apparent. changes must be made in some cases; reaffirmation and renewed commitment may occur in others. The thirties are a time for settling down, for achievement, and becoming one's own person. Time becomes more finite in the forties. The limits of success and achievement become apparent and mid-life transition is at hand. Major questions concerning priorities and values are examined. Friends, relatives, and spouse become increasingly important as restabilization occurs during the late forties and fifties. Personal interests receive more attention. Mellowing and increasing investment in personal relationships characterize the fifties.

Krupp (1981), deeply influenced by Levinson, described adult growth as a sequence of overlapping stages. Each of these periods may be stable or transitional. Krupp noted that individuals make key decisions in stable periods and that, in transitional periods, individuals question, reappraise, explore possibilities, and move toward new commitments. According to Krupp, stable and transitional periods alternate throughout life.

Bernice Neugarten has elaborated the roles of age and the timing of life events in adult development more than any other theorist (Chickering, 1976, p. 65). She has examined adult life in terms of development of the personality, age norms, sociology, and psychology. She stated that time rather than age is the critical variable in adult development. When normal events, such as children leaving home, were "on time," they were not experienced as a crisis. Therefore, the timing of life events provides some of the most powerful cues to adult personality and behavior.

Erikson (1959, 1963), a life-cycle theorist, charted the course of personality development by proposing eight universal stages of psychosocial growth for the human life span. Each stage represented a major crisis—a challenge or a turning point—faced in the normal course of life dealing with the needs to trust, to assert independence, to resolve guilt, to form bonds with others, to find solitude, to produce, to work with strength and conviction, and to know oneself. The last three stages typically occur in adulthood. Each crisis is considered to be salient at a particular age period, and optimal development is characterized by a sequence of eight successful resolutions. Although the sequence forms a logical series of stages, the stages are not hierarchial and may occur at any time in life. While not necessarily related to particular ages, Erikson indicated general time periods when the crises occur (e.g., adolescence, early adulthood, middle adulthood).

Developmental Stages. Stage theorists focus on distinct or qualitative differences in the modes of thinking at various points in development that are not necessarily age-related. The different structures or ways of thinking form an invariant sequence or progression in individual development. Bents and Howey (1981) noted that these structural changes provide insight into what information individuals tend to use, how information is used, and the type of interactions they might have with the environment.

Drawing upon Piaget's writing, Kohlberg (1973) described characteristics of stages:

1. Stages imply distinct or qualitative differences in structures (modes of thinking) which perform the same function (e.g., intelligence) at various points in development.
2. Different structures form an invariant sequence in individual development. Although factors may accelerate, slow, or stop development, the sequence does not change.
3. Each of these different and sequential modes of thought forms a structural whole.
4. Stages are hierarchial integrations. Higher stages reintegrate the structures found at lower stages.

Kohlberg's notion of stage involves changes in quality, competence, and form, as one moves from one stage to another, rather than changing in quantity, performance, and content. Structural change tells less about *what* information people process but more about *how* they use that information; less about *what* people are performing but more about *how* they are performing; and less about *what* they are thinking but more about *how* they are thinking (Willie & Howey, 1980, p. 29).

Piaget, Kohlberg, Loevinger, Hunt, and Perry are among the stage theorists who view adult development in individuals as a definite progression from concrete, undifferentiating, simple, unstructured patterns of thought to more abstract, differentiating, and complex patterns of thought. Table 1, from Sprinthall and Thies-Sprinthall (1983b), displays these theorists and the descriptions of the domains of developmental stages of human growth.

Piaget's (1963) framework provided a means of understanding cognitive growth and how people understand the physical world of time, space, and causality. Kohlberg (1969) emphasized moral development as people change in their orientations toward authority, others, and self when making decisions. Loevinger (1966) examined ego development and described how adults pass through stages as they try to understand themselves. Adults moved from conformity to emotional independence, and, finally, to a state where individuals reconcile inner conflicts, renounce the unattainable,

TABLE 1 Domains of Developmental Stages

Theorist	Piaget (1963)	Kohlberg (1969)	Loevinger (1966)	Hunt (1971)	Perry (1970)
Domains	Cognitive	Value/Moral	Ego Self	Conceptual	Epistemological Ethical
Stages	Sensori-Motor	Obedience-punishment (1)	Presocial impulsive	Unsocialized impulsive	
	Preoperational	Naively egotistic (2)	Self-protective	Concrete dogmatic	
	Concrete	Social confirmity (3)	Conformist	Dependent abstract	Dualist
	Formal Substage I	Authority maintaining (3)	Conscientious		Relativist
	Formal Substage II	Principles reasoning (5 and 6)	Autonomous	Self-directed abstract	Committed-relativist

Note. From "The Teacher as An Adult Learner: A Cognitive-Developmental View" by N. A. Sprinthall and L. Thies-Sprinthall, 1983, in G. A. Griffin (Ed.), *Staff Development, The Eighty-Second Yearbook of the National Society for the Study of Education, Part 2* (p. 17). Chicago, IL: University of Chicago Press. Reprinted by permission.

189

cherish individuality, and find their identity. Hunt (1971) reported that more advanced conceptual systems have been associated with creativity, greater cognitive flexibility, a wider range of coping behaviors, and a greater tolerance for stress.

Perry (1970) described stages of intellectual and ethical development where individuals move from dualistic thinking with a right or wrong perspective, to relativistic thinking where the world of knowledge is seen as relativistic and uncertainty becomes legitimate, and finally to the point where individuals make choices to define their identity.

Harvey, Hunt, and Schroeder (1961) developed a cognitive stage model that dealt with the pattern of beliefs, attitudes, and values through which one interprets experience. Four conceptual stages were proposed in which individuals: (a) are viewed as basically self-centered with an orientation toward external causality and the primacy of concrete rules; (b) can examine themselves apart from external standards and conditions; (c) move to an even more personal introspection; and (d) finally achieve a more integrated and truly independent set of internal standards which may or may not coincide with cultural norms and external pressures.

Effects of Adult Development on Teaching Performance. A comprehensive set of studies concerning adult teachers was conducted in natural settings by David Hunt (1971) and associates at the Ontario Institute for Studies in Education. Teachers who were assessed at more advanced (in terms of their conceptual level) developmental stages were more effective as classroom teachers. For example, teachers at higher stages of development functioned in the classroom at a more complex level. They were more adaptive in their teaching style, more flexible, and more tolerant. These teachers also were more response to individual differences and used a variety of teaching models such as lectures, small group discussions, inquiry, and role playing. These teachers also were more empathetic in that they could more accurately "read" and respond to the emotions of their students. Overall, they provided a wide and varied learning environment for their students.

Additional studies have established the relationship between conceptual level and teaching styles. Research by Harvey, Hunt, Joyce, and colleagues suggests that teachers at higher conceptual levels may be more flexible, more stress tolerant, and more adaptive than teachers at lower levels (Harvey, 1970; Hunt, Joyce, Greenwood, Noy, Reid, & Weil, 1974). Furthermore, teachers at higher stages may be able to assume multiple perspectives, use a wide variety of coping behaviors, employ a broader repertoire of teaching models, and, consequently, be more effective with a wider range of learning styles and with students from diverse cultural backgrounds (Harvey, Prather, White, & Hoffmeister, 1968; Hunt, 1966, 1975).

Hunt and Joyce (1967) found significant positive correlations between indices of reflective teaching (use of learner's frame of reference to plan, initiate, and evaluate performance) and conceptual level. Teachers at higher conceptual levels could create a great variety of learning environments and use a variety of teaching approaches. High conceptual teachers also were more helpful to students in evaluating information and generating hypotheses than low conceptual level teachers. Joyce, Weil, and Wald (1973) also reported that a teacher's ability to use a variety of educational environments was positively correlated with higher conceptual level scores.

Studies by Tomlinson and Hunt (1971) and Gordon (1976) revealed that low conceptual level preservice teachers preferred to teach using a rule/example order (general principles or rules stated first and then examples given), whereas high conceptual level teachers preferred using an example/rule order (first providing an example and then determining a rule or principle to govern the example). Other studies reported that high conceptual level teachers are more stress tolerant (Suedfeld, 1974), better able to look at a problem from multiple perspectives (Wolfe, 1963), and function best with discovery types of learning (McLachlan & Hunt, 1973).

While recognizing the relationship between higher conceptual levels and effective teaching performance, Sprinthall and Thies-Sprinthall (1980b, 1983a, 1983b) have effectively asserted that a theoretical framework must be established for educating teachers for continued cognitive development, and that consideration must be given in the training model for the teacher as an adult learner.

Teacher Development

Teacher career development deals with changes teachers experience throughout their careers in: (a) *job skills, knowledge, and behaviors*—in areas such as teaching methods; discipline techniques; curriculum; lesson plans; rules and procedures; and relationships with students, colleagues, supervisors, parents, and other members of the school community; (b) *attitudes, expectations, and concerns*—in such areas as attitudes toward self and others, images of teaching, professional confidence and maturity, commitment to teaching, satisfactions, beliefs, and concerns; and (c) *job events*—in areas such as changes in grade level, school, or district; breaks in service; involvement in additional professional responsibilities such as serving on committees or in teacher associations or as department head; involvement in professional development programs; entry into and retirement from teaching; and achieving honors, titles (e.g., master teacher), or other forms of recognition.

Reports of Teachers' Developmental Stages. A number of research studies provide descriptions of various aspects of teacher development. Motivated by a desire to make teacher education more relevant, Frances Fuller and her associates at the University of Texas at Austin (Fuller, 1969; Fuller, Parsons, & Watkins, 1973; Fuller & Bown, 1975; George, 1978) examined the nature of teacher concerns. In the original work, Fuller (1969) presented the results of two of her studies and reviewed the results of a number of related studies conducted by other researchers. When drawing conclusions about all of these reports, she proposed a 3-stage developmental model of teacher concerns in the process of becoming a teacher. First was the preteaching phase of no concerns, second was the early teaching phase of concerns about self, and third was the late phase of concerns about pupils. Based on subsequent data gathering and analysis, these stages were revised and explained by Fuller and Bown (1975) as a developmental sequence of concerns. For preteaching concerns in the first stage, preservice teachers identify realistically with pupils, but with teachers only in fantasy. In the second stage, there are early concerns about survival in which idealized concerns are replaced by concerns about their own survival as a teacher and concerns with class control and mastery of content to be taught. For the teaching situation concerns in the third stage, teachers have concerns about their teaching performance, about limitations and frustrations of the teaching situation, and about demands being made on them. In the fourth stage, teachers have concerns about the learning, social, and emotional needs of the pupils and about their own ability to relate to pupils as individuals. Fuller and Bown said these "stages" are described mainly in terms of what the teachers are concerned about rather than what they are actually accomplishing. Whether the stages were distinct or overlapping has not been established.

The theories of Fuller and her associates have been further investigated in studies (e.g., Adams, Hutchinson, & Martray, 1980; Adams, 1982; Briscoe, 1972/1973; Pantaniczek, 1978/1979) designed to document the actual concerns of teachers and how these vary according to a teacher's year of service or according to grade level of the teaching assignment. Adams (1982 reported that the results of a 5-year longitudinal study generally support Fuller's early stages of concern about self and concern about instructional tasks. But Adams suggested that there may be an error in Fuller's theory about impact or pupil concerns, because his study indicated no significant differences in impact concerns across years of experience. Adams (1982) also reported significant differences between elementary and secondary teachers for the stages of concern about self, about instructional tasks, and about pupil impact. In each case, elementary teachers reported greater concerns.

Sitter and Lanier (1982) reported that their research on student teachers supports the work of Frances Fuller in that "commonalities" of concern were expressed by people engaged in the process of learning to teach. In contrast to the Fuller research, however, the commonalities did not occur in clusters and did not occur sequentially. Concerns about self, survival, teaching tasks, pupil learning, materials, and curriculum development occurred simultaneously and were dealt with concurrently by the student teachers. They perceived the student teaching experience as a time to consolidate and integrate these concerns into a "whole," a time to "put it all together."

Other studies on the process of becoming a teacher have identified stages of development. Sacks and Harrington (1982) labeled six stages as students prepare for and move through student teaching: (a) anticipation; (b) entry; (c) orientation; (d) trial and error; (e) integration/consolidation; and (f) mastery. From this study of student teachers, Sacks and Harrington concluded that identification of the stages and the associated student behaviors and feelings would make early remediation of problems possible. They recommended intervention strategies for seminars and individual conferences that would be appropriate at each stage. These strategies would start with a focus on details of the student teaching assignment and end with a focus on specific teaching behaviors.

Based on his work with student teachers in seminars and in reading student logs, Caruso (1977) discussed phases of feelings that student teachers had about themselves and about their experiences as they continued in student teaching. These feelings affected the development of the student teachers' personal and professional identifies. Caruso noted that the phases were not mutually exclusive and that there was much overlap. He gave these phases the following labels: (a) anxiety/euphoria; (b) confusion/clarity; (c) competence/inadequacy; (d) criticism/new awareness; (e) more confidence/greater inadequacy; and (f) loss/relief.

Research by Iannaccone (1963) indicated that student teaching is a transitional period in the making of a teacher. Three stages of this transition were identified in terms of the social distance between the student teacher and the cooperating (critic) teacher. Changes in the student teachers' perceptions concerning classroom management and levels of expectations were also identified.

I reported experienced elementary teachers' perceptions of their personal and professional development for their entire careers (Burden, 1979/1980a, 1980b). Limitations of the study include the fact that the data were self-selected by the teachers as they recounted the events in their careers, that the sample included only teachers with certain demographic characteristics (e.g., elementary teachers in suburban school districts), and that only teachers who had continued to teach were interviewed. In spite of the limitations, the study contributes to an understanding of teachers' professional development by providing details of teachers' experiences. Teachers reported that they passed through three stages in their teaching careers. Stage 1, *a survival stage,* occurred during the first year of teaching. Teachers reported their limited knowledge of teaching activities and environment; they were subject-centered and felt they had little professional insight; they lacked confidence and were unwilling to try new methods; and they found themselves conforming of their preconceived image of "teacher." Stage 2, *an adjustment stage,* occurred for these teachers in the second through fourth years. The teachers reported that during this period they were learning a great deal about planning and organization and about children, curriculum, and methods. They started to see children's complexities and sought new teaching techniques to meet the wider range of needs they found. The teachers became more open and genuine with children and believed they were meeting children's needs more capably. The teachers gradually gained confidence in themselves. Stage 3, *the mature stage,* comprised the fifth and subsequent years of teaching. Teachers in this stage felt they had a good command of teaching activities and the environment. They were more child-centered, felt confident and secure, and were willing to try new teaching methods. They found they had gradually abandoned their former image of "teacher," had gained professional insight, and thought they could handle most new situations that might arise. Since teachers who dropped out of teaching were not included in the study, it is possible that they followed a different developmental pattern than those who continued to teach.

Field (1979) interviewed teachers and found three identifiable stages in their development. For each stage, broad descriptions were provided in each of the following dimensions: planning the day, arranging the classroom, planning for large groups, diagnosis, record keeping, parent conferences, unstructured time, behavior of children, self-evaluation, and self-concept. The detailed descriptions included changes in skills as well as perceptions. Stage 1 was characterized by day-to-day survival, hit-or-miss solutions to problems, and intense feelings of inadequacy. In stage 2, teachers expressed increased self-confidence and feelings of self worth. Success provided teachers with some appropriate and reliable solutions to problems, and teachers in stage 2 extended the boundaries of their planning beyond one day at a time to weeks in advance. At stage 3, teachers viewed learning as a whole process, not as something to be divided into subjects or blocks of time. Teachers felt at home in the classroom and saw children as people, not just pupils. Field indicated that transition from one stage to another is not clear —new problems may cause teachers to have feelings of regression to an earlier stage, whereas successes could have a reverse effect. The descriptions of the stages were meant to serve as a continuum for identifying where teachers are and where they are going.

Anthony Gregorc (1973) and the leadership team at University High School in Urbana, Illinois, studied the behavior of teachers to determine patterns of development. They identified four stages—becoming, growing, maturing, and the fully functioning professional—and provided a detailed chart of the teachers' professional behaviors; knowledge and techniques; and values, beliefs, and needs at each stage. Teachers in the *becoming stage* demonstrated an ambivalent commitment to teaching. They began to develop initial concepts about the purposes of education, the nature of teaching, role expectations in the educational process, and the roles of the school as a social organization. They had limited perceptions of the complexity of the work environment and felt that their job was to share knowledge with students, get through the book, do what the principal says, and be protective of their students. The level of commitment for teachers in the *growing stage* tended to be based on minimal expectations they had of the school and the school had of them. Their basic concepts and stereotypes of the educational process, of their discipline, and their responsibilities were forming. Teachers had increased knowledge about students, curricula, materials and equipment, and themselves. Gregorc suggested that teachers who reach this stage and stop developing may reject new experiences, whereas others may progress to advanced stages. Teachers in the *maturing stage* had made a strong commitment to education, functioned beyond minimum expectations, and drew upon and contributed to the varied resources of the school. Teachers reconsidered instructional objectives and altered teaching techniques, materials, and attitudes about roles played in the educational process. They reexamined concepts about education, themselves, others, subject matter, and the environment. This period of reexamination can be stressful, yet it also can be exhilarating as new insights are gained. Teachers at the *fully functioning professional stage* had made a definite commitment to the education profession, were immersed in the process of education, and tried to realize their full potential as individual teachers and as contributing members of the profession. They constantly tested and restructured their concepts and beliefs.

Newman (1978/1979) interviewed 10 public school teachers who ranged in teaching experience from 19 to 31 years to obtain their perceptions of their career development. Several stages emerged from the teachers' experiences in this cross-sectional study in the dimensions of work history, graduate study, teaching, professional membership, and satisfaction. Newman used 10-year periods of time in teaching to discuss changes that the teachers reported. The first 10 years of teaching involved several changes in schools, levels, and subjects taught. Many women took breaks in service to raise families. Graduate study was done, and there was a reconsideration and reaffirmation of the decision to teach. The teachers were highly satisfied and had achieved a feeling of professional maturity. The second 10 years of teaching found most teachers settled in one school system, grade level, and subject. They experienced highs and lows in their satisfactions. Toward the end of the second 10 years of teaching, some felt themselves "getting into a rut" and changed schools and/or grade levels in an attempt to revitalize themselves. Several experienced a decline in satisfaction. The third 10 years of teaching brought a continuation of the stability in the work situation, but the teachers felt moderately dissatisfied. As they looked back over their careers, they realized they had become more personal in their relationships with students, more flexible in their dealings with student behavior, and less energetic. They were thoughtful and troubled as they faced the early retirement decision. The teachers saw their careers being significantly affected by contemporary history.

Peterson (1978/1979) used a structured interview with 50 retired secondary school teachers to find out how teachers' attitudes and outlooks changed throughout their careers. From the personal changes the teachers described, Peterson said the teaching career could be divided into three phases. The *first phase,* from the approximate age of 20 to 40, involved considerable shifts in commitment to teaching, job morale, and other outlooks. Teachers were in the process of establishing themselves in their careers, finding the optimal school environment, and were also deeply involved in their families. This period of ups and downs for teachers appeared to end when they found a school which gave them the chance to put down roots and begin a phase of professional commitment and growth. Teachers in the *second phase,* ages 40 to 55, seemed to be at their professional peak as they exhibited high morale and commitment to teaching. The *final phase,* from age 55 to retirement, was marked by withdrawal from the teaching profession as energy and enthusiasm faded. Teachers were able to maintain high job morale but were aware of the effects of biological aging.

Based on their experiences with teachers and teacher education, Yarger and Mertens (1980) described a continuum of career stages that teachers experience. These career stages were identified based on an analysis of working conditions that teachers meet throughout their career, including the need to be evaluated, credentialed, and tenured, and the need to adjust to new policies, procedures, and innovations in both teaching and organization.

Yarger and Mertens also provided a detailed description of inservice programming that would be appropriate to meet the needs at each professional stage. The *preeducation student* at stage 1 examines the teaching career but is not yet committed. The *education student* at stage 2, typically a college upperclassman, has made a conscious decision and commitment to become a teaching professional and develops basic teaching skills. In the first year of teaching, the *initial teacher* at stage 3 moves from the relative security of a training program to the demands of the teaching profession. Concerns about classroom discipline, further development of pedagogical skills, and receiving specific, immediate feedback characterize this stage. The *developing teacher* at stage 4, during the second and third year of teaching, still has initial teacher concerns but new concerns also emerge about content and "gaps" in their previous training. These teachers start to recognize that the teaching environment continually changes. The *practicing teacher* at stage 5 (3–8 years of experience) is more stable. At this stage they are apt to have completed requirements for advanced certification, tenure, and even advanced degrees. Content expertise is a high priority as well as preparation for a new professional role such as department chairperson, team leader, or administrator. At stage 6, teachers who had at least eight years of experience were labeled by Yarger and Mertens as *experienced teachers.* These teachers had already carved out their areas of particular strength and expertise and therefore had different needs for professional activities.

Katz (1972), based on her work with preschool teachers, proposed that there may be at least four developmental stages for the professional growth of teachers. As she described the characteristics of teachers, Katz also identified the type of training assistance that would be appropriate at each stage. Teachers may vary greatly in the length of time spent in each stage. Teachers in stage 1, the *survival stage,* are mainly concerned about surviving as they realize the discrepancy between their anticipated success and classroom realities. This stage may last throughout the first year of teaching, and teachers may feel inadequate and unprepared. On-site support and technical assistance would be appropriate at this stage. Teachers in stage 2, the *consolidation stage,* consolidate the gains made in the first stage, begin to focus on individual children, and differentiate specific tasks and skills to be mastered next. This stage may occur during the second year and continue into the third year. On-site assistance would be appropriate at this stage with access to specialists, and advice from colleagues, consultants, and advisors. Teachers in the *renewal stage,* stage 3, during the third or fourth year of teaching, may tire of doing the same things and want to look for innovations in the field. Training needs could be achieved through conferences, visits to demonstration projects, teachers' centers, journals, films, and critiques of their videotaped lessons. Katz suggested that some teachers may reach *maturity,* stage 4, within three years, whereas others need five years or more. Teachers come to terms with themselves as teachers and ask deeper and more abstract questions. Training needs at this stage are met by seminars, institutes, courses, degree programs, books, journals, and conferences.

Based on their experience working with teachers, Unruh and Turner (1970) suggested that there are four periods of professional growth for teachers: (a) the preservice period—preparation at the high school and college level; (b) the initial teaching period—1 to 5 or 6 years of service similar to the probationary period, though it may vary in length; (c) the security period—roughly 6 to 15 years of service, building upon the early years of service; and (d) the maturity period—a continuing increase in competence and effectiveness.

Unruh and Turner indicated that some teachers could remain in the initial teaching period for many years, while others progress rapidly toward the maturing period. Teachers in the initial teaching period often have problems with discipline, routine and organization, scoring and marking papers, and curriculum development, while trying to gain acceptance from the rest of the staff. Teachers in the security period find security in their convictions and commitments. In this period, teachers are also devoted to seeking excellence in instruction and often seek ways to improve their background and increase personal knowledge. Teachers in the maturing period usually exhibit considerable depth in most phases of the professional life and are likely to be highly competent and feel quite secure in the performance of the teaching duties. The attitude of the mature teacher permits change to be accepted as the dominant process of life rather than a threat. The teachers recognize and accept the concept that a teacher never "arrives."

McDonald (1982) suggested four stages in the professional development of a teacher: (a) *transition stage*—during which there is a low sense of efficacy; elemental teaching; learning about pupils; and learning basic skills of managing and organizing; (b) *exploring stage*—in which there is a sense of efficacy in using basic skills of teaching; manages instruction effectively; (c) *invention and experimenting stage*—when the teacher tries major strategies, invents new strategies and techniques, seeks opportunities for development, and is developing critical judgment; and (d) *professional teaching stage*—when the teacher has problem-solving skills and is able to teach other teachers to be creative.

Summaries of many of these reports concerning stages of teachers' careers are displayed in Tables 2 and 3.

Critique of Stage Models

Helpful summaries and critiques of teacher development literature were provided by Feiman and Floden (1980a, 1980b, 1981) and Floden and Feiman (1980, 1981a, 1981b). They identified three approaches to, or conceptions of, teacher development. The first, based largely on the work of Frances Fuller and her colleagues at the Research and Development Center for Teacher Education at the University of Texas at Austin, involves attempts to construct theories of teacher development. Based on the theory, training programs would use a diagnostic-prescriptive approach to match the intervention to the teacher's current concerns. The second approach involves efforts to apply existing cognitive developmental theories to teacher development. Training programs would be built around a disequilibrium model that seeks an optimal mismatch between the teacher's current and desired stage of development. The third approach contains descriptions of practices and efforts to justify them in developmental terms. Training programs would emphasize certain enabling conditions that support self-directed learning (Feiman & Floden, 1980a, 1980b).

Despite their differences, all three approaches emphasize certain aspects of teacher education generally underestimated in conventional programs and approaches. First, they acknowledge the reality of individual differences among preservice and inservice teachers and the necessity for more individualized training opportunities. Second, they focus on changes in teachers over time, which calls for interventions and support spread over time. Third, they take into account teachers' present needs and interests in developing appropriate interventions (Feiman & Floden, 1980a, p. 16).

TABLE 2 Preservice Teachers' Developmental Stages

Theorist	Fuller & Bown (1975)	Sacks & Harrington (1982)	Caruso (1977)	Yarger & Mertens (1980)
Stages	Preteaching concerns	Anxiety	Anxiety/euphoria	Preeducation student
	Early concerns about survival	Entry	Confusion/clarity	The education student
	Teaching situation concerns	Orientation	Competence/inadequacy	
	Concerns about pupils	Trial and error	Criticism/new awareness	
		Integration/consolidation	More confidence/greater inadequacy	
		Mastery	Loss/relief	

TABLE 3   Inservice Teachers' Developmental Stages

Theorist	Burden (1979/1980)	Gregorc (1973)	Peterson (1978/1979)	Katz (1972)	McDonald (1982)	Yarger & Mertens (1980)	Unruh & Turner (1970)
Stages	Survival stage	Becoming	First attitudinal phase (ages 20–40)	Survival	Transition stage	The initial teacher	Initial teaching
	Adjustment stage	Growing	Second phase (ages 40–55)	Consolidation	Exploring stage	The developing teacher	Security
	Mature stage	Maturing	Third phase (age 55–retirement)	Renewal	Invention and experimenting stage	The practicing teacher	Maturing
		The fully functioning professional		Maturity	Professional teaching stage	Experienced teachers	

Floden and Feiman (1981a, p. 6) noted that two types of descriptions are needed when explaining developmental theory for teacher change. The first is a description of the sequence of changes, leading up to the end state, and the second is a description of the process or mechanism by which change is brought about. They concluded that most developmental theories are weakest in the descriptions of the mechanism for change (Feiman & Floden, 1980b). Floden and Feiman (1980, p. 22) also found weaknesses in the defenses of the criteria for all three approaches to teacher development. They raised questions about weaknesses in developmental stage models and the lack of clarity in the descriptions. The implied relationship between higher developmental stages and more effective instruction was also questioned.

Floden and Feiman (1981a, pp. 18–24) identified a number of uses of a theory of teacher development while recognizing that there is no single approach to development. A theory of teacher change could indicate what should be done to reach goals in a teacher education program. The theory could provide a description of the changes individuals must go through and the mechanism by which change occurs. The theory also could be used by teacher educators when arranging instructional content and sequence.

PROMOTING DEVELOPMENTAL GROWTH

When designing programs to promote teacher development, it is important to recognize how adults learn, how they prefer to learn, and what they want to learn. Principles of adult learning must be considered as aspects of instruction are developed. Furthermore, it is important to be able to assess teacher development over time.

Adult Learning Principles

There are some generally accepted principles for facilitating adult learning, regardless of one's stage of development, that need to be considered in relation to promoting teacher development. These principles are based on the recognition that adults exhibit characteristics and learning needs significantly different from children's. According to Knowles (1978), these principles constitute "the foundation stones of modern adult learning theory":

1. Adults are motivated to learn as they experience needs and interests that learning will satisfy; therefore these needs and interests are appropriate starting points for organizing adult learning activities.
2. Adult orientation to learning is life-centered; therefore, the appropriate units for organizing adult learning are life situations, not subjects.

3. Experience is the richest source for adult learning; therefore, the core methodology of adult education is the analysis of experience.
4. Adults have a deep need to be self-directed; therefore, the role of the teacher is to engage in a process of inquiry with adult learners rather than to transmit knowledge to them and then evaluate their conformity to it.
5. Individual differences among people increase with age; therefore, adult education must make optimal provision for differences in style, time, place, and pace of learning. (p. 31)

Some of Knowles's statements should be qualified since teachers may vary in the degree of self-directedness, ability and desire to work collaboratively, and competence to deal with conceptual problems and universal principles as well as practical concerns. Furthermore, teachers' orientation for professional development should be centered on professional performance.

In a study for the Ontario Institute for Studies in Education, Brundage and MacKeracher (1980) identified 36 principles of learning with respect to adults. For example, adults are more concerned that what they study fits with their idealized self-concept than with standards and objectives set by others; unlike children, they want assistance and support, not pressure or demands, from instructors or other learners; and they learn best when their study is relevant to their experience and concerns. Factors such as stress, anxiety, and even physical aging also may affect an adult's ability to learn. A similar report, prepared by the Adult Learning Potential Institute (1980) at American University, provided an overview of training practices related to adult learning, including teacher training.

In a review of principles of adult learning, Wood and Thompson (1980) concluded that there is support for training programs to include both experiential learning and informal learning situations where social interaction can take place among learners. They described experiential learning—learning by doing—as including: (a) an initial limited orientation followed by participation activities in a real setting to experience and implement what is to be learned—the skill, concept, or strategy; (b) an examination and analysis of the experience in which learners identify the effects of their actions; (c) an opportunity to generalize and summarize when the learners develop their own principles and identify applications of those principles; and (d) an opportunity to return to try out their principles in the work setting and develop confidence in what is learned. Based on these concepts, Wood and Thompson then proposed guidelines for effective staff development for adult teachers.

Andrews, Houston, and Bryant (1981, p. 11) asserted that educational programs are not properly designed for adults and that adult learning principles are often not applied. The Adult Learning Potential Institute (1980, p. 10) emphasized that adult learners are consistently approached as a homogeneous group in which every member is expected to participate and respond in like fashion.

Aspects of Instruction

Hunt (1978) noted that the developmental level of a child, adolescent, or adult is not necessarily a permanent classification, but instead is a current preferred mode of functioning. Hunt further stated that one of the greatest challenges facing educators is to create programs designed to stimulate development to a higher mode of functioning.

Programs which have been proposed by educators to stimulate this development seem to have several common features including: (a) guiding teachers' reflection of their experience; (b) matching training programs to the teachers' skills and needs; (c) enabling teachers to anticipate further development; (d) providing a supportive yet challenging environment during instruction; (e) emphasizing the individual teacher rather than large group instruction; and (f) involving teachers in planning and direction.

Newman, Burden, and Applegate (1980) asserted that teachers' understandings and interpretations of their own development could be a positive influence on their further development. They proposed that programs could be designed to help teachers reflect on their development and to anticipate future developmental stages. A number of methods were suggested to meet these objectives. First, teachers could examine their own careers—through activities such as writing autobiographies, charting one's career in terms of stages or experiences, and making a comparison of present and past attitudes and behaviors. Second, teachers could view other teachers' careers—through activities such as befriending an experienced teacher and reading about other teachers' experiences and teacher career development. Third, teachers could compare personal and professional development—including reading about stages of adult lives and considering lifelong learning needs.

Watts (1982) used staff development programs occurring in teacher centers as the context for discussing some of Kohlberg's suggestions for promoting developmental growth. These included association with ideas or people whose thinking is slightly ahead of one's own; practical experience; and the opportunity to reflect on one's own experience, talk it over, and develop greater understanding and new insights.

Feiman and Floden (1981, pp. 27–28) suggested that helping teachers reflect on their experiences and providing support during times of change may be effective practices in promoting development, regardless of the developmental status of the learner. They further suggested that it makes sense to pay attention to what teachers are motivated to learn when determining the appropriate starting point for learning.

Devaney (1977) identified four conditions that summarize what practitioners believe teachers need in order to develop and what teachers' centers try to provide—warmth, concreteness, time, and thought. Warmth means a responsive, nonjudgmental setting that promotes sharing, a sense of community, and support for the risks of change. Concreteness refers to the hands-on, real-life curricular material that teachers explore and construct in center workshops. Thought means increased understanding of children and the subject matter that is required for curricular decision making. Development takes time, and teachers' centers structure activities to give teachers time to discover their own needs and their students' needs.

Kelly and DeMarte (1981) investigated the effects of reflective writing on the personal and professional development of inservice teachers. While the changes in professional development on most scales were not statistically significant, Kelly and DeMarte concluded that the reflective writing had helped create a supportive environment for development. After reviewing their own research and the literature on reflective writing, they asserted that those responsible for staff development, teacher education, and supervisory functions must be trained in ways of establishing supportive, challenging environments to promote teachers' developmental growth.

Cognitive Complexity. After reviewing developmental stage theory, Willie and Howey (1980, p. 30) concluded that teacher edcuation should focus on instructional designs to promote more psychological growth in terms of increased cognitive complexity.

Sprinthall and Thies-Sprinthall (1980a) examined how adult development theory could be used to help prepare adults for new roles as teachers. They concluded that behavior modification, skills training, and academic acquisition training models each appear to be inadequate, single-variable solutions to complex training needs for trying to promote development. They further indicated that training programs should focus on the teachers' cognitive development. This training approach is based on Dewey's contention that a central goal of education is to promote developmental growth, with psychological maturity as a primary indicator of this development. Developmentally mature humans can perform the requisite complex tasks of adulthood, whereas less mature, less complex adults process experience and behave less adequately. Sprinthall and Thies-Sprinthall strongly urged tryouts of a developmental instructional model for adults, even though all the answers are not yet in from basic research. Tryouts or field-based experiments are themselves basic research. Interaction of theory and practice were suggested to go hand-in-hand.

Based on their review of the developmental literature, Sprinthall and Thies-Sprinthall (1983b, pp. 27–31) identified and discussed elements of training programs that are designed to stimulate developmental stage growth. The elements of the training programs for preservice and inservice teachers were: (a) *role-taking experiences*—requiring direct and active experience in a variety of professional roles (such as cross-role teaching and internships); (b) *qualitative role taking*—matching the level of complexity in the role to the level of development in the students; (c) *guided reflection*—teaching how to ask questions and examine one's experience from a variety of views through structured learning; (d) *guided integration*—providing a balance between real experience and discussion/reflection/teaching; (e) *continuity*—arranging for continuous programs that extend over at least a 1-year period; (f) *personal support and challenge*—providing for both support and challenge during instruction; and (g) *assessment level*—identifying an individual's level of development through a variety of test instruments.

Matching Training Models. Teachers at different stages in their careers have different skills, concerns, and needs and may operate at different conceptual levels which would affect what they learn in training programs. Therefore, matching training programs to individual developmental needs and specific learning styles has been proposed by a number of educators (e.g., Burden & Wallace, 1983; Christensen, Burke, & Fessler, 1983; Joyce, 1980; Krupp, 1981; Wilsey & Killion, 1982; Yarger & Mertens, 1980). Based on their research with adult teachers, Hunt (1971) and Hunt and Sullivan (1974) proposed a matching model to facilitate adult learning and enhance developmental growth. They demonstrated that less developmentally mature individuals—those at more concrete levels—profit most from highly structured training environments. More developmentally mature individuals at more abstract levels can profit from either highly or lowly structured environments. Bents and Howey (1981, pp. 21–27), drawing upon Santmire, considered the theoretical treatment of matching teachers' conceptual level to training programs and translated that in terms of the kinds of orientations found in teachers' day-to-day experience. Drawing from Joyce (1980) and Bents and Howey (1981), Wilsey and Killion (1982) identified four distinct stages of adult development and provided a detailed description of the training environment appropriate at each stage.

For each of the six stages they identified in a teacher's career, Yarger and Mertens (1980) described the training programs in terms of appropriate content and delivery. They further recommended a model for integrating stages of teachers' careers, program agenda types (content), and program development issues (authority, credibility, finance, and governance) in teacher education.

In a similar way, Burden and Wallace (1983) proposed a 3-dimensional model for teacher training in staff development programs which integrates teachers' developmental stages with different types of content and different delivery approaches. In the model, the plane for teachers' developmental stages represents stages through which teachers might advance (i.e., from an early survival stage to an advanced mature stage, or from a low to a high conceptual level). The content plane represents the content that would be offered in staff development programs (e.g., programs on microcomputers, gifted students, or classroom management). The plane for the delivery mode represents the type of supervisory or administrative approach that would be used in delivering the staff development program. This approach might range from a directive to a collaborative to a nondirective supervisory or administrative style. In an effort to be responsive to the various instructional preferences of teachers at different developmental levels, Burden and Wallace recommended that programs be offered with a variety of delivery modes so that teachers could select the type of delivery mode that was best suited to them.

After reviewing the literature on teacher career development, Watts (1980) described three stages of teacher development. The survival or beginning stage was characterized by the teacher struggling with problems of personal and professional competence. Teachers in the middle stage showed an increased sense of comfort and shifted toward more child-centered activities. In the mastery stage, they functioned smoothly within the context of the school and his/her own experience. Watts stated that the teacher center experience indicated that the formal and traditional forms of inservice programs decreased in value as teachers increased in mastery. Workshops and how-to courses were valuable to most first and second stage teachers but helpful only occasionally for third-stage teachers.

Techniques for Determining Teachers' Stages of Development

In the effort to match the complexity or the content of an instructional program to the teacher, it is important to first determine the teacher's stage of development. Sprinthall and Thies-Sprinthall (1980a, p. 48) indicated that indices of psychological development should form an important core of the selection procedure. They suggested that assessment might range from very informal measures such as open-ended question interviews, as proposed by Hunt and Perry, to formal measures such as Hunt's Conceptual Levels test, Loevinger's Ego Development test, or Kohlberg's Moral Judgment test.

McNergney and Carrier (1981, pp. 154–176) also proposed using both informal and formal assessment of teacher characteristics and provided a detailed review of the measuring instruments that had been developed by others. Brief descriptions of the instruments they reviewed are listed.

1. Embedded Figures Test—measures field dependence, involves the identification of simple geometric figures which are embedded within complex figures.
2. Paragraph Completion Test—measures conceptual level; involves the completion of 6 open-ended topic stems.
3. Washington University Sentence Completion Test—measures ego development; involves the completion of 36 sentence completion items.
4. Defining Issues Test—measures moral judgment development; involves 6 stories and the multiple-choice rating and ranking of responses in relation to the stories.

5. Minnesota Teacher Attitude Inventory—measures attitudes which predict how well teachers will get along with pupils and the degree of satisfaction with teaching as a vocation; involves the completion of 150 items with a 5-point rating scale.
6. Teacher Preference Scale—measures an individual's unconscious motivations for teaching; involves the completion of 200 items with a 6-point rating scale.
7. Manifest Anxiety Scale—measures anxiety; involves the true or false rating of 50 anxiety-related items.
8. Teaching Anxiety Scale—measures anxiety directly related to teaching; involves the completion of 29 items with a 5-point rating scale.
9. Stages of Concern About an Innovation Questionnaire—measures teachers' concerns about change; involves the completion of 35 items on an 8-point rating scale.
10. Role Construct Repertory Test—measures the complexity of an individual's system for describing other people; involves the identification and comparison of people in 12 different roles.

In assessing inservice teachers' developmental growth, Kelly and DeMarte (1981) used the Loevinger Sentence Completion Test, Hunt's Conceptual Systems test, and George's (1974) Teacher Concern Checklist.

Another method of gathering development-related information is through the analysis of questions received at teacher centers. Apelman, cited in Feiman and Floden (1980b), observed that teacher developmental stages are reflected in the type of requests for curriculum aid: first, for immediate, practical help; second, for how-to-use aid when exposed to new curricular materials; and third, self-initiated questions for aid in curriculum development and enhancement.

Based on a review of literature (Christensen, Burke, & Fessler, 1983) of adult development, teacher development, and inservice education, Burke, Fessler, and Christensen (1983) developed a 60-item instrument to identify stages of teacher growth. The next phase of their research is to test the importance of items or categories in the instrument to individuals in certain career stages. With reliable measures of teachers' professional development, Burke et al. suggested that planners of staff development programs could begin to individualize such programs.

IMPLICATIONS OF THE CAREER STAGE MODEL

Developmental stage theory of teacher growth appears to hold promise for (a) improving preservice teacher education programs; (b) improving staff development programs; (c) improving the supervision of teachers; (d) providing a longitudinal framework for teachers when making decisions about their careers; (e) helping in institutional planning; and (f) providing the basis for making decisions about differentiated staffing plans or career ladder plans for teachers.

Preservice Programs

Information on teacher career development could be used to improve preservice teacher education programs by (a) serving as the basis for revising instructional content and learning experiences to better meet preservice teachers' developmental needs and to promote further growth; and (b) providing preservice teachers with information on how teachers change throughout their careers.

Revising Instructional Content and Procedures. Preservice teachers go through several stages of development in the process of becoming a teacher (e.g., Caruso, 1977; Fuller & Bown, 1975; Sacks & Harrington, 1982). Fuller and Bown (1975) suggested that teacher educators could use this developmental information to select appropriate training content and learning experiences for preservice teachers at a given developmental stage to meet their current needs and to promote further development.

Since research on teacher career development provides details about the unique needs and problems of first-year teachers, teacher educators could revise content to better prepare preservice teachers to meet these needs (Burden, 1982–1983). For instance, more emphasis could be placed on topics such as classroom management, discipline, time management, and evaluation and record keeping. In a review of the stages and problems of teacher development, Cruickshank and Callahan (1983) indicated that novices can be helped to make the transition from students to teachers. Cruickshank and Callahan further suggested that preservice teachers "can anticipate and cope successfully with the stages of teacher development and with the problems of practice, thus achieving personal satisfaction as well as student achievement and satisfaction" (p. 257).

Sprinthall and Thies-Sprinthall (1983a, pp. 93–94) proposed a theoretical framework for educating teachers using a cognitive-developmental perspective. They suggested that a series of differentiated learning environments and different supervision techniques be applied to groups of student teachers according to their entry developmental level. The initial training stage would represent the individual's current preferred style. Matching the general instruction (content and process) to the initial training level would be nothing more than Dewey's original dictum of starting where the learner is. Readings, homework assignments, and even examinations could represent different developmental levels and could be selected to be congruent with the developmental level of the student. With careful assessment through formative evaluation, the preservice training program could continually be refined.

Including Content on Teacher Career Development. There are several advantages for including content in preservice programs on how teachers change thoughout their careers. First, preservice teachers would have more information about teachers and the teaching career on which to base a career decision. With this additional information on teacher career development, some preservice teachers may choose to switch majors before finishing their college training. Those who continue in the teacher education program would presumably be more certain of their career selection and have more commitment. The dropout rate in the early years of service would likely be lower. Second, detailed information on teacher career development would present preservice teachers with a realistic view of various aspects of the job and the teaching career, consequently helping to minimize the disequilibrium that many first-year teachers experience. Third, this career development information would provide a foundation for the preservice teacher's self-assessment of professional skills. Areas of weakness would be identified and corrected before entering the public classroom.

To obtain this information on teacher career development, preservice teachers could conduct interviews with experienced teachers, and readings could be assigned to help students recognize changes that teachers experience throughout their careers (Burden, 1983a). Readings might include career descriptions written by teachers themselves, research reports, or brief career descriptions on teacher development. Sources for the readings could include authors such as Fuller and Bown, Burden, Gregorc, Newman, Katz, Yarger and Mertens, Ryan and others, Loevinger, Hunt, and Perry.

Staff Development Programs

The premise that the stages of teacher development are important in planning effective professional development programs is well accepted in the literature (e.g., Andrews et al., 1981; Bents & Howey, 1981; Brundage & Mackeracher, 1980; Burden, 1982; Hall & Loucks, 1978). In these reports, there are many similarities in the recommendations to match staff development content and delivery modes to the teachers' stage of development. In general, teachers in the early stages need much assistance with the technical skills of teaching and would benefit most from a highly structured, directive staff development program. Practical information and applications would be most useful. Teachers who are a little more advanced developmentally would seek information to add variety in their teaching and would prefer a collaborative approach to staff development and supervision. Teachers at the highest developmental levels would focus on more complex and crosscutting concerns and would prefer more team types of arrangements and staff development programs that are nondirective. Tailoring staff development programs to individual developmental needs and specific learning styles has the potential for making teachers more effective (Bents & Howey, 1981, p. 20).

Applications of the "conceptual systems" theory as described by Bents and Howey (1980), Joyce (1980), and Wilsey and Killion (1982) provide useful guidelines for matching learning environments in staff development programs to teachers at different developmental stages. Krupp's (1981) handbook on adult development also provides useful guidelines for designing staff development programs based on the stages of adult's lives.

In an effort to provide optimal environments for teacher growth, Yarger and Mertens (1980) described teachers' career stages with matching content and program types for training.

Supervision of Teachers

One responsibility of school administrators and supervisors is to help classroom teachers improve their instruction and facilitate their development. With knowledge of teacher career development, supervisors could provide different types of supervisory assistance and vary their supervisory strategies with teachers at different developmental levels.

After examining teacher development studies, Glickman (1981) suggested developmental supervision as a means for helping teachers at various points in their careers. He proposed three orientations to the supervision of teachers, each with differing degrees of teacher and supervisor responsibility when meeting the objectives of the supervision. First, with the directive approach, the supervisor assumes a high degree of responsibility when delineating standards. Definite, immediate, and concrete assistance is provided when the supervisor demonstrates, clarifies, directs, and reinforces teacher behaviors. Second, the collaborative approach includes supervisory behaviors such as listening, presenting, problem solving, and negotiating. The end result would be a mutually agreed upon contract by supervisor and teacher that would delincate the structure, process, and criteria for subsequent instructional improvement. Third, the nondirective approach rests on the premise that teachers are capable of analyzing and solving their own instructional problems. The supervisor helps channel the teacher toward self-discovery.

Supervisors can assess an individual teacher using the two variables of *level of teacher commitment* (drawing largely from the literature on adult development and teacher career development) and *level of abstraction* (based largely on cognitive development theory) (Glickman, 1981, p. 47). The assessment is accomplished by a simple paradigm with two intersecting lines, one for the line of commitment and one for the line of abstraction. Then the teacher can be matched to the supervisory approach most suited to that teacher, using the paradigm.

Since many teachers' changes in job skills, knowledge behaviors, attitudes, and concerns appear to follow a developmental sequence, I have suggested using one developmental line representing stages of teacher career development to be used for assessment in developmental supervision rather than the two intersecting lines proposed by Glickman (Burden, 1982). Using three stages of teacher career development (Burden, 1980b), I proposed that teachers at stage 1, concerned with self-adequacy, might profit most from a directive supervisory approach which would include modeling, directing, and measuring by the supervisor. Teachers at stage 2, concerned with improving the learning environment for their students, might be approached using the collaborative supervisory model which would include presenting, interacting, and contracting by the supervisor. Teachers at stage 3, concerned with helping other students and teachers, may need only the minimal influence of a nondirective supervisory approach where the supervisor would listen, clarify, and encourage (Burden, 1982).

Teachers' Career Decisions

Knowledge of teacher career development can help teachers recognize where they are in terms of their development and serve as a basis for making professional growth plans.

Information on teacher career development provides a reference point for teachers to compare their development to that of other teachers. Field (1979) stated that her descriptions of teachers' career stages were "meant to provoke a sense of community for the teacher who often feels so very much alone" (p. 2). First-year teachers, for instance, may feel that they are the only ones experiencing problems with planning, discipine, or time management. They may feel more at ease by knowing that the problems they experience are common for first-year teachers, that they will develop and refine their teaching skills, and that the initial problems will be overcome.

Teachers can be aware of and anticipate changes they might experience with a knowledge of teacher career development. Field (1979) described the stages in the teaching career as a continuum for identifying where one is and where one is going. Taking it one step further, Gregorc (1979) said this career perspective could be used in professional development goal setting.

The concept of career stages can help teachers think more clearly not only about what they should be doing and learning at their current level of development but also about what they should do if they want to continue their development.

Institutional Planning

School districts could use information on teacher career development to aid in planning a differentiated program for assisting teachers in their professional development. To meet teachers' needs and learning styles at different points in their careers, these programs should include a variety of topics and be conducted in learning environments ranging from high to low structure. Planning for financial support for professional development programs would be simplified when details of the programs have been identified.

Differentiated Staffing and Career Ladders

Because of limitations in salary, status, gains, recognition, job responsibilities, and growth possibilities, many competent and knowledgeable teachers leave teaching and go into administration or other occupations. In an effort to address these issues and promote teacher retention, differentiated staffing plans (Dempsey & Smith, 1972; English & Sharpes, 1972), and career ladder plans have been proposed which provide promotion opportunities for teachers. These plans provide a variety of stages in the teaching career with different duties and possibly different pay at each stage. As teachers climb the career ladder, they may become eligible to become involved in curriculum development, staff development, and departmental leadership. Information on teachers' developmental needs and abilities could be used to aid school districts in determining criteria and duties for each step of the career ladder.

A RESEARCH AGENDA

Additional research could be conducted to define and clarify many aspects of teacher development. Research strategies should be selected carefully to meet the objectives of the investigations, and researchers should publish results to add to the data base in this area.

Research Topics

One desirable result of the investigation of teacher development would be increased efforts to promote teacher development. With that objective in mind, research efforts should focus on (a) changes with teachers experience, and (b) ways teacher development could be promoted.

Changes That Teachers Experience. There are many possible areas of investigation that would help define and clarify teachers' changes. Some of the most useful topics include:

1. Changes in teachers' cognitive, conceptual, ego, moral, and ethical development.
2. Changes in teachers' professional behaviors, attitudes, and job events.

3. Effects of personal and professional changes on teacher behavior and teacher effectiveness.
4. Effects of reassignment or relocation to new schools on teacher development.
5. Differences in development for elementary, middle school, junior high, and high school teachers; men and women teachers; and teachers of different ethnic and cultural backgrounds.
6. Relationships between teachers' developmental characteristics and student otucomes.
7. A comparison between the developmental and career patterns for those who quit teaching compared to those who continue teaching.
8. Relationships between adult development and teacher development.

Ways to Promote Teacher Development. Teacher development may be positively influenced in a variety of ways. Some useful areas for research include the following items.

1. The content, instructional approach, and timing of training programs for preservice and inservice teachers.
2. Effects of supervision on teacher development.
3. Effects of various incentives and rewards on development.

Research Approaches

A multifaceted research approach is needed for examining teacher development. The ultimate aim of *hypothesis-generating* research designs (often using ethnographic and qualitative approaches) is to seek meaning and to generate hypotheses. *Hypothesis-testing* research designs (often using experimental, quasiexperimental, correlational, or survey methods) are used to test the truthfulness or accuracy of predetermined hypotheses. These two approaches help answer different types of questions and serve different purposes. In terms of teacher development, the use of hypothesis-generating designs can lead to descriptions and hypotheses of teachers' developmental characteristics and influences. Further testing could be conducted with hypothesis-testing research designs (Burden, 1983b).

SUMMARY

While recognizing that adult development and teacher development are not fully articulated concepts, teachers' personal and professional characteristics were described in this chapter. Accepting the premise that teachers are different in some important ways is a prerequisite to supporting their development differentially. A number of strategies were discussed to promote teacher development, but it is clear that much work needs to be done before a fully articulated education program for teacher development will be ready for implementation. Training programs should have continual, developmental evaluation. There needs to be clarification of the nature of teacher changes and the process by which this change is brought about.

REFERENCES

Adams, R. D. (1982, March). *Teacher development: A look at changes in teacher perceptions across time.* Paper presented at the meeting of the American Educational Research Association, New York.

Adams, R. D., Hutchinson, S., & Martray, C. (1980, April). *A developmental study of teacher concerns across time.* Paper presented at the meeting of the American Educational Research Association, Boston, MA.

Adult Learning Potential Institute (1980). *Overview of training practices incorporating adult learning: Adult learning in inservice training and staff development.* Washington, DC: Author. (ERIC Document Reproduction Service No. ED 198 365)

Andrews, T. E., Houston, W. R., & Bryant, B. L. (1981). *Adult learners (A research study).* Washington, DC: Association of Teacher Educators.

Baltes, P. B., & Goulet, L. R. (1970). Status and issues of a life-span developmental psychology. In L. R. Goulet & P. B. Baltes (Eds.), *Life-span developmental psychology: Research and theory.* New York: Academic Press.

Bents, H. R., & Howey, K. R. (1981). Staff development—Change in the individual. In B. Dillon-Peterson (Ed.), *Staff development/Organizational development.* Alexandria, VA: Association for Supervision and Curriculum Development.

Briscoe, F. G. (1973). The professional concerns of first year secondary teachers in selected Michigan public schools: A pilot study (Doctoral dissertation, Michigan State University, 1972). *Dissertation Abstracts International, 33,* 4786A.

Brundage, D. H., & MacKeracher, D. (1980). *Adult learning principles and their applications to program planning.* Toronto: The Ontario Institute for Studies in Education. (ERIC Document Reproduction Service No. ED 181 292)

Burden, P. R. (1980a). Teachers' perceptions of the characteristics and influences on their personal and professional development (Doctoral dissertation, The Ohio State University, 1979). *Dissertation Abstracts International, 40,* 5404A.

Burden, P. R. (1980b). *Teachers' perceptions of the characteristics and influences on their personal and professional development.* Manhattan, KS: Author. (ERIC Document Reproduction Service No. ED 198 087)

Burden, P. R. (1982, February). *Developmental supervision: Reducing teacher stress in different career stages.* Paper presented at the meeting of the Association of Teacher Educators, Phoenix, AR. (ERIC Document Reproduction Service No. ED 281 267)

Burden, P. R. (1982–1983, Winter). Implications of teacher career development: New roles for teachers, administrators, and professors. *Action in Teacher Education, 4,* (4), 21–25.

Burden, P. R. (1983a). Confidence in career choice: Preservice teachers interview experienced teachers. *The Teacher Educator, 18* (4), 19–23.

Burden, P. R. (1983b). Research designs used to examine teacher development. *College Student Journal, 17* (2), 116–120.

Burden, P. R., & Wallace, D. (1983, October). *Tailoring staff development to meet teachers' needs.* Paper presented at the Association of Teacher Educators Mini-Clinic, Wichita, KS. (ERIC Document Reproduction Service No. ED 237 506)

Burke, P. J., Fessler, R., & Christensen, J. (1983, April). *Teacher life-span development: An instrument to identify stages of teacher growth.* Paper presented at the meeting of the American Educational Research Association, Montreal.

Caruso, J. J. (1977). Phases in student teaching. *Young Children, 33,* 57–63.

Charlesworth, W. R. (1972). Developmental psychology: Does it offer anything distinctive? In W. R. Looft (Ed.), *Developmental psychology: A book of readings.* Hinsdale, IL: Dryden Press.

Chickering, A. W. (1976). Developmental change as a major outcome. In M. Keeton, and Associates (Eds.), *Experiential learning: Rationale, characteristics, and assessment.* San Francisco, CA: Jossey-Bass.

Christensen, J., Burke, P., & Fessler, R. (1983, April). *Teacher life-span development: A summary and synthesis of the literature.* Paper presented at the meeting of the American Educational Research Association, Montreal.

Cruickshank, D. R., & Callahan, R. (1983). The other side of the desk: Stages and problems of teacher development. *The Elementary School Journal, 83* (3), 251–258.

Dempsey, R. A., & Smith, R. P., Jr. (1972). *Differentiated staffing.* Englewood Cliffs, NJ: Prentice Hall.

Devaney, K. (1977). Warmth, concreteness, time, and thought in teachers' learning. In K. Devaney (Ed.), *Essays on teachers' centers.* San Francisco, CA: Teachers' Center Exchange, Far West Laboratory for Educational Research and Development.

English, F. W., & Sharpes, D. K. (1972). *Strategies for differentiated staffing.* Berkeley, CA: McCutchan.

Erikson, E. H. (1959). *Identity and the life cycle.* New York: International Universities Press.

Erikson, E. H. (1963). *Childhood and society* (2nd ed.). New York: Norton.

Feiman, S., & Floden, R. E. (1980a, April). *Approaches to staff development from conceptions of teacher development.* Paper presented at the meeting of the American Educational Research Association, Boston, MA.

Feiman, S., & Floden, R. E. (1980b). *What's all this talk about teacher development?* (Research Series No. 70). East Lansing, MI: Institute for Research on Teaching, Michigan State University. (ERIC Document Reproduction Service No. ED 189 088)

Feiman, S., & Floden, R. E. (1981). *A consumer's guide to teacher development* (Research Series No. 94). East Lansing, MI: Institute for Research on Teaching, Michigan State University. (ERIC Document Reproduction Service No. ED 207 970)

Field, K. (1979). *Teacher development: A study of the stages in development of teachers.* Brookline, MA: Brookline Teacher Center.

Floden, R. E., & Feiman, S. (1980, April). *Basing effectiveness criteria on theories of teacher development.* Paper presented at the meeting of the American Educational Research Association, Boston, MA.

Floden, R. E., & Feiman, S. (1981a). *A developmental approach to the study of teacher change: What's to be gained?* (Research Series No. 93). East Lansing, MI: Institute for Research on Teaching, Michigan State University.

Floden, R. E., & Feiman, S. (1981b). *Problems of equity in developmental approaches* (Research Series No. 91). East Lansing, MI: Institute for Research on Teaching, Michigan State University.

Fuller, F. F. (1969). Concerns of teachers: A developmental conceptualization. *American Educational Research Journal, 6,* 207–226.

Fuller, F. F., & Bown, O. H. (1975). Becoming a teacher. In K. Ryan (Ed.), *Teacher education,* the *Seventy-fourth yearbook of the National Society for the Study of Education* Pt 2. Chicago, IL: University of Chicago Press.

Fuller, F. F., Parsons, J. S., & Watkins, J. E. (1973). *Concerns of teachers: Research and reconceptualization.* Austin, TX: Research and Development Center for Teacher Education, University of Texas.

George, A. (1974). *Analysis of five hypothesized factors on the teacher concerns checklist, form B.* Austin, TX: Research and Development Center for Teacher Education, University of Texas.

George, A. (1978). *Measuring self, task, and impact concerns: A manual for the use of the teacher concerns questionnaire.* Austin: TX: Research and Development Center for Teacher Education, University of Texas.

Glickman, C. D. (1981). *Developmental supervision: Alternative practices for helping teachers.* Alexandria, VA: Association for Supervision and Curriculum Development.

Gordon, M. (1976, April). *Choice of rule-example order used to teach mathematics as a function of conceptual level and field dependence-independence.* Paper presented at the meeting of the American Educational Research Association, San Francisco, CA.

Gould, R. (1972). The phases of adult life: A study in developmental psychology. *American Journal of Psychiatry, 129,* 521–531.

Gould, R. (1978). *Transformations.* New York: Simon & Schuster.

Gregorc, A. F. (1973). Developing plans for professional growth. *NASSP Bulletin, 57,* 1–8.

Hall, G. E., & Loucks, S. F. (1978). Teacher concerns as a basis for facilitating and personalizing staff development. *Teachers College Record, 80,* 36–53.

Harvey, O. J. (1966). *Experience structure and adaptability.* New York: Springer.

Harvey, O. J. (1967). Conceptual systems and attitude change. In C. W. Sherif & M. Sherif (Eds.), *Attitude, ego-involvement, and change.* New York: Wiley.

Harvey, O. J. (1970, December). Beliefs and behavior: Some implications for education. *The Science Teacher, 37,* 10–14, 73.

Harvey, O. J., Hunt, D. E., & Schroeder, H. (1961). *Conceptual systems and personality organization.* New York: Wiley.

Harvey, O. J., Prather, M., White, B., & Hoffmeister, J. (1968, March). Teachers' beliefs, classroom atmosphere, and student behavior. *American Educational Research Journal, 5,* 151–166.

Hunt, D. E. (1966). A model for analyzing the training of training agents. *Merrill-Palmer Quarterly of Behavior and Development, 12,* 137–156.

Hunt, D. E. (1971). *Matching models in education.* Toronto: Ontario Institute for Studies in Education.

Hunt, D. E. (1975, Spring). Person-environment interaction: A challenge found wanting before it was tried. *Review of Educational Research, 45,* 209–230.

Hunt, D. E. (1978). In-service training for persons in training. *Theory Into Practice, 17,* 239–244.

Hunt, D. E., Joyce, B. R. (1967). Teacher trainee personality and initial teaching style. *American Educational Research Journal, 4,* 253–259.

Hunt, D. E., Joyce, B. R., Greenwood, J. A., Noy, J. E., Reid, R., & Weil, M. (1974). Student conceptual levels and models of training: Theoretical and empirical coordination of two models. *Interchange, 53,* 19–30.

Hunt, D. E., & Sullivan, E. V. (1974). *Between psychology and education.* Hinsdale, IL: Dryden.

Iannaccone, L. (1963). Student teaching: A transition stage in the making of a teacher. *Theory Into Practice, 2,* 73–81.

Joyce, B. R. (1980). Learning how to learn. *Theory Into Practice, 19,* 15–27.

Joyce, B. R., Weil, M., & Wald, R. (1973). The teacher-innovator: Models of teaching as the core of teacher education. *Interchange, 4,* 47–59.

Katz, L. G. (1972). Developmental stages of preschool teachers. *Elementary School Journal, 73,* 50–54.

Kelly, M. K., & DeMarte, P. J. (1981). *Reflective writing—An effective look for the professional and personal development of teachers.* Paper presented at the meeting of the American Educational Research Association, Los Angeles, CA.

Knowles, M. S. (1978). *The adult learner: A neglected species.* Houston, TX: Gulf.

Kohlberg, L. (1969). Stage and sequence: The cognitive developmental approach to socialization. In D. Croslin (Ed.), *Handbook of Socialization Theory and Research.* New York: Rand-McNally.

Kohlberg, L. (1973). Continuities in childhood and adult moral development revisited. In P. B. Baltes & K. W. Schaie (Eds.), *Life-span developmental psychology: Personality and socialization.* New York: Academic Press.

Krupp, J. A. (1981). *Adult development: Implications for staff development.* Manchester, CT: Author. 40 McDivett Drive.

Levinson, D. J., Darrow, C. N., Klein, E. B., Levinson, M. H., & McKee, B. (1978). *The seasons of a man's life.* New York: Knopf.

Loevinger, J. (1966). The meaning and measurement of ego development. *American Psychologist, 21,* 195–206.

McDonald, F. J. (1982, March). *A theory of the professional development of teachers.* Paper presented at the meeting of the American Educational Research Association, New York.

McLachlan, J. F. C., & Hunt, D. E. (1973). Differential effects of discovery learning as a function of student conceptual level. *Canadian Journal of Behavioral Science, 5,* 152–160.

McNergney, R. F., & Carrier, C. A. (1981). *Teacher development.* New York: Macmillan.

Newman, K. K. (1979). Middle-aged experienced teachers' perceptions of their career development (Doctoral dissertation, The Ohio State University, 1978). *Dissertation Abstracts International, 39,* 4885A.

Newman, K. K., Burden, P. R., & Applegate, J. H. (1980). Helping teachers examine their long-range development. *The Teacher Educator, 15* (4), 7–14.

Oja, S. N. (1980). Adult development is implicit in staff development. *Journal of Staff Development, 1,* (2), 7–56.

Pataniczek, D. (1979). A descriptive study of the concerns of first year teachers who are graduates of the secondary pilot program at Michigan State University (Doctoral dissertation, Michigan State University, 1978). *Dissertation Abstracts International, 39,* 5916A.

Perry, W. (1970). *Forms of intellectual and ethical development during the college years.* New York: Holt, Rinehart, & Winston.

Peterson, A. R. (1979). Career patterns of secondary school teachers: An exploratory interview study of retired teachers (Doctoral dissertation, The Ohio State University, 1978). *Dissertation Abstracts International, 39,* 4888A.

Piaget, J. (1963). *Psychology of intelligence.* Paterson, NJ: Littlefield Adams.

Ryan, K., Newman, K. K., Mager, G., Applegate, J. H., Lasley, T., Flora, V. R., & Johnston, J. (1980). *Biting the apple: Accounts of first-year teachers.* New York: Longman.

Sacks, S. R., & Harrington, G. N. (1982, March). *Student to teacher: The process of role transition.* Paper presented at the meeting of the American Educational Research Association, New York.

Sheehy, G. (1976). *Passages: Predictable crises of adult life.* New York: Dutton.

Sitter, J. P., & Lanier, P. E. (1982, March). *Student teaching: A stage in the development of a teacher or a period of consolidation?* Paper presented at the meeting of the American Educational Research Association, New York.

Sprinthall, N. A., & Thies-Sprinthall, L. (1980a). Adult development and leadership training for mainstream education. In D. C. Corrigan & K. R. Howey (Eds.), *Concepts to guide the education of experienced teachers.* Reston, VA: Council for Exceptional Children.

Sprinthall, N. A., & Thies-Sprinthall, L. (1980b). Educating for teacher growth: A cognitive developmental perspective. *Theory Into Practice, 19* (4), 278–286.

Sprinthall, N. A., & Thies-Sprinthall, L. (1983a). The need for theoretical frameworks in educating teachers: A cognitive-developmental perspective. In K. R. Howey & W. F. Gardner (Eds.), *The education of teachers.* New York: Longman.

Sprinthall, N. A., & Thies-Sprinthall, L. (1983b). The teacher as an adult learner: A cognitive-developmental view. In G. A. Griffin (Ed.), *Staff development,* the *Eighty-second yearbook of the National Society for the Study of Education* Pt 2. Chicago, IL: The University of Chicago Press.

Suedfeld, P. (1974). Attitude manipulation in restricted environments: Conceptual structure and response to propaganda. *Journal of Abnormal and Social Psychology, 68,* 242–247.

Tomlinson, P. D., & Hunt, D. E. (1971). Differential effects of rule-example order as a function of learner conceptual level. *Canadian Journal of Behavioral Science, 3,* 237–245.

Unruh, A., & Turner, H. E. (1970). *Supervision for change and innovation.* Boston, MA: Houghton Mifflin.

Watts, H. (1980). *Starting out, moving on, running ahead, or how the teachers' center can attend to stages in teacher's development.* San Francisco, CA: Far West Laboratory for Educational Research and Development. (ERIC Document Reproduction Service No. ED 200 604)

Watts, H. (1982). Observations on stages in teacher development. *MATE Viewpoints, 4,* 4–8.

Willie, R., & Howey, K. R. (1980). Reflections on adult development: Implications for inservice teacher education. In W. R. Houston & R. Pankratz (Eds.), *Staff development and educational change.* Reston, VA: Association of Teacher Educators.

Wilsey, C., & Killion, J. (1982). Making staff development programs work. *Educational Leadership, 40,* 36–38, 43.

Wolfe, R. (1963). The role of conceptual systems in cognitive functioning at varying levels of age and intelligence. *Journal of Personality, 31,* 108–123.

Wood, R. H., & Thompson, S. R. (1980). Guidelines for better staff development. *Educational Leadership, 37* (5), 374–378.

Yarger, S. J., & Mertens, S. K. (1980). Testing the waters of school-based teacher education. In D. C. Corrigan & K. R. Howey (Eds.), *Concepts to guide the education of experienced teachers.* Reston, VA: Council for Exceptional Children.

10

Teacher Education Program Evaluation: Organizing or Agonizing?

Gary R. Galluzzo
Western Kentucky University

INTRODUCTION

With the publication of Sandefur's *An Illustrated Model for the Evaluation of Teacher Education Graduates* in 1970, the practice of educational evaluation was first applied to the programs that prepare beginning teachers. During the years since this publication, educational evaluation slowly, yet consistently, garnered the attention of schools, colleges, and departments of education across the country and many state departments of education as well. A more recent article by Sandefur (1982) counted no fewer than 36 states which had implemented, or were planning to implement, some form of teacher competency assessment. No doubt the recent demand by the public and the legislatures for the evaluation of educational programs extends to the evaluation of teacher education programs.

The purpose of this chapter is to review the literature and practice of the evaluation of teacher education program. Two national groups currently require program evaluations as part of the accreditation process. The National Council for the Accreditation of Teacher Education (NCATE, 1981) includes a standard which requires that programs seeking accreditation conduct an evaluation of their program. The National Association of State Directors of Teacher Education and Certification (NASDTEC, 1981) includes in its guidelines, standards which require that evaluation become an integral component of a teacher education program. Thus with two national and influential agencies representing two distinct constituencies and requiring that an evaluation component be built into teacher education, a growing body of literature is emerging on teacher education program

evaluation. This chapter will review the literature on teacher education program evaluation which has been made available through the ERIC Document Collection and education journals. In addition, this chapter includes
an examination of some issues in teacher education program evaluation, a
review of exemplary efforts of four institutions, and a discussion of what is
included and excluded from the literature to date.

THE LITERATURE ON TEACHER EDUCATION PROGRAM EVALUATION

While it is difficult to delineate an area unambiguously by using a definition, unless teacher education program evaluation is defined, debates will
ensue as to what actually is an example of program evaluation. Adams,
Craig, Hord, and Hall (1981) underscored the problems of identifying examples of teacher education program reports and the pitfalls in analysis
which may result. Stufflebeam (1982) has best stated a definition for teacher
education program evaluation.

> Evaluation is the process of delineating, obtaining, and applying de-
> scriptive and judgmental information concerning the worth and merit of
> some program's goals, design, implementation, and impacts in order to
> promote improvement, serve needs of accountability, and foster under-
> standing. (p. 138)

In his own words, the definition is "complex," but includes many
techniques that program evaluators can use. This definition includes data
collection, description, the judgment of the worth and merit of a program,
and meeting three important purposes: judgments about program improvement, issues in accountability, and understanding the nature of a program.
This definition, then, allows for measures of outcome, e.g., teacher knowledge or teaching performance as well as evaluation of the processes of
becoming a teacher, an account of the costs of a program, and overall judgment of the effort expended to operate the teacher education program.

Thus, with a functional definition to guide the selection of the evaluation studies included in this chapter, it is possible to turn to the literature on
teacher education program evaluation.

ISSUES IN LANGUAGE AND DESIGN

While teacher education program evaluation can be traced back some 40
years (Troyer & Pace, 1944), it was revived by Sandefur's (1970) monograph. The model he suggested assumes a product-orientation posture, i.e.,
a program can be evaluated by measuring the degree to which graduates

demonstrate the selected competencies which serve as its objectives. Thus, the follow-up study was initiated to assume a product or outcome assessment orientation. The competencies/objectives are drawn from the research on teaching literature. Rather than spend time describing the model here, it will be discussed as it was implemented at Western Kentucky University later in the chapter.

Much of the literature since 1970 has focused on issues related to teacher education program evaluation. It does not take long to realize that the terms model, method, technique, strategy, and approach are used loosely and interchangeably in the teacher education program evaluation literature. Philosophers of science would probably question such casual parlance. *Model,* the predominant term used for describing an evaluation "design" in the literature, is probably a candidate for philosophical analysis, but it is not the purpose of this paper to present such an analysis. A model, as defined by Borich (1983) is "a guide or heuristic for thinking about how an evaluation could be conducted" (p. 61). He stated that a model does not provide methods for evaluating, just a framework for thinking about evaluation methods and the selection of those methods. Not one of the data collection procedures described in this chapter yet meets the notion of a model, strictly defined. Rather than taking time to treat an issue as important as model-building, the term *approach* will be used. While this may beg the question, it is the opinion of this author that evaluations are value-laden, site-specific endeavors which reflect the orientations of the evaluators and the primary audience. At best, the "models" for teacher education program evaluation are exploratory approaches to data collection which have yet to withstand the tests of time and manipulation. Whereas, Stake (1981) may label these "persuasions" and not models, this author will use the term approach(es), suggesting a site-specific plan for evaluation.

As an example of the problem of nomenclature, De Voss and Hawk (1983) argued that product-oriented teacher education program evaluation, as described by Sandefur (1970), fails to capture the full range of information available about a program that can be used for evaluation. They present a rival "model" to conducting program evaluation that is based not solely on outcome assessment, but one that assumes a documentation orientation, i.e., in this approach, evaluation begins when the student enters the teacher education program and follows the experiences through which the preservice teacher passes. Their point of view was in concert with Reed's position (1978), that the behavioral science models of research and evaluation limit the full array of information available to program evaluators. By ascribing to the behavioral science models, some evaluators will inevitably preclude the use of other equally valuable anthropological or sociological models, which yield very different types of information that can be used for making decisions. It is problematic that there is anything more implied here than data collection procedures. It is doubtful that what constitutes teacher education program evaluation "models" would be the same as Stufflebeam's CIPP model, Stake's transactional model, or Eisner's connoisseurship model.

Another issue that has received some treatment in the literature concerns who may be in the best position to conduct program evaluations. Floden (1980) has argued that lay people rather than professional associations may be best suited to evaluate teacher education programs; Stedman (1980) claims that state departments of higher education are the most appropriate evaluators; and Galluzzo (1982) has argued that the institution itself should plan and implement rigorous evaluations for its own purposes.

The issue of designing effective evaluation plans has received some attention in the literature. Hord, Savage, and Bethel (1982) reported the proceedings of a symposium that sought to identify what they label strategies that could be used to evaluate teacher education programs. Five different strategies are included in their volume with responses from three nationally recognized educational evaluators. The strategies include comments on the viability and utilization of follow-up studies (Sandefur, 1982); problems and solutions for the NCATE process of program evaluation (Gardner, 1982); the concerns of a state department of education regarding program evaluation and approval (Roth, 1982); the needs of a local education agency for program evaluation data (Erly, 1982); and a discussion of program evaluation as more than follow-up studies (Galluzzo, 1982).

It is not the intention of this author to undervalue the importance of Sandefur's monograph. To the contrary, it is an extremely important document; it started the wheels in motion. However, history is beginning to indicate that the model moved practice ahead 10 years and then kept it there. That is, the institutions that followed in developing program evaluation plans used Sandefur's ideas without embellishment. Follow-up studies became the status quo. Sandefur's approach filled a gap; however, the assumptions underlying his approach remained unchallenged. As Sandefur (1982) noted some 12 years later, "the practice of evaluation of graduates has made little advance in the past ten years" (p. 13). Teacher education program evaluators and users have not yet looked to the issues raised in recent years, and practice, as evidenced by the evaluation reports available, has not changed much. The follow-up survey remains the dominant, and arguably the predominant, approach to teacher education program evaluation.

RESEARCH LITERATURE ON
TEACHER EDUCATION PROGRAM EVALUATION

When reviewing the literature on teacher education program evaluation, one cannot avoid noticing the lack of published evaluation reports. While the evaluation method used seems to be common across institutions (follow-

up surveys), there are numerous idiosyncracies which render the aggregation of studies for purposes of synthesis and analysis a rather imposing
challenge. However, two attempts have been made to analyze the state of
practice in teacher education program evaluation, and each deserves brief
discussion.

Katz, Raths, Mohanty, Kurachi, and Irving (1981) reviewed 26 program evaluation reports in an effort to examine some of the main problems
connected with conducting follow-up studies and the value they bring to the
improvement of practice. They concluded that teacher education program
evaluation lacks the precision and the sophistication of tightly designed
studies, and that the resultant data are difficult to interpret and rarely useful. They argued that the response rate across the 26 studies was less than
adequate for drawing valid conclusions. They also found that only 15 of the
reports they reviewed included recommendations for future practice. A
total of 70 recommendations was found in the reports, and few of them
were specific enough to be acted upon directly. In fact, they noted that all of
the recommendations were for additions to the program, and that not one
recommendation suggested deleting an activity or course from the teacher
education program that was rated as less than adequate, e.g., discipline and
management.

The authors offered some suggestions for the improvement of program evaluation studies. These included: identifying accurately the target
population so as to increase the probability of getting usable responses,
e.g., survey graduates who took a teaching position rather than all graduates; the inclusion of anecdotes in the evaluation report to enhance the presentation of numbers; the use of specific rather than broad and general
recommendations that designate a course of action, and expending more effort on the study of teacher socialization and the effects that years of service in teaching has on the subjects' opinions of their preparation.

Somewhat concerned about the review, Adams et al. (1981) responded
to the comments of Katz, et al. While there was agreement between both
groups of writers that the praxis of program evaluation could be improved,
Adams and his colleagues took exception with some of the comments of
Katz et al.

It was the position of Adams et al. that program evaluation is more
sophisticated than Katz et al. allowed. Adams et al. argued that the studies
reviewed were not all evaluation studies and that by focusing only on follow-up surveys, Katz et al. (1981) ignored key aspects such as classroom
observation, principal/supervisor ratings, and teacher characteristics which
appeared in some of the evaluation efforts, hence presenting "a very limited
view of program evaluation efforts being conducted in colleges of education
across the country" (p. 21).

Adams et al. argued that to review evaluation studies using a paradigm
more appropriate for reviewing research affects the results of the review.

The guidelines for research reports may be too stringent for reviewing evaluation reports; however, they offer no procedures which are acceptable for reviewing evaluation reports but not acceptable for reviewing research reports. Much can be learned from the point-counterpoint between the two positions, particularly in the area of evaluation methodology and data analysis, however, the debate also highlighted the need for a common ground for a practice which is as institution-specific as teacher education program evaluation.

The second attempt to describe the state of practice was through the analysis of a survey of teacher education programs (Adams & Craig, 1983). Seven hundred seventy-nine (779) institutions affiliated with the American Association of Colleges for Teacher Education (AACTE) comprised the sample for this study. Four hundred forty-five (445), or 57%, of the questionnaires returned were usable. Among their results, Adams and Craig reported that 381, or 85.6%, of the institutions reported that they were conducting some form of program evaluation. The dominant data collection procedures according to Adams and Craig was the follow-up study of one variety or another, ranging from one to four or more years. The most common areas covered by the evaluations were teaching skills, knowledge of subject matter, relationships with students, and relationships with peers/colleagues, and the most common methods for conducting follow-up studies were mailed questionnaires, personal interviews, and direct observation. Adams and Craig noted that many institutions responded that evaluation reports were written; however, the reports were used within each institution and tended not to be used for publication or presentation at professional meetings. The picture created by the Adams and Craig study was that program evaluations were being conducted and that any resultant reports were used for local concerns and not to contribute to a body of knowledge.

In sum, many institutions claimed to be conducting program evaluation studies, primarily follow-up studies. However, few of the reports were submitted for publication. If the reports were used at all, one can only speculate that the reports were applied to meeting the various accreditation standards and for internal review.

A LOOK AT FOUR EXAMPLES

While the data gathering techniques employed at most institutions are similar (follow-up questionnaires), there are great variations among the instruments. For instance, a Likert scale may be used by one institution, a semantic-differential by another, open-ended questions by a third, and some combination of these by a fourth.

The broad categories of dependent variables found by the Adams and Craig survey, such as teaching skills, subject matter knowledge, etc., are about the most generalizable content that can be synthesized from the literature. A meta-analysis of the program evaluation studies may be helpful to understanding the practice, but more likely than not, would yield results indicating that beginning teachers rate their programs favorably in the "preactive" areas of teaching, e.g., lesson and unit planning, the evaluation and selection of materials, and subject matter knowledge, etc., and unfavorably in the "interactive" areas, e.g., management and discipline, question asking, and giving feedback. These are generalizations that are not new in teacher education.

It may also be helpful to use a framework for analysis which is derived from the *Standards for Evaluations of Educational Programs, Projects, and Materials* (Joint Committee on Standards for Educational Evaluation, 1981). The *Standards* are an attempt to offer guidelines to a broad spectrum of educators and policy makers who "commission, conduct, or employ the results of evaluations to improve education" (Joint Committee, 1981, p. 1). The volume contains 30 standards that can be used in evaluating programs, projects, and materials. They are divided into four areas about program evaluation: (a) utility, the practical information needs of the audience; (b) feasibility, the prudent and diplomatic aspects of evaluation procedures; (c) propriety, the ethical aspects; and (d) accuracy, the precision and comprehensiveness of the assessment. However, many of the teacher education program evaluation reports, published and unpublished, fail to approach many of the standards. For example, it is rare to find in many reports the identification of an audience, be it an NCATE team, a dean, or the education faculty. No report reviewed for this study included a discussion of cost effectiveness, and in only a few reports were attempts made to assess or discuss the reliability and validity of the data collection instruments (Flowers, 1978; Ayers, 1982). While teacher education program evaluation practice should strive to attain each of the standards, it is premature and less than productive to aggregate studies for review and hold them to the standards.

One should not get the impression that because teacher education program evaluation does not meet the 30 criteria included in the Joint Committee's *Standards* that teacher education program evaluation lacks substance. To the contrary, those institutions which have conducted program evaluation studies over a period of years have identified techniques and instruments that yield usable data which, at the least, describe the status quo of an institution's program. This chapter will review four programs which have developed a workable evaluation model.

One of the most outstanding characteristics of teacher education program evaluation reports is the lack of analysis and discussion of the data and therefore the lack of specific conclusions and recommendations for program modification. As mentioned earlier, teacher education program evaluations are highly individualistic, institution-specific endeavors which are used primarily for internal purposes. However, some institutions have sought to design evaluation plans which meet their needs and contribute to a body of knowledge, e.g., methodology, performance assessment, model building. The four institutions whose efforts in teacher education program evaluation are presented in this section of the chapter are unique in that they collected data that described not only the status quo of their programs but relationships among the data as well. They sought to gain summative evaluation data on performance competencies/program objectives, and they also sought other data, e.g., characteristics of their trainees or beginning teachers which helped explain the summative results through correlation. The four programs cited below are variations on an evaluation theme. Their efforts can guide the efforts of others.

Western Kentucky University

Based upon the outline in Sandefur's (1970) monograph, Western Kentucky University designed and implemented a longitudinal follow-up study of the graduates of its program (Adams, 1974, 1978). The data were collected over a 9-year period. Surveys were mailed to graduates during the first, third, and fifth years of employment. The teachers responded to questions about various personal characteristics. They were also observed by trained supervisors using Ryans' Classroom Observation Record and a modified form of the Flanders Interaction Analysis Category System. Perceptions about the teaching ability of each of the teachers were also collected from supervisors and students. The teachers also completed three other measures: the F-Scale, a measure of authoritarian/democratic tendencies, the Rokeach Dogmatism Scale, and the Teacher Concerns Checklist, a measure of problem areas for practicing teachers.

With so much data collected, Western Kentucky University was in the unique position to gain an evaluation of its graduates hence its program in various domains and also to use the data to answer other questions about beginning teachers. For example, in the evaluation report used for review in this chapter (Adams, 1978), three questions were posed: What are the factors related to perceived problems of first-year teachers? What are the probable factors which are related to entry into and retention in teaching? Does teacher behavior change with experience? In answer to the first question, the first-year teachers perceived "teaching disrespectful students," "discipline," and "motivating students" as major concerns. Correlations were computed to identify which personality variables, e.g. dogmatism, authoritarianism, etc., related to these problem areas. Significant correlations were found with observed teacher behavior and supervisor ratings. The teachers had difficulty performing these areas of concern, and rated them as problems. To answer the second question, regarding entry and retention, data on attrition from teaching were collected. Adams found that 55% of the graduates entered teaching after graduation. After three years, 91% of the beginning teachers remained in teaching, and after five years, 42% remained in teaching, showing a distinct pattern of beginning teachers leaving the profession. To answer the third question, stability of teaching behavior, classroom observation data were used. Using the Classroom Observation Record, Adams noted a shift away from "desirable" teaching behavior over the five years. While not a significant difference among mean scores on those behaviors over the five years, Adams did note a pattern in the data that there were effects of years of experience on teaching behavior. The teachers demonstrated "less than desirable" teaching behavior as defined by the Classroom Observation Record. Adams concluded that the teaching behavior of beginning teachers slowly changes with longevity.

The Western Kentucky University effort was broad, and as Sandefur (1982) noted later, expensive. However, this approach to program evaluation demonstrated that there was valuable information which could be collected and used to answer not only program evaluation questions but questions about beginning teachers as well such as the stability of the teaching behavior of beginning teachers and attrition from the field. However, even after collecting data for nine years, Western Kentucky University could only speak with greater accuracy about its program. Not all of the data were conclusive and provided direction for program modification or program revision. Perhaps the most salient contribution to the literature after pioneering was the comprehensive approach to follow-up studies in teacher education program evaluation.

Bowling Green State University

One of the criticisms of follow-up studies leveled by Katz et al. was the failure of many evaluators to identify the target population accurately. Pigge (1978), using an evaluation approach that is built solely on follow-up survey, employed a procedure which ensured that the respondents were actually teaching. By coordinating its efforts with the Ohio State Department of Education, Bowling Green State University identified its graduates who took a position as a teacher and used them as the subjects for its evaluation study. Nonteaching graduates were excluded from this follow-up study.

A major emphasis was the effort to determine beginning teachers' perceived need for selected competencies. Using what was labeled a needs-assessment orientation as the basis for the evaluation, Pigge sought to address four areas about the Bowling Green State University program. Given a list of 26 competencies, the graduates rated: (a) their need for each competency; (b) their use of the competency; (c) their proficiency in the competency; and (d) where the proficiency was developed. The principal of each beginning teacher was also requested to rate his/her beginning teacher(s) from Bowling Green State on the competencies. The data were analyzed by major. Among the findings, Pigge reported: a high correlation between the teachers' need for a competency and their proficiency in it, e.g., individualizing instruction; a tendency to rank competencies for which they expressed a high need as being learned on the job and not during the training program, e.g., discipline, motivation, and evaluation; a high correlation between the teachers' and principals' ordering of the need for certain competencies; and a tendency to credit the teacher education program with developing proficiencies in competency areas which are not needed on the job. It appears that the teacher education program did not emphasize sufficiently those competencies or skills required most by their graduates' work settings. Bowling Green State University's approach to program evaluation yielded data that not only highlighted areas in need of program modification, e.g., individualizing instruction, classroom management, and student motivation, but also helped set an agenda for inservice teacher education program development.

The University of Toledo

In 1975, The University of Toledo began a program evaluation effort that sought to measure teacher performance and teaching competence in its competency-based teacher education program. The literature that undergirded the approach employed by the University of Toledo is the teacher effectiveness/process-product research. Using this literature as the knowledge base, Dickson and Wiersma (1982) defined program evaluation as the demonstration by student teachers of selected research-based performance competencies in the classroom using both high- and low-inference observation instruments.

Two instruments were used for data collection: the Teacher Performance Assessment Instrument (TPAI) developed at the University of Georgia, a high-inference classroom observation instrument and the Classroom Observations Keyed for Effectiveness Research (COKER), a low-inference classroom observation instrument. Both instruments required the extensive training of faculty to ensure interrater reliability during observations. The two instruments were used to measure teacher competence on the 49 competency statements that the faculty identified as the expected outcomes of its curriculum. What set the University of Toledo apart from the institutions previously cited was that it employed a highly behavioral approach, using objective observation, and the subjects were preservice teachers observed during student teaching and not graduates who were teaching. The aggregation of the classroom observation data from all subjects indicated that the student teachers generally demonstrated the competencies of the program. However, the data also revealed a set of competencies on which the student teachers received lower scores. This study yielded data that indicated that the student teachers were less effective on two competencies; modifying instructional activities to accomodate the different abilities of the learners and student evaluation and feedback to learners on their performance. Dickson and Wiersma recommended that the curriculum be examined for program effectiveness, with the possibility that new curricula may need to be developed that seek to promote teacher competence in these two areas. The faculty then can place greater emphasis on these competencies in the program. An advantage of the University of Toledo approach was that this work contributed not only to the literature on program evaluation but on performance assessment, measurement using direct observation, and process/product research as well.

Glassboro State College

The purpose of the approach to program evaluation employed at Glassboro State College (NJ) was to collect data on the preservice teachers from admissions through the first year of teaching. Whereas other approaches discussed in this chapter have been based upon product assessment, needs assessment, or teaching competence, the approach used at Glassboro State College took a process-product orientation (Galluzzo, 1982), based ostensibly on Stufflebeam's (1971) CIPP (context, input, process, product) model. That is, the inputs to a program, e.g., students, were as essential to evaluating a program as were product assessments, e.g., teacher knowledge. As well, the students were monitored along the way to evaluate the processes of becoming a teacher.

Under the Glassboro State College approach, data collection began when the students were admitted into the professional education program as freshmen. Demographic characteristics and other data such as high school rank, SAT scores, and state basic skills tests were obtained. A gross measure of student attitude toward teaching, using the Minnesota Teacher Attitude Inventory, and the Rokeach Dogatism Scale was also collected in a repeated measures design to assess both the changes over time, and the relationship of these variables to other independent and dependent variables.

Process evaluation was characterized by an interview of juniors who were entering the professional semester of prestudent-teaching practicum. The students were asked to comment on their preparation to date, the sequence of courses, and their perceptions of the relationship between field experiences and campus course work. The students also took the National Teachers Exam (NTE) during the spring of each year in an effort to monitor changes in academic achievement during teacher preparation, or while the preservice teachers were in the process of becoming teachers. Attrition data were collected in an attempt to understand why students leave teacher education. The reasons offered most were uncertain life plans and a lack of interest in teaching. Interviews with students identified some other problems in course sequence in workload (Galluzzo, 1981).

Product evaluation included the final administration of the attitude and personality measures and the NTE in the completion of a longitudinal study. The results of this evaluation indicated that the students' attitudes toward teaching became more positive from the freshman through the junior year and declined after student teaching. These preservice teachers also became less dogmatic from the freshman through the junior years. There were no changes after the junior year. An analysis of the four administrations of the NTE scores showed a steady and significant increase in the group means over the four years on the Weighted Common Examination Tests. However, when the Professional Education Test was removed from the total score, leaving a measure of liberal arts (written English expression; social studies, literature, and fine arts; and math and science), the analysis revealed no significant differences among the four means.

The results were explained by generating three other hypotheses which can be used for future research. First, the general studies subtests of the NTE may not be an accurate measure of the general studies curriculum which these students experienced. Second, the 60 credit hours of general studies required by this teacher education program were not enough to induce a change that can be detected by a standardized test. This explanation is further complicated by the fact that general studies courses are typically a potpourri affair. For example, the general studies programs of any two students may vary widely given the array of options available to students when selecting courses. A third reason for the lack of significance on the general studies subtests related to a notion of "selective attention." It may best be captured by the question, "Did these students concentrate primarily on the courses within their major at the expense of their other nonmajor courses?" In this case, these students would have had a career orientation to study for their education courses first, and then, if time was available, review the work for their electives and general studies. This would explain the differences on the NTE when the Professional Education Test was included. Little is known about the transition from student to teacher. From these results two larger questions emerge: "What are the effects of a teacher education curriculum on student achievement?" and, "Can the effects be measured on a paper and pencil test?" (Galluzzo, 1983).

It is not the intention of the author to slight other institutions by identifying a handful who have implemented exemplary evaluation efforts. These are four among numerous others. The purpose of this section of the chapter was, however, to cite some of those institutions which have conducted evaluations, have written evaluation reports which described the methods they selected, have discussed the data, and have drawn conclusions and recommendations for decision making. Again, using the works of Katz et al. (1981) and Adams and Craig (1983), what exists in the literature under the rubric, teacher education program evaluation, is scant. One can find in the literature evaluation reports, however, many are brief, unsophisticated reports prepared to address local concerns. The good ones are few, and drawing generalizable conclusions from such a small sample is difficult at best.

WHAT IS NOT THERE

This chapter has briefly examined the expository exhortations regarding teacher education program evaluation and described the evaluations of four programs from institutions whose efforts have not only been productive for local review of programs but have also contributed to the literature on methods and practice. However, besides there being few published reports and a need for evaluation reports that would be useful to others, there are other gaps in the literature. It is helpful to highlight a few.

Felder, Hollis, and Houston (1981), by the publication of their monographs, identified an area of need in the literature. Papers that reflect on the processes and commitments necessary for conducting an evaluation are noticeably missing. Felder et al. described and discussed in some depth, the problems encountered during the years the University of Houston conducted program evaluations. They described the steps taken to plan and conduct their evaluation. They outlined some impediments that they met, e.g., obtaining and retaining subjects for follow-up studies; the development of competencies which reflect the tasks performed routinely by experienced teachers. However, besides the Felder et al. monograph and other than brief comments at the end of an evaluation report by Adams (1978), there are no discussions in the literature of the problems of implementing program evaluations which yield usable information.

A second area that has not been treated in the literature is knowledge utilization, or the degree to which programs have been influenced by the results of an evaluation. Katz et al. commented on the weak substance of most recommendations included in the reports they reviewed. However, a larger question is, "What happens to the data and recommendations in the report?" This issue includes, not only, "Are they discussed or used?" but "How are they disseminated?" and, "How closely is program evaluation linked to program modification or faculty development?" It would seem that program evaluation would be tied to efforts that seek program modifications or revision, and/or faculty development if necessary. Adams (1978) and Sandefur (1982) address this point in their analyses of Western Kentucky University's studies; however, this author could find no other discussions of the implementation of a recommendation and its evaluation in a subsequent report. Oftentimes, curricula are changed, either within the institution or by an external agency. Yet, in no report was there an evaluation of a "new" component. For instance, some institutions have learned through evaluations that teacher preparation in the area of management and discipline is rated by graduates as inadequate and is reported as such. But in no subsequent evaluation report did an institution evaluate a new training experience in management and discipline. One could draw the conclusion that the faculty nods in agreement when the evaluation data are presented but continues to offer the same program that apparently had been failing. The use of the results or recommendations included in the evaluation report is an area of consideration which has not been addressed in the literature.

A third gap in the literature is meta-evaluation, or the evaluation of an evaluation. This author found no reports of meta-evaluations. While external evaluation, i.e., bringing in an outsider to review a program, may be practiced and even advisable when the state department of education calls, meta-evaluation, or bringing in an outsider to review the evaluation report constitutes a "null set." There are standards available (Joint Committee, 1981), for conducting meta-evaluations, yet in such a new phenomenon as teacher education program evaluation, meta-evaluation is not formally included in current practice.

Finally, and it may be obvious to the reader by now, there are no replication studies, i.e., nowhere in the literature is there the report from one institution which used the data collection procedures tested at another institution. Knowledge is built systematically through insight, intuition, by analysis of the work of others, and the replication of the work of others. The production of knowledge in teacher education program evaluation is characterized more precisely by the first two, insight and intuition, and less by the latter two, analysis and replication.

The author does not wish to convey the impression that by standardizing the measurement devices used for teacher education program evaluation that practice will improve. To the contrary, the individual flavor that each evaluation approach offers to the literature is valuable, but, program evaluations which are limited to site-specific studies will tend to forestall the development of the field. As the practice of program evaluation presently stands, institutions planning an evaluation are destined to visit the same problems and obstacles that some have already encountered, and in some instances, have overcome. Without the testing of models that will guide thinking, the spirit of discussion and refinement that characterizes academic pursuit will be lost. With almost 400 institutions reporting that they are conducting evaluation studies, it would seem that replication studies and the discussion of method would be occurring with greater frequency. When debate and discussion about program evaluation models begins, the development of an identified field can follow. Insight and intuition are necessary, but program evaluation will continue to grow haphazardly without practitioners building on the work of each other, sharing experiences, and refining techniques. Teacher education program evaluation lacks tested guides for thinking about designing a plan.

Final Thought

The purpose of this discussion was to explore the literature and practice of teacher education program evaluation. The practice is just beginning to emerge and lacks the guidance of theory, methodology, and model development that will make teacher education program evaluation a field of inquiry. In an attempt to provide some direction, this chapter identified key literature and exemplary practice, but by no means is this review exhaustive. By describing the state of program evaluation literature and by identifying some aspects that have not been treated to a great extent in the literature, some boundaries that can define the field of teacher education program evaluation may become evident.

The practice of teacher education program evaluation is very young and in need of guiding principles. Various approaches are available, and through analysis and replication program evaluation can advance from a practice into a field and eventually into a study that others who are charged with program development and evaluation can examine. Teacher education program evaluation models should be valuable for their contribution to an organizing body of literature as well as for use by individual institutions. This author hopes that by providing a brief review of the present state of practice that a coherent agenda for a field of teacher education program evaluation will ensue.

REFERENCES

Adams, R. D. (1974). *Follow-up and evaluation of teacher education graduates: A pilot study. Final report.* Bowling Green, KY: Western Kentucky University, Office of Educational Research.

Adams, R. D. (1978). Western Kentucky follow-up evaluation of teacher education graduates. In S. M. Hord & G. E. Hall (Eds.), *Teacher education program evaluation: A collection of current efforts.* Austin, TX: Research and Development for Center Teacher Education.

Adams, R. D., & Craig, J. R. (1983). A status report of teacher education program evaluation. *Journal of Teacher Education, 34*(2), 33–36.

Adams, R. D., Craig, J. R., Hord, S. M., & Hall, G. E. (1981). Program evaluation and program development in teacher education: A response to Katz et al. (1981). *Journal of Teacher Education, 32*(5), 21–24.

Ayers, J. B. (1982). *Tennessee Technological University teacher evaluation model-year IX.* (Report 82-2). Cookeville, TN: Tennessee Technological University, College of Education.

Cooper, J. M. (1983). Basic elements in teacher education program evaluation: Implications for future research. In K. R. Howey & W. E. Gardner (Eds.) *The education of teachers: A look ahead.* New York: Longman.

De Voss, G., & Hawk, D. (1983). Follow-up models in teacher education. *Educational Evaluation and Policy Analysis, 5*(2), 163–171.

Dickson, G. E., & Wiersma, W. (1982). *Research and evaluation in teacher education: Measurement of teacher competence.* Toledo, OH: The University of Toledo, College of Education.

Erly, M. C. (1982). A practitioner's perceptions regrading problems in assessing the effectiveness of teacher education programs. In S. M. Hord, T. V. Savage, & L. J. Bethel (Eds.), *Toward usable strategies for teacher education program evaluation.* Austin, TX: Research and Development Center for Teacher Education.

Felder, B. D., Hollis, L. Y., & Houston, W. R. (1981). *Reflections on the evaluation of a teacher education program: The University of Houston experience.* Washington, DC: ERIC Clearinghouse on Teacher Education.

Floden, R. E. (1980). Flexner, Accreditation, and Evaluation. *Educational Evaluation and Policy Analysis, 2*(2), 35–46.

Flowers, J. D. (1978). *Measuring beginning teacher satisfaction with pre-professional training.* Biloxi, MS: Augusta College. (ERIC Document Reproduction Service No. ED 177 098)

Galluzzo, G. R. (1981). *An evaluation of EPIC: Annual report.* Unpublished manuscript.

Galluzzo, G. R. (1982). Program evaluation in teacher education: From admissions through follow-up. In S. M. Hord, T. V. Savage, & L. J. Bethel (Eds.), *Toward usable strategies for teacher education program evaluation.* Austin, TX: Research and Development Center for Teacher Education.

Galluzzo, G. R. (1983). *An evaluation of a teacher education program.* Glassboro, NJ: Glassboro State College (ERIC Document Reproduction Service No. ED 229 373)

Gardner, W. E. (1982). NCATE accreditation: Problems, issues, and needed research. In S. M. Hord, T. V. Savage, & L. J. Bethel (Eds.), *Toward usable strategies for teacher education program evaluation.* Austin, TX: Research and Development Center for Teacher Education.

Hord, S. M., Savage, T. V., & Bethel, L. J. (1982). *Toward usable strategies for teacher education program evaluation.* Austin, TX: Research and Development Center for Teacher Education.

Joint Committee on Standards for Educational Evaluation. (1981). *Standards for evaluations of educational programs, projects, and materials.* New York: McGraw-Hill.

Katz, L., Raths, J., Mohanty, C., Kurachi, A., & Irving, J. (1981). Follow-up studies: Are they worth the trouble? *Journal of Teacher Education, 32*(2), 18–22.

Kirk, E. L. (1982). *Follow-up studies of teacher education program graduates.* Abilene, TX: Abilene Christian Univeristy. (ERIC Document Reproduction Service No. 221 544)

National Association of State Directors of Teacher Education and Certification. (1981). *Standards for state approval of teacher education.* Salt Lake City, UT: Author.

National Council for the Accreditation of Teacher Education. (1981). *Standards for the accreditation of teacher education.* Washington, DC: Author.

Pigge, F. L. (1978). Teacher competencies: Need, proficiency, and where proficiency was developed. *Journal of Teacher Education, 29*(4), 70–76.

Reed, H. B. (1978). *The accuracy-meaning tensions in teacher education evaluations.* Paper presented at the F. G. Watson Festschrift Conference, Cambridge, MA. (ERIC Document Reproduction Service No. 205 524)

Roth, R. A. (1982). Requirements of a data base for effective program evaluation. In S. M. Hord, T. V. Savage, & L. J. Bethel (Eds.), *Toward usable strategies for teacher education program evaluation.* Austin, TX: Research and Development for Teacher Education.

Sandefur, J. T. (1970). *An illustrated model for the evaluation of teacher education graduates.* Washington, DC: American Association of Colleges for Teacher Education.

Sandefur, J. T. (1982). Teacher education's evaluation of graduates: Where are we going and how do we know when we get there? In S. M. Hord, T. V. Savage, & L. J. Bethel (Eds.), *Toward usable strategies for teacher education program evaluation.* Austin, TX: Research and Development for Teacher Education.

Stake, R. (1981). Persuasions, not models. *Educational Evaluation and Policy Analysis, 3*(1), 83–84.

Stedman, D. J. (1980). *Improving teacher education: Academic program review.* Atlanta, GA: Southern Regional Education Board. (ERIC Document Reproduction Service No. 205 467)

Stufflebeam, D. L. (1982). Explorations in the evaluation of teacher education. In S. M. Hord, T. V. Savage, & L. J. Bethel (Eds.), *Toward usable strategies for teacher education program evaluation.* Austin, TX: Research and Development for Teacher Education.

Stufflebeam, D. L., Foley, W. J., Gephart, W. J., Guba, E. G., Hammond, R. L., Merriman, H. O., Provus, M. M. (1971). *Educational evaluation and decision-making.* Itasca, IL: Peacock.

Troyer, M. E., & Pace, C. R. (1944). *Evaluation in teacher education.* Washington, DC: American Council on Education.

11

Issues in Student Teaching: A Review*

Gary A. Griffin
University of Illinois at Chicago

INTRODUCTION

Student teaching has existed throughout the development of teacher preparation in this country (Hughes, 1981) and is presently incorporated in several forms in nearly all teacher education programs. The importance of student teaching is voiced often by teacher educators, inservice teachers, and many others (Griffin, 1982). Despite the importance of the topic to educators there have been few attempts to synthesize and critique research on student teaching so as to identify major findings and pose further questions. The current state of the literature reflects the tendency in research to focus on isolated aspects of student teaching (e.g., attitude change, supervision, etc.) without considering the interaction of other aspects. To overcome this limitation, the present review seeks to develop an overall framework to consider the multiple issues that exist in examining student teaching, as well as to scrutinize the research literature within each problem area. This framework can provide an heuristic model for further examination of student teaching.

* This work was supported in part by Grant #NIE-G-80-0116 from the National Institute of Education, Department of Education. However, the opinions expressed do not necessarily reflect the position or policy of the National Institute of Education, and no official endorsement should be inferred. Appreciation is expressed to Maria E. Defino and Robert Hughes, Jr., who participated in the preparation of an earlier version of this paper and to Alicia Salinas who located additional sources for the current version.

PURPOSES

This review serves the primary purpose of critically surveying much of the available literature pertaining to student teaching. In doing so, issues and themes related to the student teaching experience are noted and discussed. While the quantity of literature on student teaching is vast, very little of it is empirical in nature, and few instances of large-scale research exist. Therefore, generalizations are made within the context of this somewhat limited research.

A second purpose of the review is to provide an organizational framework for considering student teaching literature. This organization, beginning in the center with the principal triad (student teacher, cooperating teacher, and university supervisor) moves outward to the contexts in which they are embedded. It indicates the people who are participants in student teaching, together with the factors in their work environments which may influence their behavior. At the personal level, individual and professional characteristics may influence the student teaching experience.

At the next level, the influences of each participant upon the others can be examined. Questions about the interactive processes between student teacher, cooperating teacher, and university supervisor may be considered, as well as those concerning substantive changes in attitudes and/or skills that may occur as a result of the interactions.

Finally, all of these individuals conduct their work within several environments, including the school, the university, the school district, the community, and so on. Thus, individual behavior can be affected by the nature of these work places.

A recent large-scale study of student teaching conducted by the present author and colleagues provides additional information regarding the components of the organizational framework (Griffin, Barnes, Hughes, O'Neal, Defino, Edwards, & Hukill, 1983). These findings, in contrast to others reported here, are directly related in that they emerged from the same sample at the same point in time. The insights about student teaching that emerged from this comprehensive inquiry are noted throughout the review.

The review of literature is organized around this framework. The organizing topics are (a) individual characteristics in student teaching; (b) the student teaching experience; (c) contextual influences; and (d) a summary and overview of emergent issues.

THE ROLE OF INDIVIDUAL CHARACTERISTICS IN STUDENT TEACHING

Two basic questions emerge when one considers student teaching: Who are the participants? What are their characteristics? These may be answered from either of two distinct perspectives, demographics or individual differences. Information pertaining to student teaching from each of these perspectives is reviewed.

Demographics

Yarger, Howey, and Joyce (1977) have provided demographic profiles of the typical preservice student and teacher educator based upon a sample of 2,200 students and 420 faculty members from 175 teacher training institutions. The "typical" preservice teacher, in 1977, was a single, Anglo woman in her early twenties. In contrast, the "typical" university education faculty member was a 43-year-old Anglo male with experience working in the public schools. Approximately half of the teacher educators were full professors and roughly the same number had supervisory duties.

Little demographic information characterizing either cooperating teachers or university supervisors, as distinct groups, is available. Other demographic variables such as age, sex, or ethnicity have not been well researched in relation to preservice training outcomes in teacher education. Generally more women than men (especially at elementary levels) enter the teaching profession and are thus involved in greater numbers in preservice experiences. (No conclusions have been reached regarding differential efficacy between men and women in education or in preservice activities.)

Griffin et al. (1983) noted the persistence of the Anglo female dominance of the student teacher population. In their sample, however, the university supervisor role was filled more often by nonprofessorial persons (e.g., graduate students) than by male professors of education. Although the sample was much smaller than that of Yarger et al., the difference is striking. This difference may be a function of the institutions included in the two samples. The Griffin et al. study included universities that are considered research-oriented and with major emphasis on graduate study. The larger Yager study included a larger number of teacher training-oriented institutions.

Individual Differences

Individual differences in student teaching occur at levels other than simple demographics. Among the psychological characteristics or traits which have been investigated in relation to student teaching and its outcomes are: teacher concerns; self-concept and self-esteem; empathy; interest in people; scholastic aptitude; cognitive levels of processing; and, flexibility and creativity. Research on the role of each of these traits in the student teaching experience is examined here.

Teacher Concerns. Fuller (1969) studied the concerns of preservice and inservice teachers. Three areas of concerns were identified: self, teaching tasks, and impact of teaching on pupil learning. A developmental transition through these three concern areas was theorized as a function of greater teaching experience. According to the theory, teachers are able to be concerned primarily with the impact of their teaching on students only after resolving concerns about their own socialization into the teaching field and ameliorating concerns about how to teach. The Teacher Concerns Questionnaire (TCQ) has been used to measure concerns in these three areas. To date, however, research has not supported the validity of hierarchical movement through levels of concerns as a function of teaching experience (George, 1978). Nevertheless, the TCQ does identify concerns among cooperating teachers, university supervisors, and student teachers which may be sources of conflict. The Griffin et al. (1983) study discovered a pattern of teacher concerns that is in some conflict with the theory. Although student teachers demonstrated higher self concerns than did either cooperating teachers or university supervisors, consistent with the theory, the student teachers had higher impact concerns than the theory would predict. Also, again in some conflict with the theory, all participants' concerns scores decreased over the semester. The finding related to student teachers' higher-than-expected impact concerns can be understood in relation to the "conservative" environment of the placements where cooperating teachers maintained strict control of the classroom, thereby probably lessening the possibility of high task concerns. The uniform decrease in concerns scores over all participants remains an issue for further study.

Self-Concept and Self-Esteem. While some investigators have used self-concept and self-esteem interchangeably, Coopersmith and Feldman (1974) defined self-esteem as evaluative in overall degree (high or low) and self-concept as referring to various attributes of self. Positive teacher self-concepts have been related to overall teacher mental health (Milgram & Milgram, 1976) and to their students' achievement (Rayder, Abrams, & Larson, 1978). Soares and Soares (1968) noted that student teachers' self-concepts were related more to their university supervisors' ratings rather than to their cooperating teachers' ratings of them. They also found elementary-level student teachers to have more positive self-concepts than secondary-level student teachers. Walberg (1968) reported that males majoring in elementary education had poorer self-concepts than males majoring in secondary education or women in education. Garvey (1970) found positive self-concept as measured by the Tennessee Self-Concept Scale to be related to higher student teaching ratings. She concluded that student teaching success is affected, but not necessarily determined, by a positive view of oneself. It is possible, of course, to speculate that a causal relationship might be the reverse.

Doherty (1980) echoed these findings by discovering a link between low self-esteem among student teachers and lower competency ratings as student teachers. In 1965, Wright and Tuska reported that significant changes in self-image occurred in student teachers after preservice and first-year teaching experiences. With greater experience in the classroom, preservice and new teachers saw themselves as increasingly more demanding, "meaner," and less inspiring to students. Smith and Smith (1979) considered the effect of teaching in lower-socioeconomic-level schools on the self-concepts of student teachers. Those student teachers placed in poverty areas were likely to have unfulfilled expectations about the achievement levels of their pupils that contributed to a lack of perceived success for the student teachers. Similar findings have been reported by Wagenschein (1950) and Smith and Adams (1973).

Walberg (1968) concluded that observed declines in self-concept self-ratings from student teachers during preservice was a result of the conflict between personal needs (to establish rapport with individual children) and role demands (to establish authority and discipline in the classroom). The research appears to support the view that higher levels of self-esteem and positive self-concepts are related to many experiences in teaching. Thus, they are likely to be of significance in the preservice period of teacher education.

The Griffin et al. (1983) sample demonstrated few differences in self-concept and self-esteem among student teachers, cooperating teachers, and university supervisors. As with other personality measures, the findings suggest that the persons entering teaching are quite similar to those already in teaching.

Empathy. Research in a variety of people-oriented professions has concluded that empathy is related to growth, development, or health. Carkhuff (1971) reported that counselors who exhibit high empathic listening skills have more successful theapy outcomes. Similarly, LaMonica (1980) in a study of empathy in nurses reported that more empathic nurses are viewed as more caring and helpful by patients. In education, craft knowledge and conventional wisdom have held that teachers who are more caring and concerned about their students will be more effective. This idea has rarely been examined by educational researchers, although it has received attention from developers of curriculum materials.

Another important place where empathy may be an especially important concept is in supervision. Goldhammer's (1977) and Cogan's (1973) descriptions of clinical supervision clearly acknowledge the need for supervisors to consider the thoughts and feelings of the supervisee (e.g., the student teacher).

Griffin et al. (1983) reported that of all personality constructs, empathy was the only consistent predictor of success in student teaching. That is, the more empathic the student teacher, the more likely that s/he would be rated highly by cooperating teachers and university supervisors, the more likely that s/he would be satisfied with the experience, and the more likely that s/he would receive high performance ratings from colleagues.

Prior Work with Children. One background characteristic that has been the focus of attention regarding student teachers is past experience with children. Some investigations have claimed that previous experience with children is of major importance in successful student teaching (Ryans, 1960; Ducharme, 1970). Schalock (1979), writing on teacher selection, noted that three Oregon College of Education studies failed to find any relationship between previous experience with children and student teaching competencies. Examining this issue from the perspective of the relation of prior experience to choosing teaching as an occupation, Wood (1978) found that previous experience with children was the highest ranked reason for entering teaching.

Interest in People. Interest in people is considered characteristic of members of the teaching profession. It is often assumed that teachers should be warm and empathetic in interacting with children. A study by Yarger, et al. (1977) acknowledged that student teachers and teacher educators expressed interest in working with pupils. Other researchers have reported that persons entering the teaching profession cite their desire to work with people as most important in their occupational decision. Haurich (1960) found this true of students, and Isham, Carter, and Stribling (1981) have confirmed this finding among teacher educators.

Scholastic Aptitude. Verbal ability in teachers has been found important to the instructional skill of communicating (Taylor, Ghiselin, & Yagi, 1967). Intellectual ability would seem essential in teaching, although intelligence and academic grade-point average have correlated only modestly with teacher performance ratings (Ducharme, 1970; Ferguson, 1977. It has been argued by Vernon (1965) that high correlations between intellectual ability and teaching performance are unlikely, because teachers are relatively homogeneous as to intellectual ability (scoring between 110 and 120 on most traditional intelligence tests). With this restricted range of ability, higher correlations with other variables are not likely to be found.

The Griffin et al. (1983) study found sharp differences in verbal facility among groups participating in the student teaching experience. Using a standardized measure of vocabulary with norms established through administration to recent college graduates, university supervisors scored at the 63rd percentile, cooperating teachers at the 50th percentile, and student teachers at the 14th percentile. This finding confirms many of the expressed concerns regarding the language ability of recent additions to the teaching force.

Cognitive Levels of Processing. The interest in cognitive developmental stages, sparked by the work of Piaget (1970) and Kohlberg (1969), has been noted in teacher education. Murphy and Brown (1970) found that the encouragement of student self-expression by teachers was related to the teachers' higher conceptual level. Lower conceptual levels on the part of teachers were related to more rote questioning of their students. Hunt and Joyce (1967) and Glassberg and Sprinthall (1980) have examined levels of information processing among preservice teachers as they affect student teaching processes. Hunt and Joyce (1967) reported that higher conceptual levels in preservice teachers were associated with a teaching style in which children are assisted in evaluating information, raising hypotheses, and making inferences. Glassberg and Sprinthall (1980) concluded that experiences in role taking and various reflections exercises (e.g., systematically thinking back upon one's own practice) could result in increased ego and ethical development.

Despite these results, other research has noted that such higher-order teaching skills as probing, redirection, and higher cognitive questioning had little effect on increasing the conceptual skills of pupils. Nevertheless, these somewhat conflicting results leave open the precise relationship between conceptual levels and teaching behavior, especially as it affects pupils. Some developmental research (Kohlberg, 1969) has speculated that persons must be challenged by others at more complex levels of development to produce growth, suggesting that differences in the cooperating teachers' and student teachers' levels of development may result in some change.

Flexibility/Creativity. The constructs of flexibility and creativity have been rather consistently identified as important in teacher education (Ekstrom, 1976). Hunt and Joyce (1967) found that student teachers displaying a wider range of teaching styles were considered more effective as teachers than student teachers engaging in fewer teaching styles. Earlier, Bond (1959) found that 90% of student teachers rated as creative before beginning preservice teaching were judged outstanding by their teaching supervisors. Crocker (1974) found significant relationships between creativity test scores and student teaching performance; flexibility, as measured by the creativity tests, was found to be the strongest single predictor of performance.

Ishler (1973) examined differences in verbal behavior among student teachers classified as either high or low in creativity on the Torrance (1962) Tests of Creative Aptitude. Those student teachers with higher creative aptitude scores used more open-ended and varied activities in the classroom, as recorded on the Flanders (1970) Interaction Analysis. Generally, the literature suggests that flexibility and creativity are important predictors of teaching competency.

Yet, it remains unclear what particular student outcomes might be most affected by measures of flexibility and creativity. Flexibility as a construct is not unidimensional, for academic problem-solving flexibility is not necessarily manifested in the same way as interpersonal, social flexibility. Nor is creativity a unidimensional construct; different measures of creative aptitude do not correlate positively with one another (Durio, 1979).

However, flexibility and creativity variables are continually found to be related to teaching effectiveness in studies. Social flexibility is related to teaching effectiveness in studies. Social flexibility is related to constructs such as empathy and communication skills and is important to the human interactions of those engaged in teaching and teacher education.

THE STUDENT TEACHING EXPERIENCE

The interaction of the student teacher, cooperating teacher, and university supervisor is the core of the student teaching experience and the area that has received the most attention. Here are considered the selection and training of each member of the triad as well as changes in attitudes and philosophies, role conflicts, socialization, acquisition of teaching behavior, and supervision. The reciprocal influences of the student teacher, cooperating teacher, and university supervisor upon one another provide means to better understand the student teaching experience.

Career Selection and Placement of Student Teachers

A prevailing theme in the literature regarding the selection of student teachers was stated succinctly by Muente (1974): "Let's be more selective with student teachers" (p. 236). Writing from the perspective of cooperating teacher and field supervisor, she urges that "poor risks" and students who are "unsuited for teaching" be "weeded out" prior to student teaching. Given such a critical perspective of the status quo, it is important to know the characteristics that are prevalent in the population of prospective teachers.

By contrasting responses of prospective teachers in 1960 with those in 1975, Fox (1976) investigated the question of why students major in education. he noted that students in 1975 were significantly more likely to indicate humanistic reasons (e.g., desire to work with young children, dissatisfaction with poor teachers, etc.) than the 1960 subjects. They were significantly less influenced by factors such as higher salaries, job security, or social prestige.

These findings may reflect systematic differences in the two populations; however, the changes may be due to the context in which the decision to teach is made rather than the individuals making the decision. Teaching in the 1970s and 1980s may no longer be characterized as a relatively high-paying, secure, or prestigious profession. This is reinforced by the popular press such as *Newsweek* ("Why Public Schools are Flunking," April 20, 1981, April 27, 1981; May 4, 1981). Therefore, it is unlikely that contemporary preservice teaching would cite these reasons for their career choice, whereas they might have been quite plausible ones 20 years ago.

There is some indication that the decision to enter teaching is not made or acted upon hastily. Van Patten (1977) and Seiforth and Samuel (1979) stress that the first education course in the professional sequence may be critical in the selection process. Zeichner (1980) has proposed that many preprofessional experiences may contribute to selection into (or out of) the profession.

Clearly, no profession relies exclusively on self-selection for determining its membership, particularly when there are clear and pressing supply–demand forces operating in the societal context. Ellsworth, Krepelka, and Kear (1979) and Haberman (1974) address the selection process from this perspective.

Ellsworth et al. (1979) emphasize that the core issue should be the fairness and appropriateness of candidate screening procedures vis-à-vis the role of the teacher. They concede that substantial variation in screening criteria exists across teacher education institutions but note that the differences may be a reasonable reflection of the differing goals in those institutions. This should not excuse, however, a lack of systematic investigation of institutional processes, especially those relating entry skills of teaching to the institutional goals. Among screening procedures, Ellsworth et al. found that grade-point averages (GPAs) and personal interviews are used most frequently. Other criteria used somewhat less often included evidence of good health, language proficiency, and profiles derived from personality inventories. Also, the authors point out that there is a trend toward increasing demand for, and reliance upon, various competency tests. The tests being developed and/or used pertain to subject matter competency and general reading, language, and mathematics proficiency.

Haberman (1974) would support the use of such testing, to the extent that the tests could predict teaching success rather than success as a student. Lack of predictive validity is an essential element of the arguments of those who criticize the use of GPAs and interviews for selection purposes.

Given the apparent need for more careful selection of student teachers and the demand for systematic and appropriate selection criteria, it is surprising to find so little current research relating the use of selection criteria to different student teacher outcomes. Leslie (1970) and Wilk (1964) studied possible relationships between placement selection variables, student teacher performance, and student teacher attitudes. Whereas Wilk's student teachers performed better when their grade-level preferences and area of experience were considered in the placement process, Leslie's student teachers did not perform better (the matching efforts here were far more extensive). However, Leslie concluded that certain within-group comparisons supported the general theoretical advantages of matching for placement practices.

Selection of Cooperating Teachers and University Supervisors

It is easy to document the need for careful selection of student teachers while, at the same time, believing that cooperating teachers should be chosen carefully for their role. Yet, as Brodbelt (1980) notes, the selection of supervising teachers is ironically among the more neglected aspects of student teaching programs. Participants at a 1981 national conference on student teaching agreed with Brodbelt's opinion that it is too easy to become a co-operating teacher (Griffin, 1982).

The criteria which seem to be used most often (Brodbelt, 1980) for selection include the act of volunteering to supervise a student teacher, satis-factory ratings from one's building principal, and a certain number of years of teaching experience. The point is also made that neither partner in the university–public school collaboration wishes to antagonize the other by re-quiring high teaching-performance standards—the implicit assumption is that a professional operating in the field should be capable of providing the novice with an adequate induction experience.

The Griffin et al. (1983) investigation found that there were wide varia-tions in regard to the selection of cooperating teachers. The variation ranged from assignment of volunteers with no apparent use of criteria to guide the selection to systematic selection procedures guided by criteria and imple-mented through multiple observations of prospective cooperating teachers' work in classrooms. The degree to which more rigorous procedures were used appeared to depend upon the importance placed by the university on the characteristics of an "ideal" cooperating teacher.

As far as the selection of university supervisors is concerned, it is diffi-cult to locate published literature explaining or guiding this process. This may very well be a function of the vast differences across institutions in the assignment of the supervisory role/functions to individuals.

Similarly, Griffin found that university supervisors were selected in a variety of ways. This variety included appointment of graduate students at the last minute as well as the joint appointment of career public-school edu-cators through a system of collaboration between the university and the schools.

Cooperating Teacher Training and Experiences

Most of the literature regarding the training of cooperating teachers is craft-oriented. While many authors (Blair, 1960; Painter & Weiner, 1979; Quick, 1967) agreed that special training and skills are needed, there was less agree-ment as to the precise content of that training. Blair (1960) emphasized a need for self-reflection. Quick (1967) specified different categories of assets for cooperating teachers, including professional attitudes, professional abilities, human relations skills, and personal habits. Quick also listed nine supervisory activities with which cooperating teachers need to be familiar. Among these are evaluating student teachers through observation, providing specific feedback and constructive criticism, pointing out strengths and weaknesses, and relinquishing classroom control to the student teacher.

Because these skills are stated clearly, it becomes relatively simple to operationalize them as criteria for selecting cooperating teachers and as training objectives for individuals serving as cooperating teachers. The idea that cooperating teachers can or should be given some inservice education for their expanded instructional/supervisory role is widespread in the literature.

Painter and Weiner (1979) described an inservice, competency-based program for cooperating teachers (competencies were those set forth by AACTE and the teaching competencies established by the State of North Carolina). At least three sessions between cooperating teachers and university supervisors were included in the inservice model, together with campus visits by the cooperating teachers. Informal evaluations of the inservice program were quite favorable. The student teachers tended to feel that communication with cooperating teachers was improved, and the university supervisors gained increased respect for the cooperating teachers' role.

These results may be interpreted as an indirect consequence of the intervention, as well as a direct effect. Garner (1971) found that student teachers reported experiencing improved relations with their cooperating teachers, because the student teachers were allowed to assume greater responsibility for teaching.

Under Painter and Weiner's system, student teachers had to assume increased teaching responsibility to free cooperating teachers to attend university sessions. The improved communication may have been as much a function of this shift in responsibilities as of the nature of inservice training provided. Similarly, Chun (1979) and Shiraki (1979) emphasized the need for active participation on the part of the student teacher.

Other research has been equivocal. Amidon (1967, cited in Tittle, 1974) experimentally manipulated the training given to groups of student teachers and cooperating teachers. Experimental groups received training in interaction analysis while control groups were taught learning theory. Although the student teachers demonstrated improved interaction skills (e.g., were more indirect, accepting, and supportive) with the classroom pupils, no systematic effects were observed with the cooperating teachers. Because there were no reported changes in attitudes of either set of teachers, one might infer that student teachers' improved communication skills with pupils were not transferred to interactions with colleagues. As yet, there has been little conclusive information about the effects of training on cooperating teachers or its impact on student teachers.

The Griffin et al. (1983) study included a small subset of cooperating teachers who had participated in a master's degree program designed specifically with their needs in mind. The content of this program could be characterized as being an adaptation of the clinical supervision model. Thus, cooperating teachers were taught to work with student teachers toward identifying and acting upon perceived problems in ongoing and systematic ways. These cooperating teachers' interactions with their student teachers in the Griffin study demonstrated three differences from the larger sample. First, they implemented a process for working with student teachers, whereas other cooperating teachers appeared to be acting with less structure. Second, the student teachers with whom they worked participated a great deal more in the supervision conferences than did other student teachers. Third, there was evidence that the student teachers were more aware of their own progress than were other student teachers.

University Supervisor Training and Experiences

There is little literature related to formulating a way to prepare supervisors. In a craft-oriented article, Hanke (1967) noted "individuals invariably have no specific preparation for this job" (p. 37), although it seems desirable for the person to have a broad range of experience. It is also believed important for the supervisor to have a thorough knowledge of the college's teacher education sequence. In this manner s/he will be prepared to fulfill the public relations demands of the supervisor's role, to provide for inservice needs of cooperating teachers, and to provide feedback and evaluations regarding the student teacher's performance. Some background in interpersonal relations also seems desirable to enable the supervisor to assist student teachers with anxiety reduction and reality-checking of goals, perspective, and enthusiasm (Hanke, 1967). S/he should be prepared to make appropriate placements by being sensitive to the needs of both the student teacher and the cooperating teacher.

Jones (1980), Copeland and Atkinson (1978b), and Junell (1969) all focused on the elements of human relations and/or communication training and skills of supervisors. Junell argued compellingly that the standard practice of requiring supervisors to grade student teachers has a negative effect on communication. Jones listed a series of potential communication problems between supervisors and cooperating teachers.

Jones's emphasis was a reflection of how extensively the supervisor will need to make use of specialized training. Hence, through training, supervisors should become aware of their own styles, of the reinforcing nature and content of their interactions with teachers, and of the nature of their nonverbal cues. All of the authors mentioned emphasize the need for supervisor training in self-awareness.

Copeland and Atkinson (1978a) manipulated the style of presentation of a supervisor, together with his use of professional jargon, in relation to student teachers' perceptions of the supervisor's perceived credibility and utility. Some support was found for the theoretically based hypothesis of a relationship between perceived expertness and perceived supervisor utility. Thus, student teachers' perceptions of the usefulness of a supervisor were seen by the authors as tied to student perceptions of the extensiveness of supervisor background experiences and training. Research concerning supervisors' training and background is generally inconclusive regarding their effects on student teachers.

Cooperating Teacher and University Supervisor Roles

There are many variations in the roles and activities of the cooperating teacher and the university supervisor. These variations may be due to the university, school district, or schools in which these people work. There has been very little research conducted regarding the actual models of practice despite the numerous theoretical models that have been proposed (e.g., Andrews, 1964; Conant, 1963; Slay, 1974). A few studies exploring the role of the university supervisor note some of the key variables regarding roles and activities in student teaching.

The value of the university supervisor in the usual triadic model has been open to question. Monson and Bebb (1970) view the role as unnecessary, and Zimpher, De Voss, and Nott (1980) regard it as extremely complex. At least two studies have investigated the effects of changing or eliminating the role of the university supervisor (Morris, 1974; Smith, 1969).

In these cases, alteration or elimination of contacts with a university supervisor led only to differences in student teachers' self-reports of satisfaction and ease of communication with cooperating teachers.

Another possible role for university supervisors is that of working directly with the cooperating teacher. Monson and Bebb (1970) described a pilot program in which the only function of the supervisor was a weekly inservice meeting. The results of this program indicated that student teachers, cooperating teachers, and university supervisors were all quite satisfied with this arrangement; however, these results indicated little about what was lost or gained by this model of supervision in comparison to other more traditional models.

A contrasting study by Zimpher et al. (1980) suggested that the university supervisor's influence is very important. From their descriptive study they concluded that without the university supervisor, student teachers would have little input in setting requirements, evaluating or assessing the overall experience. Apparently, these supervisors provided most of the impetus to the student teachers to advance beyond concerns for daily chores to concerns for self-analysis and improvement.

The Griffin et al. (1983) inquiry did not confirm or deny these positions beyond noting that the cooperating teacher and university supervisor roles were not clearly defined either through institutional policies or through individual reflection and decision. Members of both role groups reported little systematic orientation to their functions in the student teaching experience except to note that they were there to somehow help the student teachers. The nature of that help was seldom clarified with any precision.

Socialization or Enculturation of the Student Teacher

Much of what takes place during student teaching can be generally described as socialization. Most of the studies of socialization have focused on particular aspects of the process such as attitude change or acquisition of teaching behaviors. Lortie (1966), Zeichner (1979, 1980), and others have broadened the study of student teacher enculturation to include consideration of other socializing factors such as early childhood experience and peer influences. Zeichner (1979, 1980) and Griffin (1982) have also criticized much of the past work on this topic because of the often implicit assumption that the student teacher was a passive recipient in the process. Zeichner has argued that studies of socialization must take into consideration the reciprocal influences of the cooperating teacher, university supervisor, and student teacher.

Studies of socialization include those that provided various conceptualizations of induction (Iannacone, 1963) and studies that sought to identify the key individuals and their functions in the socialization of newcomers to the profession (Friebus, 1977; Karmos & Jacko, 1977; Manning, 1977; Ryan, 1981). Closely related to this work are studies which identify conformity effects (Haberman, 1978) and critical incidents in successful and unsuccessful student teacher enculturation (DeVoss, 1979).

Iannacone (1963) and Lortie (1966) have both analyzed the teacher socialization process. Iannacone (1963) confined his focus to the changes in student teachers' perceptions of teaching over the course of a semester-long placement. The preliminary concerns reflect student teacher "horror" and "indignation" over cooperating teacher behaviors, and they correspond to an entry stage in which student teachers act only as observers. A transition stage occurs when student teachers and cooperating teachers begin to establish collaborative relationships dependent upon mutual concern for individual learning. However, the relationships are still clearly superordinate–subordinate in nature.

In the final phase, the relationship between student teachers and cooperating teachers becomes more collaborative in nature. The student teachers' perspective toward disruptive behavior, the operationalization of learning goals, and learning problems more closely resemble those set forth by the cooperating teachers (except in the rare case of a student teacher whose socialization may have been unsuccessful; Iannacone, 1963). This is consistent with Haberman's (1978) thesis that student teachers are particularly susceptible to control by group norms, especially those espoused by the classroom teachers.

Several researchers have looked more specifically at the socializing agents (Friebus, 1977; Karmos & Jacko, 1977; Manning, 1977). Manning (1977) reported that the student teachers indicated that professional contacts (cooperating teachers, supervisors, and other college professors) exerted the most significant influence upon their beliefs. Other groups of people such as parents and friends had a less significant influence. Setting and training variables had some effect on the perceived nature of influence exerted by each group. Student teachers who were placed in an inner-city environment without having been trained specifically about that environment were more likely to indicate that their pupils' parents and the community were sources of negative influence on their attitudes. Also, their perceptions of student discipline and beliefs about children's learning, generally, were negatively affected by being in the inner city and by not being prepared for that setting.

Other studies have failed to make direct comparisons of setting and training variables to perceived influences of significant others. The work of Karmos and Jacko (1977) focused only on positive influences on the student teaching experience. Both professional and nonprofessional sources of influence were mentioned more often than any of the others. In addition, the cooperating teachers' most critical functions, in descending order, were perceived to be: (a) promoting the student teachers' role development; (b) providing the student teachers with personal support; and (c) assisting the student teachers to gain professional skills.

Karmos and Jacko (1977) also found that student teachers reported that pupils served two critical functions. First, the pupils' responses to student teachers worked to legitimize the latter's place in the classroom. Second, their task-related behaviors worked to determine the success or failure of student teachers' lessons. In neither the Karmos and Jacko (1977) study nor the Friebus (1977) study were university supervisors given any significant mention, unlike Manning's (1977) work.

De Voss (1979) examined student teachers' enculturation from an even broader perspective. Through observations and a series of open-ended interviews, he was able to select case studies demonstrating the impact of different settings (classroom, university, school, home) acting upon the student teachers. By contrasting the "best" and "worst" cases and sifting through the series of critical incidents they contained, De Voss reached several conclusions. First, when student teachers and cooperating teachers were mutually supportive and similar in philosophy, orientation, and attitudes, the student teachers were more likely to report having successful experiences. Second, the student teachers' ability to focus personal energy on the experience was associated with success. Those student teachers who had large portions of their time, energy, and attention consumed by the demands of unrelated settings (e.g., spouses and children, other jobs, etc.) were less likely to experience success in their placements.

Other investigators have explored critical incidents in student teaching. Southall and King (1979) were able to identify a lack of student teacher–cooperating teacher communication and unrealistic cooperating teacher expectations as the two most important and frequent problems with which supervisors had to contend. Differing expectations were also identified by Campbell and Williamson (1973) as a problem. Other problem areas were tied to a failure in interpersonal relations.

These problems indicate that multiple factors influence the socialization process. De Voss (1979) emphasized the importance of considering the student teachers as active agents in their own socialization, because satisfaction with the experience was directly tied, in part, to the students' own abilities to utilize the opportunities for learning.

Attitude and Philosophy Changes

Traditionally, the study of student teacher socialization has focused on changes in students' philosophy and attitudes. A review of this work substantiates the following two generalizations. First, student teachers' attitudes toward students and teaching tend to change negatively during the course of student teaching. Second, student teachers' attitudes, values, and/or philosophies tend to shift toward increasing conformity with those of their cooperating teachers.

Tittle (1974) reviewed at least five studies of attitude change in student teachers. Two (Butcher, 1965; Jacobs, 1968) documented a decrease in positive educational attitudes during student teaching, even though the instrumentation differed. Four others (Clarke, 1956; Corrigan & Griswold, 1963; Price, 1960; Tabachnick, 1980) yielded sets of data consistent with the general notion that student teachers' attitudes more closely approximated those of their cooperating teachers by the end of the placement. Two other studies (Leslie, 1970; Ringness, 1966) failed to find any significant impact of cooperating teachers upon attitudes and self-ideal image discrepancies of student teachers, respectively.

Boscher and Prescott (1978) considered educational philosophies of cooperating teachers as they impact student teachers during preservice training. They found no apparent cooperating teacher influence. Of the predictor variables considered, only preservice philosophical positions of the student teachers predicted their poststudent-teaching philosophical views, if the student teacher had come into the preservice experience with perennialism or essentialism biases. Thus, changing attitudes did occur during preservice, but they were not influenced by the supervising teacher.

However, Yee (1969) pointed out a major shortcoming in most prior studies of attitude change, particularly those using the Minnesota Teacher Attitude Inventory (MTAI). Most of the research failed to take into account the possibility that in a dyad influences on attitudes can be either mutual or bidirectional in causality. Further, the influences may effect increased congruity across the attitudes of each member of the dyad. When statistical manipulations were performed to allow for multiple outcomes, Yee (1969) reached three major conclusions. First, cooperating teachers exerted an influence that caused student teachers attitudes to become more like their own. Second, student teachers' attitudes shifted toward increasing conformity with cooperating teachers' attitudes. Third, when the attitude shifts in a dyad led to greater incongruity, there was no difference in the frequency of influence across cooperating and student teachers. These results were consistent with Yee's (1968) earlier study, which indicated that few stable relationships (in terms of attitudes) across dyads existed and that most attitude shifts were negative in nature.

From a different, theoretically based perspective, Mahan and Lacefield (1978) also examined the possibilities of mutual influence and greater congruity or incongruity in attitude changes as a function of student teaching. Their review of available descriptive research indicated that, generally, student teachers' values on several dimensions were more "emergent," or liberal, than those of cooperating teachers. This information, together with the observed trends toward increasing congruity and similarity to the cooperating teachers' attitudes, enabled the authors to explain student change on the basis of cognitive dissonance theory. If a student teacher is exposed to a cooperating teacher's set of beliefs that are moderately different from his/her own, the resultant dissonance should be resolved over time by a shift in student attitudes. Moreover, given the limited discrepancy between student beliefs and the situational/organizational constraints surrounding the dyad, the shift should be one of increased similarity to the beliefs of the cooperating teacher. Finally, the extent of the shift should be a function of the duration of exposure to the cooperating teacher. In this study, student teacher perceptions did become more compatible with local reality over time. These findings were confirmed in the 1974 and 1975 studies reported by Mahan and Lacefield (1978).

The Mahan and Lacefield (1978) studies support the contention that time plays a role in the magnitude of the shifts in student teacher attitudes. Lipka and Goulet (1979) also investigated age- and experience-related changes in teacher attitudes toward the profession. Using a self-report questionnaire based upon the "technique of retrospection," teachers served as their own historical comparison group. Lipka and Goulet failed to obtain significant differences between teachers' perceptions of values across chronological age (even when experience was used as a covariate). Significant differences were observed, however, in the perceived importance of values over time, independent of age.

The Griffin et al. (1983) study also used the Mahan and Lacefield methodology to determine educational preferences. The findings were consonant with previous studies in that student teachers (as well as cooperating teachers and university supervisors) became more traditional over the course of the experience. That is, initial self-reports of progressivism shifted to more conventional views.

Interpersonal Communication and Role Conflict

Other factors can be a source of difficulty in the communication and interpersonal relationships of the student teachers, cooperating teachers, and university supervisors. A few studies have examined role conflict and interpersonal communication.

Gettone (1980) looked at differing expectations about the roles and duties of student teachers as perceived by school administrators, master teachers, and student teachers. Student teachers saw themselves as more ready to assume a professional role than did school personnel, who saw student teachers as more similar to assistants, aides, or apprentices. Farley (1973) found that cooperating teachers and student teachers differed in opinions on the importance of instruction time, discipline policies, and educational innovations as well as the duties of the student teachers.

Kaplan (1967) investigated the perceptions of student teachers, cooperating teachers, and college supervisors regarding the role of college supervisors and found that there was a lack of agreement about the valuation and resource consultant functions of college supervisors. Prokop (1973), Simms (1975), Clemons (1973), and Campbell and Williamson (1973) have all declared that such differing expectations are central to role conflict.

Lasley (1980) found differences between student teachers and experienced teachers in terms of beliefs held about teaching. Preservice teachers expressed beliefs that teaching was a fulfilling career, whereas many experienced teachers were disillusioned with teaching, citing low prestige, low pay, and student misbehavior as reasons. Preservice teachers tended to believe that their preservice courses did not prepare them for the reality of student teaching, and experienced teachers seemed to share this view.

The effects of cooperating teachers in the general areas of interpersonal relations and communications have been investigated in several studies. Close matching of student teachers and cooperating teachers on conceptual levels has been advocated often in the literature (Thies-Sprinthall, 1980). The assumption behind matching appears to be that those pairs working from a similar frame of reference will interact more effectively and smoothly.

The importance of the interpersonal relationship between student and cooperating teachers has been supported by some research findings. Supervisors asked to identify the problems encountered in working with cooperating and student teachers identified lack of communication between cooperating teachers and student teachers as their most frequent problem (Southall & King, 1979). Other problem areas were failure of the student teachers to meet expectations of the cooperating teachers and failure of the student teachers to follow through on suggestions from the cooperating teachers. These problems clearly relate to the interpersonal communication realm. Furthermore, they may be related to the different conceptual levels and different personal reference points for judging effective teaching.

Wide variation between student teachers and cooperating teachers was described by two studies. Thies-Sprinthall (1980) measured stages of both moral judgment and conceptual levels in cooperating and student teachers and investigated their relationship to ratings of student teacher effectiveness. When student teachers with high ratings were paired with cooperating teachers with low ratings, the latter rated the student teacher as being average or below average in teaching effectiveness. Thies-Sprinthall suggested that this rating might occur because the cooperating teachers misperceived the performance of the student teachers. The "mismatched" cooperating teachers may lack a common frame of reference to adequately communicate analyses and suggestions to the student teachers.

Teacher Behavior

A major issue regarding student teachers is the way in which they acquire their teaching behavior. Several studies have found that cooperating teachers play an important role in the student teachers' classroom performance (Price, 1961; Seperson & Joyce, 1973; Zevin, 1974). However, McIntyre and Morris (1977) found studies that may qualify those findings. Individual characteristics of both the cooperating teachers and the student teachers may mediate the influence of the cooperating teachers on student teachers' classroom performance (McIntyre, Buell, & Casey, 1979).

Evidence that student teachers were affected by the teacher practices of the cooperating teacher was found by Price (1961), Seperson and Joyce (1973), and Zevin (1974). Zevin used an adaptation of Flanders Interaction Analysis to measure the change in inquiry or lecture styles of teaching by student teachers in relation to the style of the cooperating teachers. In the case of lecture, this change occurred despite input by the university supervisor.

Copeland (1977) acknowledged that the cooperating teacher effects were not always clear-cut and direct. When student teachers were exposed to different combinations of microteaching and modeling of a target skill by the cooperating teachers, there was an interactive effect between the microteaching and modeling. That is, "When either direct intervention provided by the cooperating teacher was augmented by training in Instructional Supervision techniques or indirect intervention was characterized by high exhibition of the target skill, the student teachers who received microteaching training evidenced a significantly higher rate of exhibition of the target skill in their classrooms" (Copeland, 1977, p. 154). As a partial explanation, Copeland suggested that the cooperating teachers' influence was mediated by the context of the classroom: Student teachers exhibited target skills taught through microteaching to a significantly higher degree in classrooms where the classroom teachers exhibited those skills.

However, conflicting results have been reported for cooperating teacher influence on student teacher classroom performance. Prospective teachers studied by McIntyre et al. (1979) did not model the verbal behavior of their cooperating teachers. There are many possible explanations for this finding: (a) the experimenters may not have waited long enough for the modeling effects to be visible; (b) pupil behavior may not have permitted the student teachers to demonstrate the targeted verbal behaviors; and/or (c) the student teachers may have been instructed by their supervisors to behave in a particular manner.

Recent research on teaching effectiveness provides some guidelines for teaching practice in some grades and content areas (Good & Grouws, 1979; Soar & Soar, 1972; Brophy & Evertson, 1974; McDonald, Elias, Stone, Wheeler, Lambert, Calfee, Sandoval, Ekstrom, & Lockheed, 1975; Stallings & Kaskowitz, 1974). The guidelines can be useful to student teachers in their new role, especially at the elementary level for reading and math instruction. Competencies in giving academic feedback and keeping students academically engaged, for example, seem to be valuable skills for student teachers to acquire. Other findings may be equally valuable in areas of direct and indirect teaching, task structuring, classroom management, and questioning practices.

Medley (1977) stated that no one particular skill or competency is consistently related to effective teaching behavior across different learning outcomes and different groups of students. Instructional functions such as cuing, reinforcement behaviors, and maintaining student time on task are considered by Burke, Hansen, Houston, and Johnson (1975) and Doyle (1977) to be a more appropriate conceptualization for studying teacher competencies than singular teacher abilities. Knowing what teaching strategy to use in the appropriate context, and how to follow through on it, seems to be paramount (Brophy & Evertson, 1976; Schalock, 1979).

Research on effective teaching does reveal clusters of teacher behaviors important to student learning. However, there has been little attempt to date to coordinate this line of research endeavor with what occurs in teacher preparation. The question of whether effective teachers (those able to produce gains in pupil achievement) are also the most effective cooperating teachers in working with student teachers has not been addressed, yet this clarifying link is essential to the purposes of teacher education.

Supervision

The topic of supervision cuts across several of the previous sections, and certainly many of the previous topics (e.g., attitudes and teaching behaviors) are clearly influenced by the variable of supervision. Several recent studies demonstrate clearly the role that supervision plays in student teaching.

Recalling the notion that the best plans may fail, Copeland (1977) and Doyle and Ponder (1975) have analyzed the distinction of performance versus acquisition of sets of behaviors in the context of student teaching. The latter two authors contend that most empirical investigations of the effectiveness of skills training in teacher education are based upon an assumption which may be erroneous. They question the premise that teachers can behave independently of or control the many contingencies operating in the classroom context.

Copeland (1977) conducted an investigation which addressed the performance/acquisition distinction. Findings indicated that when cooperating teachers were trained in supervision, regardless of how often they utilized a particular skill, the student teachers found enough support to risk trying out laboratory-learned skills. When cooperating teachers utilized a target skill quite often, regardless of whether or not they were trained in supervision, the student teachers were likely to adopt the skill. Lastly, when the cooperating teachers were neither trained in supervision nor exhibited a target skill with much frequency, the student teachers were unlikely to complete, and/or be rewarded for, the transfer of laboratory-learned skills to the classroom.

The question of directive and nondirective techniques of supervision of student teachers was investigated by Copeland (1980) and Copeland and Atkinson (1978b). In the earlier study, student teachers were asked to view videotapes of directive and nondirective supervisors in conference and then rate the supervisors according to eight concepts. The student teachers rated the directive supervisors significantly differently on seven of the concepts and clearly preferred the directive behavior. The later study by Copeland and Atkinson (1980a) added the variables of supervisor sex and student-teacher sex to the analysis. Again the directive approach was preferred, and student teachers appeared to prefer supervisors of the opposite sex. Women gave higher ratings to nondirective male supervisors than to nondirective female supervisors.

Griffin and colleagues (1983) noted several patterns in terms of supervision of student teachers. First, cooperating teachers dominated these interactions significantly from the beginning of the experience through to the end. Second, student teachers utterances during supervision conferences were confined almost exclusively to short confirming statements (e.g., "Yes," "I see," etc.). Third, specific evaluative comments about student teachers were seldom made by cooperating teachers or university supervisors. Furthermore, the content of the supervision conferences was dominated by concerns about classroom management. In addition, there was an almost total absence of talk regarding affective dimensions of classroom life. Moreover, the supervision conferences dealt with situation specific, time bound issues such as what to do with a certain student regarding a certain problem at a certain time. Finally, there was very little attention given to instructional planning beyond the scope of a particular lesson.

Clearly, the style of supervision and preferences of student teachers interact in a complicated manner. A preference on the part of student teachers for directive supervision has strong support in these studies. Keeping in mind the pressures on the student teachers to perform at an acceptable level within a certain time period and within various contexts, a preference for concrete, professional advice is not surprising. Conversely, the student teachers may feel that they are being needlessly frustrated by the requirement to self-analyze, self-diagnose, and self-evaluate under the watchful eye of the nondirective supervisor.

CONTEXTUAL INFLUENCES

It is axiomatic that the contexts in which people live and work are instrumental in shaping and modifying behaviors. With few exceptions, the influence of the school/university context upon teachers and students in these settings has been studied from the perspective of the practicing inservice educator rather than from the vantage point of the teacher in preparation. Of necessity, then, this section of the review depends upon information believed to be related to, although not directly drawn from, the interactions of cooperating teachers/student teachers/university supervisors and the contexts in which they execute their roles. Two contexts are considered: the university and the elementary or secondary school.

The University Context

This section of the review attends to the formal organizational properties of the university setting as they impact upon the student teaching experience. Such properties include rules and regulations, policies regarding evaluation and recommendation for certification, evaluation of student teachers, and assignment of student teachers.

In addition to the direct influences the university exerts on teachers in training through courses and supervision, the academic environment also has an indirect impact on the student teaching experience. This indirect impact occurs through the university community's values, beliefs, and standards. Teacher education evolved independently of the academic community and has only gradually, in the last century, emerged as a function of higher education (Hughes, 1981). Through the years, several authors have commented about teacher education as being the "stepchild" of the university (Goldhammer, 1977). There is some question as to whether the values and standards necessary for effective teacher education are compatible with typical academic values. Goldhammer (1977) argues strongly that the "culture of higher education often runs counter to skill-building and professional development programs" (p. 12). Specifically, he mentions the lack of values, prestige, and recognition given by the academic community to persons engaged in the clinical aspects of teacher education.

This criticism has been a constant theme through the history of teacher education. Conant (1963) sought to solve this same problem through the creation of "clinical professorships" on an equal status with the more typical discipline-oriented professorships. Individuals who assumed these new professorships were to be evaluated in terms of their clinical skills and their training of preservice education students rather than the more typical criteria of research productivity or conventional scholarship. This proposal has not received widespread acceptance, and no general, satisfactory resolution to the problem of different values across institutional systems or contexts has been found.

The degree to which this conflict is resolved by the education department of a university can influence both the teacher education program and the perspectives of students in the program. The university community provides some very potent socializing influences, with regard to students' perceptions of the importance of skill-building and academic preparation. The influence may be felt through the type of program in operation or through the philosophies and value positions held by faculty members.

Perhaps the most obvious way in which the value of practice and skill-building is upheld occurs through the degree to which the university provides a supportive environment for practice (Goldhammer, 1977; Hunter, 1980). Often supervision of clinical education is an added responsibility for an already overburdened staff. As such, it is assigned to graduate students and assistants who must "pay their dues." For them it is often a low-priority task with little benefit. The degree to which they function effectively as supervisors depends heavily on support, encouragement, and rewards available for that service. Therefore, the student teaching experience may be affected sharply by the degree to which the university provides a supportive environment for those charged with supervision of student teachers.

In summary, the university has an indirect influence on student teaching through its value system and its support role. The values that become incorporated into teacher education programs and are articulated by faculty provide some primary socialization experiences for preservice teachers. Likewise, student teaching is influenced by the supportive role played by the university in its assistance to basic supervisory personnel.

The Public School Context

While it is generally agreed that cooperating teachers exert a great deal of influence on student teaching, there has been little examination of the impact of the public school environment or context on the student teaching experience. Some general advice from the field suggests that this context may be important. Several of the guidelines developed for student teachers include recommendations that students be exposed to children of various backgrounds and levels of ability. And, recently, educators have placed more emphasis on student teaching experiences that include various ethnic groups. Despite these suggestions, little is known about the effects of these experiences.

Poole (1972) suggests that school context is quite important to student teachers' perceptions of adequate training. In this study student teachers were asked to rate 30 statements about their experiences with their cooperating teacher, the principal, and other staff; physical arrangements within the school; and contacts with fellow student teachers. They were also asked to rate the value of the student teaching experience.

The questions about experiences in the school were factor analyzed, yielding six factors: (a) experience in well-organized, supportive situations; (b) experience of criticism; (c) good working relationships with other staff; (d) lack of support; (e) good working relationships with fellow students; and (f) good, informal, working relationships with the children. When these factors were correlated with the student teachers' perceived value of the experience, the strongest predictor of each student's rating (that s/he had learned a great deal from student teaching) was having experienced a well-organized, supportive environment.

Those students who indicated that their present program had provided adequate preparation for student teaching felt that they had made a contribution to the school and that they had experienced good informal working relationships with the cooperating teacher and the students. Those students who reported that student teaching appeared to be merely an evaluative experience indicated that they had experienced considerable criticism and lack of support.

Another very significant part of the public school influence on student teachers is what Hoy and Rees (1977) call "bureaucratic socialization," which they define as an organization's "attempt to mold role ideology and role performance of personnel through a variety of procedures and mechanisms designed to make individual beliefs, values, and norms correspond with those of the organization" (p. 23). In their study the authors assessed students' bureaucratic orientation before and after their clinical experiences. They found that student teachers' beliefs and orientations were more bureaucratic following the student teaching experience. They were more likely to state that orders were to be followed without challenge and that one should be loyal to superiors without questioning their authority.

Pruitt and Lee (1978) commented that it is not surprising that teachers are subordinate and traditional in their outlooks. These authors note that most teachers, especially cooperating teachers, are caught in a web of conformity. "They are often rewarded for conformity through promotions, salary increases, light schedules and subtle administration favors" (Pruitt & Lee, 1978, p. 71). Likewise, student teachers find themselves trapped in this bureaucratic net. If they conform to the demands, they find the teaching experience rewarding. Pruitt and Lee (1978) note that "innovative and idealistic student teachers often meet stern opposition, become frustrated, and then conform in a last ditch effort to salvage a grade" (p. 71). The combined pressures of certification, graduation, and approval from the cooperating teacher and university supervisor usually result in a high degree of conformity.

It is important to consider both the supportive and bureaucratic influences of the public schools. The same system of colleagues that can serve a support role to the student teachers can also create pressure to conform to the rules of the school organization. The student teachers' active participation in this process needs to be examined more fully so as to develop a greater understanding of the various public school characteristics and their effects upon the student teaching experience.

In addition to the separate influences of the university and the public school, their interaction has considerable influence on the functioning of student teaching. Several writers have indicated that a collaborative university–public school relationship is an important determining factor in a successful student teaching program (Andrews, 1964; Howey, 1977; MacNaughton, Johns, & Rogus, 1978). There has been little research of institutional relationships other than reviews of various practices (Slay, 1974).

The Griffin et al. (1983) study found that the primary influence on the student teaching experience is the public-school classroom context. The dominant theme expressed by cooperating teachers was that what the student teachers had experienced in their preservice preparation programs would be of little, if any, help in doing the work of teaching. Although some university supervisors in the study attempted to maintain ideological and pedagogical links with preservice methods courses, those attempts were not observed as being influential upon the student teaching experience. Further, there was little evidence from the data collected for the study that any systematic efforts were being expended toward the end of building institutional linkages between the schools and the university.

SUMMARY AND OVERVIEW OF EMERGENT ISSUES

It was noted at the beginning of this review that most of the literature pertaining to student teaching is nonempirical, craft-oriented, and scattered widely across different perspectives and topic areas. In an effort to collect and systematically present the information, this review has focused on student teaching as the experience of a basic triad (student teacher, cooperating teacher, and university supervisor) embedded in several overlapping contexts. To better understand the processes and outcomes of the experience, the demographics and individual differences characterizing each of the three central participants were reviewed.

Available data pertaining to several psychological constructs such as teacher concerns, empathy, scholastic aptitude, flexibility, cognitive complexity, and creativity were discussed. More questions were discovered than answered in these instances also. For example, empathy is a construct often mentioned in the contexts of supervision and consultation, but it has rarely been applied or investigated in the domain of student teaching—despite the logical inclusion of such activities in student teaching. Much of the dilemma rests on the debate as to whether such characteristics should be entry "sorting devices" or should be somehow taught during preservice teacher education sequences. Similarly, factors such as flexibility and cognitive complexity warrant further investigation of their poorly understood roles in student teaching, particularly with regard to the outcomes of the experience. It would be useful for practitioners and teacher educators to know, for example, whether or not matched levels of cognitive complexity enhance the success of student teaching either through student teacher "satisfaction" and/or in terms of teacher practice.

In the second section of the review, general constraints determining who may fill each of the roles in the triad were examined. Thus, the focus was on the preparatory experiences, training, and selection of student teachers, university supervisors, and cooperating teachers. Several problems in practice and unexplored topics in the literature were highlighted. For example, there appears to be a prevailing imprecision and dissatisfaction in the selection processes applied to cooperating teachers and university supervisors; yet few researchers or practitioners have set forth operational standards for selection which can be evaluated for their appropriateness and utility vis-à-vis student teaching outcomes. Reasons for the "selection by default" process which sometimes seems to be in effect pertain to the institutional contexts in which selection is occurring. The selection of student teachers appears to suffer from parallel problems.

Reviewing the roles and functions of cooperating teachers and university supervisors was equally telling of practical problems and new research questions. First of all, evidence for the value of the traditional university supervisor role has been equivocal. Second, the cooperating teacher role of socialization agent has been both analyzed and researched, but there is still only a minimal understanding of the dynamics of student teacher socialization. This is probably reflective of the tendency on the part of educational researchers to be overly constricted in their research foci. Third and perhaps most ironic is the dearth of carefully constructed investigations of the *in situ* acquisition of teaching behaviors, particularly with regard to the presumed influences of the cooperating teacher. Finally, styles of supervision, student teacher preferences for supervision, and their interaction effects have not been well-investigated. In view of the obvious complexity of the student teaching experience, it seems essential that future research include at least minimal evidence of how the participants were selected, of what sorts of training experiences they received, and of the nature of the participants' interactions—all as they relate to the likelihood of success or failure of student teaching.

In the closing section the contextual influences impinging upon and coloring the student teaching experience were reviewed. This included some consideration of the university or teacher training institution which establishes and regulates the student teaching experience, together with the public schools which permit the mission to be fulfilled. Further exploration of the ways in which each institution regulates student teaching and the consequences of the institutional interactions needs to be conducted to assess which conditions, regulations, communication norms, etc., are associated with positive student teaching experiences.

Several issues arise from this review. They can best be put forth as questions.

First, who should participate in the student teaching experience? There seems to be a prevailing view that the student teaching experience should be made available to all but the most obviously inept. This mentality further promotes the practice, once a student is placed in a student teaching setting, that all student teachers must succeed. This "mastery learning" approach sometimes results in certification of student teachers who are acknowledged as being somehow inadequate to teaching tasks (Griffin et al. 1983). Although a certain amount of public controversy has centered on the qualifications of persons about to begin teaching (student teachers), less attention has been given to the "ideal" cooperating teacher and university supervisor.

Second, what skills are necessary for cooperating teachers and university supervisors in relation to providing the best possible experience for novice teachers? Although there have been several programs for the professional education of these persons, none appear to have been developed as a consequence of prior research activity. Rather, they tend to be adaptations of already intact programs (e.g., clinical supervision). Is it possible that certain bodies of knowledge can be brought together to develop a new program of instruction? For instance, should cooperating teachers be aware of and skillful in techniques for working with adult learners?

Third, what should be the content of the student teaching experience? Several of the studies identified in this review noted the domination of classroom management as content. Yet, there is little evidence that the considerably expanded body of research knowledge regarding that classroom phenomenon has become a part of the student teaching experience. Rather, cooperating teachers and university supervisors tend to depend on those things that "have worked for me." In like vein, the literature regarding effective schools seems to have not made any headway into the knowledge base that supports student teaching. Further, is it enough to use only the situation specific phenomena found in individual classrooms as the primary content of student teaching? In that student teaching tends to be typically carried forth in schools that are somewhat more manageable than the majority of schools in which students may eventually be placed, should student teaching experiences be guided by the expectation that alternate solutions to persistent problems should be presented? That is, although it may satisfy immediate needs to tell or show student teachers how to deal with this child at this moment in this classroom, is it desirable (or possible) to also tell or show them alternate courses of action given different situational variables?

Fourth, is it desirable that the public elementary or secondary school classroom context be the primary (if not sole) driving force for the experience? The provision of student teaching opportunities could be a very effective means toward achieving some sort of congruence between public school and university expectations for teaching, learning, and schooling. Yet, the studies noted here and elsewhere indicate the persistence of the sharp division between "methods courses and theory taught in the college or university" and "the real world of teaching." There appears to be a well-established gulf between what higher education tells its students about teaching and what the public schools expect of teachers.

Fifth, is the dominance of the public school viewpoint, influenced as it is by influential political and social realities, the appropriate "capstone" experience for prospective teachers? It is possible that the long-decried socialization of teachers toward the norms of the public school is a consequence of bad timing on the part of teacher education programs. Should student teaching be followed by periods of guided reflection and analysis conducted by college and university persons? Ought this reflection also be guided by public school persons? Is it possible to somehow blunt the apparent lowering of teacher expectations through this or another such process?

Sixth, how can participants in student teaching experiences be guided by *shared* understandings of the processes, expectations, and outcomes of the experience? There is a significant amount of information suggesting that student teaching is understood differently by different participants. Is it time for teacher educators, university- and school-based, to begin again the dialogue regarding what student teaching should be about? And, importantly, is it time to engage student teachers in that dialogue?

Finally, what strategies can be used to promote the rigorous inquiry of student teaching by qualified researchers? Certainly, if student teaching is as important as participants, past and present, assert it to be, it deserves careful and systematic study. Although there is considerable talk about student teaching, there is a surprisingly small body of research that helps us to understand it. There is a host of questions to be answered about student teaching.

REFERENCES

Andrews, L. O. (1964). *Student teaching.* New York: The Center for Applied Research in Education.

Blair, L. C. (1960). Are you good enough to be a supervising teacher? *Teacher's College Journal, 32,* 25–29, 45–46.

Bond, J. (1959). Analysis of observed traits of teachers rated superior in demonstrating creativeness in teaching. *Review of Educational Research, 53,* 7–12.

Boscher, F., & Prescott, D. R. (1978). Do cooperating teachers influence the educational philosophy of student teachers? *Journal of Teacher Education, 29,* 57–61.

Brodbelt, S. (1980). Selecting the supervising teacher. *Contemporary Education, 51*(2), 86–88.

Brophy, J., & Evertson, C. (1974). *Process-product correlations in the Texas teacher effectiveness study: Final report* (Res. Rep. 74-4). Austin, TX: The University of Texas at Austin, Research and Development Center for Teacher Education.

Brophy, J., & Evertson, C. M. (1976). *Learning from teaching: A developmental perspective.* Boston, MA: Allyn & Bacon.

Burke, J. B., Hansen, J. H., Houston, W. R., & Johnson, C. (1975). *Criteria for describing and assessing competency-based programs: A position paper of the Consortium of CBE Centers.* Albany, NY: The Multi-State Consortium for Performance-Based Teacher Education, Syracuse University.

Buskin, M. (1975). *Parent power.* New York: Walher.

Butcher, H. J. (1965). The attitudes of student teachers to education: A comparison with the attitudes of experienced teachers and a study of changes during the training course. *British Journal of Social and Clinical Psychology, 4,* 17–24.

Campbell, L. P., & Williamson, J. A. (1973). Practical problems in the student teacher-cooperative teacher relationships. *Education, 94,* 168–169.

Carkhuff, R. (1971). *The development of human resources.* New York: Holt, Rinehart, & Winston.

Chun, J. H. N. (1979). The host teacher in the observation-participation program. *Educational Perspective, 18*(3), 12–14.

Clarke, A. A. (1956). A study of the validity of the Minnesota Teacher Attitude Inventory as an instrument to aid in the selection of directing teachers (Doctoral dissertation, Florida State University). *Dissertation Abstracts, 16,* 1404.

Clemons, W. H. (1973). Variations in role expectations and role realizations as perceived by teacher aide trainees, teachers of teacher aide trainees, teacher aides, and teachers utilizing teacher aides. *Dissertation Abstracts, 34,* 1160A.

Cogan, M. L. (1973). *Clinical supervision.* Boston, MA: Houghton Mifflin.

Conant, J. B. (1963). *The education of American teachers.* New York: McGraw-Hill.

Coopersmith, S., & Feldman, R. (1974). Fostering a positive self concept and high self-esteem in the classroom. In R. H. Coop & K. White (Eds.), *Psychological concepts in the classroom.* New York: Harper & Row.

Copeland, W. D. (1977). Some factors related to student teacher classroom performance following microteaching training. *American Educational Research Journal, 14,* 147–157.

Copeland, W. D. (1980). Affective dispositions of teachers in training toward examples of supervisory behavior. *Journal of Educational Research, 74,* 37–42.

Copeland, W. D., & Atkinson, D. R. (1978a). Prestigious introduction, professional jargon, and perceived supervisor credibility and utility. *College Student Journal, 12,* 420–428.

Copeland, W. D., & Atkinson, D. R. (1978b). Student teachers' perceptions of directive and nondirective supervisory behavior. *Journal of Educational Research, 71,* 123–127.

Corrigan, D., & Griswold, K. (1963). Attitude changes of student teachers. *Journal of Educational Research, 57,* 93–95.

Craft, D. J. (1979). *Parents and teachers: A resource book for home, school, and community relations.* Belmont, CA: Wadsworth.

Crocker, A. C. (1974). *Predicting teaching success.* London: National Foundation for Educational Research.

De Voss, G. (1979, April). *Student teaching as studentship: An ethnographic investigation.* Paper presented at the meeting of the American Educational Research Association, San Francisco, CA.

Doherty, J. (1980). An exploratory investigation into the relationship between self-esteem and teaching performance in a group of student teachers. *Educational Review, 32,* 21–35.

Doyle, W. (1977). Paradigms for research on teacher effectiveness. In. L. S. Shulman (Ed.), *Review of Research in Education* (Vol. 5). Itasca, IL: Peacock.

Doyle, W., & Ponder, G. A. (1975). Classroom ecology: Some concerns about a neglected dimension of research on teaching. *Contemporary Education, 46,* 183–187.

Ducharme, R. J. (1970). *Selected preservice factors related to success of the beginning teacher.* Unpublished doctoral dissertation, Louisiana State University, Baton Rouge, LA.

Durio, H. F. (1979). A factor analysis of response task constraint in measure of creative aptitude. *Gifted Child Quarterly, 23,* 829–836.

Ekstrom, R. (1976). Teacher aptitude, knowledge, attitudes, and cognitive style as predictors of teaching behavior. *Journal of Teacher Education, 27,* 329–331.

Ellsworth, R., Krepekla, E., & Kear, D. (1979). Teacher education and dilemmas of selecting teachers for teacher training. *Teacher Educator, 15,* 21–31.

Farley, T. W. (1973). Comparisons of perceptions of elementary student teaching as perceived by cooperating teachers and student teachers. *Dissertation Abstracts International, 34,* 654B.

Ferguson, J. (1977, November). *Personality characteristics, setting characteristics, and academic ability as predictors of teaching performance.* Paper presented at the First Oregon Conference on Research in Teacher Education, Oregon State University, Eugene, OR.

Flanders, W. R. (1970). *Analyzing teacher behavior.* Reading, MA: Addison-Wesley.

Fox, R. B. (1976). Factors influencing the career choice of prospective teachers in 1960–1975. *Illinois School Research, 12,* 19–24.

Friebus, R. J. (1977). Agents of socialization involved in student teaching. *Journal of Educational Research, 70,* 263–268.

Fuller, F. F. (1969). Concerns of teachers: A developmental conceptualizations. *American Educational Research Journal, 6,* 207–226.

Garner, A. E. (1971). The cooperating teacher and human relations. *Education,* *92*(2), 99–106.

Garvey, R. (1970). Self-concept and success in student teaching. *Journal of Teacher Education, 21,* 357–361.

George, A. A. (1978). *Measuring self, task, and impact concerns: A manual for use of the teacher concerns questionnaire.* Austin, TX: The University of Texas at Austin, Research and Development Center for Teacher Education.

Gettone, V. G. (1980). Role conflict of student teachers. *College Student Journal, 14,* 92–100.

Glassberg, S., & Sprinthall, N. A. (1980). Student teaching: A developmental approach. *Journal of Teacher Education, 31,* 35–38.

Goldhammer, K. (1977). Premises and context of collegiate-based teacher education. *Journal of Teacher Education, 28,* 10–14.

Good, T. L., & Grouws, D. (1979). The Missouri mathematics effectiveness project: An experimental study in fourth grade classrooms. *Journal of Educational Psychology, 71,* 355–362.

Gordon, I., & Brievogel, W. F. (Eds.). (1976). *Building effective home/school relationships.* Boston, MA: Allyn & Bacon.

Griffin, G. (1982). *Student teaching: Problems and promising practices.* Austin, TX: The University of Texas at Austin, Research and Development Center for Teachers Education.

Griffin, G., Barnes, S., Hughes, R., Jr., O'Neal, S., Defino, M., Edwards, S., & Hukill, H. (1983). *Clinical preservice teacher education: Final report of a descriptive study.* Austin, TX: The University of Texas at Austin, Research and Development Center for Teacher Education.

Haberman, M. (1974). Needed: New guidelines for teacher candidate selection. *The Journal of Teacher Education, 20,* 234–235.

Haberman, M. (1978). Toward more realistic teacher education. *Journal of the Association of Teacher Educators, 1,* 8–17.

Hanke, D. (1967). The college supervisor: The unsung hero. *Teacher's College Journal, 39,* 35–37.

Haurich, V. F. (1960). The motives of prospective teachers. *Journal of Teacher Education, 11,* 381–386.

Howey, K. R. (1977). Preservice teacher education: Lost in the shuffle? *Journal of Teacher Education, 28,* 26–28.

Hoy, W. K., & Rees, R. (1977). The socialization of student teachers. *Journal of Teacher Education, 28,* 23–26.

Hubbell, N. S. (1979). Some things change—some do not. In R. Brandt (Ed.), *Partners: Parents and schools.* Alexandria, VA: Association for Supervision and Curriculum Development.

Hughes, R., Jr. (1981, April). *Student teaching: The past as a window to the future.* Paper presented at RITE conference, Student Teaching: Problems and Promising Practices. Austin, TX: The University of Texas at Austin, Research and Development Center for Teacher Education.

Hunt, D. E., & Joyce, B. R. (1967). Teacher trained personality and initial teaching style. *American Educational Research Journal, 4,* 253–259.

Hunter, E. (1980). A collaborative, connected, completely organic, all natural teacher education program. *Journal of Teacher Education, 31,* 7–10.

Hymes, J. J. (1974). *Effective home–school relations.* Sierra Madre, CA: Southern California Association for the Education of Young Children.

Iannacone, L. (1963). Student teaching: A transitional stage in the making of a teacher. *Theory into Practice, 2,* 73–80.

Isham, M. N., Carter, H. L., & Stribling, R. (1981). *A study of the entry mechanisms of university-based teacher educators.* Unpublished manuscript, The University of Texas at Austin, Research and Development Center for Teacher Education.

Ishler, M. (1973). *A study of the verbal behavior of creative and less creative English and social studies student teacher* (Res. Bull. 12). Washington, DC: Association of Teacher Educators.

Jacobs, E. B. (1968). Attitude change in teacher education: An inquiry into the role of attitudes in changing teacher behavior. *The Journal of Teacher Education, 19,* 410–416.

Jones, R. E. (1980). The supervisor and the teacher: An effective model of communication. *Clearinghouse, 53*(9), 433–437.

Junell, J. S. (1969). Abolish letter grades for student teaching activities. *Education, 89,* 255–256.

Kaplan, L. (1967). An investigation of the role expectations in college supervisors of student teaching as viewed by student teachers, supervising teachers, and college supervisors. (Doctoral dissertation, The University of Rochester.) *Dissertation Abstracts, 28,* 517A.

Kappelman, M. M., & Ackerman, P. R. (1977). *Between parent and child.* New York: Dial Press.

Karmos, A. H., & Jacko, C. M. (1977). The role of significant others during the student teaching experience. *Journal of Teacher Education, 28,* 51–55.

Kohlberg, L. (1969). Stage and sequence: The cognitive developmental approach to socialization. In D. A. Gosline (Ed.), *Handbook of socialization theory and research.* Chicago, IL: Rand McNally.

LaMonica, E. (1980). *Construct validity of an empathy instrument.* Unpublished manuscript, Teachers College, Columbia University, New York.

Lasley, T. J. (1980). Preservice teacher beliefs about teaching. *Journal of Teacher Education, 31,* 38–41.

Leslie, L. L. (1970). *Improving the student teaching experience through selective placement of students.* (ERIC Document Reproduction Service No. ED 034 718)

Lightfoot, S. L. (1978). *Worlds apart: Relationships between families and schools.* New York: Basic Books.

Lipka, R. P., & Goulet, L. R. (1979). Aging—and experience-related changes in teacher attitudes toward the profession. *Educational Research Quarterly, 4,* 19–28.

Lortie, D. C. (1966). Teacher socialization: The Robinson Crusoe model. In *The Real World of the Beginning Teacher.* Report of the Nineteenth National TEPS Conference, Washington, DC, National Education Association.

MacNaughton, R., Johns, F., & Rogus, J. (1978). Alternative needs for revitalizing the school–university partnership. *Action in Teacher Education, 1,* 18–29.

Mahan, J. M., & Lacefield, W. E. (1978). Educational attitude changes during year-long student teaching. *Journal of Experimental Education, 46,* 4–15.

Manning, D. T. (1977). The influence of key individuals on student teachers in urban and suburban settings. *The Teacher Educator, 13,* 2–8.

McDonald, F. J., Elias, P., Stone, M., Wheeler, P., Lamber, N., Calfee, R., Sandoval, J., Ekstrom, R., & Lockheed, M. (1975). *Final report on Phase III: Beginning teacher evaluation study.* Princeton, NJ: Educational Testing Service.

McIntyre, D. J., & Morris, W. R. (1977). Research on the student teaching triad. *Contemporary Education, 51,* 193–196.

McIntyre, J., Buell, M., & Casey, J. (1979). Verbal behavior of student teachers and cooperating teachers. *College Student Journal,* 220–224.

Medley, D. M. (1977). *Teacher competence and teacher effectiveness: A review of process-product research.* Washington, DC: The American Association of Colleges for Teacher Education.

Milgram, R. M., & Milgram, N. (1976). Self-concept differences in student teachers in primary, secondary, and special education. *Psychology in the Schools, 13,* 439–441.

Miller, M. S. (1980). *Bring learning home.* New York: Harper & Row.

Monson, J. A., & Bebb, A. M. (1970). New roles for the supervisor of student teaching. *Educational Leadership, 28,* 44–47.

Morris, J. R. (1974). The effects of the university supervisor on the performance and adjustment of student teachers. *The Journal of Educational Research, 67*(8), 358–361.

Muente, G. (1974). Let's be more selective with student teachers. *Journal of Teacher Education, 20,* 236–238.

Murphy, P., & Brown, M. (1970). Conceptual systems and teaching styles. *American Educational Research Journal, 7,* 529–540.

Painter, L. H., & Weiner, W. K. (1979). Developing competent cooperating teachers. *Improving College Education and University Teaching, 27,* 13–15.

Piaget, J. (1970). *Science of education and the psychology of the child.* New York: Viking.

Poole, C. (1972). The influence of experiences in the schools on students' evaluation of teaching practice. *The Journal of Educational Research, 66*(4), 161–164.

Price, R. D. (1961). Relations between cooperating teachers and student teachers' attitudes and performances (Doctoral dissertation, The University of Texas). *Dissertation Abstracts, 21,* 2615.

Prokop, M. (1973). *Role conflict in student teaching.* Washington, DC: ERIC (ERIC Document Reproduction Service No. ED 080 498)

Pruitt, W. K., & Lee, J. F. (1978). Hidden handcuffs in teacher education. *Journal of Education, 29,* 69–72.

Quick, A. F. (1967). Supervising teachers do need special skills! *Michigan Education Journal, 44,* 16–17.

Rayder, N. F., Abrams, A. L., & Larson, J. C. (1978). Effect of socio-contextual variables on child achievement. *Journal of Teacher Education, 29,* 58–63.

Rich, D. (1979). Families as educators of their own children. In R. Brandt (Ed.), *Partners: Parents and schools.* Alexandria, VA: Association for Supervision and Curriculum Department.

Ringness, T. A. (1966). Effects of supervisor's knowledge of student teacher personality evaluations. Washington, DC: ERIC (*ERIC Abstract*, ED 014 442) (Abstract)

Roberts, F. (1980). You and your child's teacher: How to get along. *Parents, 55*(3), 56.

Ryan, K. (1981, April). *The cooperating teacher: Who, what, why, when, how and whither?* Paper presented at RITE conference, Student Teaching: Problems and Promising Practices. Austin, TX: University of Texas at Austin, Research and Development Center for Teacher Education.

Ryans, D. G. (1960). *Characteristics of teachers*. Washington, DC: American Council on Education.

Schalock, D. (1979). Research of Teacher selection. *Review of Research in Education, 7,* 364–417.

Seiforth, B., & Samuel, M. (1979). The emergence of early field experiences. *Peabody Journal of Education, 57,* 10–16.

Seperson, M., & Joyce, B. (1973). Teaching styles of student teachers as related to those of their cooperating teachers. *Educational Leadership, 31,* 146–151.

Shiraki, L. Y. (1979). Why become a cooperating teacher? *Educational Perspective, 18*(3), 15–17.

Simms, F. M. (1975). Role of the elementary and secondary student teachers as determined by current practices in student teaching. *Dissertation Abstracts International, 36,* 2755A.

Slay, J. L. (1974, April). *Public school-college cooperation in the field-based education of teachers: A historical perspective.* Paper presented at the meeting of the Field-Based Teacher Education for the 80's Conference, St. Simon's Island, GA.

Smith, F., & Adams, S. (1973). *Changes in self-concept during the student teaching period* (Res. Rep. Vol. 2, no. 5). Baton Rouge, LA: Louisiana State University.

Smith, P. M. (1969). *Experimentation to determine the feasibility of remote supervision of student teachers.* Washington, DC: ERIC. (ERIC Document Reproduction Service No. 033 203)

Smith, S. D., & Smith, W. D. (1979). Teaching the poor: Its effect on student teacher self-concept. *Journal of Teacher Education, 30,* 45–49.

Soar, R. S., & Soar, R. M. (1972). An empirical analysis of selected Follow Through Programs: An example of a process approach to evaluation. In I. J. Gordon (Ed.), *Early Childhood Education*. Chicago, IL: National Society for the Study of Education.

Soares, A. T., & Soares, L. M. (1968). Self-perceptions of student teachers and the meaningfulness of their experience. *The Journal of Teacher Education, 19,* 187–191.

Southall, C., & King, D. (1979). Critical incidents in student teaching. *Teacher Educator, 15,* 34–36.

Stallings, J., & Kaskowitz, D. (1974). *Follow through classroom observation 1972–1973.* Menlo Park, CA: Stanford Research Institute.

Tabachnick, B. R. (1980). Intern-teacher roles: Illusions, disillusions, and reality. *Journal of Education, 62,* 122–137.

Taylor, C. W., Ghiselin, B., & Yagi, K. (1967). *Exploratory research on communication abilities and creative abilities.* Salt Lake City, UT: University of Utah.

Terwilliger, R. I. (1965). Assessing the cooperating teachers' influence on the student teacher using Withall's technique (Doctoral dissertation, Pennsylvania State University). *Dissertation Abstracts, 26,* 6537.

Thies-Sprinthall, L.(1980). Supervision: An educative or miseducative process? *Journal of Teacher Education, 31,* 17-20.

Tittle, C. K. (1974). *Student teaching: Attitude and research bases for change in school and university.* Metuchen, NJ: Scarecrow Press.

Torrance, P. E. (1962). *Guiding creative talent.* Englewood Cliffs, NJ: Prentice-Hall.

Van Patten, J. J. (1977). The role of the first education course in selection and education of prospective teachers. *Journal of Teacher Education, 28,* 9-14.

Vernon, P. E. (1965). Personality factors in teacher training selection. *British Journal of Educational Psychology, 35,* 140-149.

Wagenschein, M. (1950). *Reality shock: A study of beginning student teachers.* Unpublished masters thesis, University of Chicago.

Walberg, H. J. (1968). Personality-role conflict and self-conception in urban practice teachers. *The School Review, 76,* 41-48.

Wallat, C., & Goldman, R. (1979). *Home/school/community interaction: What we know and why we don't know more.* Columbus, OH: Merrill.

Why public schools are flunking? (1981, April 20; 1981, April 27; 1981, May 4). *Newsweek.*

Wilk, R. E. (1964). An experimental study of the effects of classroom placement variables on student performance. *Journal of Teacher Education, 55,* 375-380.

Wood, K. E. (1978). What motivates students to teach? *Journal of Teacher Education, 29,* 48-50.

Wright, B., & Tuska, S. (1965). The effects of institution on changes in self-conception during teacher training and experience. *Proceedings of the 73rd Annual Convention of the American Psychological Association,* 299-300.

Yarger, S.J., Howey, K., & Joyce, B. (1977). Reflections on preservice preparation: Impressions from the national survey. *Journal of Teacher Education, 28,* 34-37.

Yee, H. (1968). Interpersonal relationships in the student-teaching triad. *Journal of Teacher Education, 19,* 95-112.

Yee, H. (1969). Do cooperating teachers influence the attitudes of student teacher? *Journal of Teacher Education, 60,* 327-332.

Zeichner, K. M. (1979, February). *The dialects of teacher socialization.* Paper presented at the annual meeting of the Association of Teacher Educators, Orlando, FL.

Zeichner, K. M. (1980, April). *Key processes in the socialization of student teacher: Limitations and consequences of oversocialized conceptions of teacher socialization.* Paper presented at the meeting of the American Educational Research Association, Boston, MA.

Zevin, J. (1974). *In thy cooperating teachers' image: Convergence of social studies student teachers' behavior patterns with cooperating teachers' behavior patterns.* Washington, DC: ERIC. (ERIC Document Reproduction Service No. ED 087 781)

Zimpher, N. L., De Voss, G. G., & Nott, D. L. (1980). A closer look at university student teacher supervision. *Journal of Teacher Education, 31,* 11-15.

Author Index

Subject Index